DR. SHAPIRO'S

PICTURE PERFECT
WEIGHT LOSS
COOKBOOK

More Than 150 Delicious Recipes
for Permanent Weight Loss

Dr. Howard M. Shapiro

RODALE

Notice

This book is intended as a reference volume only, not as a medical manual. It is not intended as a substitute for any treatment that may have been prescribed by your doctor. If you suspect that you have a medical problem, we urge you to seek competent medical help. Keep in mind that nutritional needs vary from person to person, depending upon age, sex, health status, and total diet. The information discussed and the recipes given here are designed to help you make informed decisions about your diet and health.

Mention of specific companies, organizations, or authorities in this book does not imply endorsement by the publisher, nor does mention of specific companies, organizations, or authorities imply that they endorse the book.

Interior design by Christina Gaugler
Food styling by Diane Vezza

Library of Congress Cataloging-in-Publication Data

Shapiro, Howard M., date.
   Dr. Shapiro's picture perfect weight loss cookbook : more than 150
delicious recipes for permanent weight loss / Howard M. Shapiro.
      p.   cm.
   Includes index.
   ISBN 1–57954–437–1   hardcover
   1. Reducing diets—Recipes.   I. Title.
RM222.2 .S4694   2002
613.2'5—dc21   2002011484

Distributed to the book trade by St. Martin's Press

  4 6 8 10 9 7 5 3   hardcover

RODALE

WE INSPIRE AND ENABLE PEOPLE TO IMPROVE
THEIR LIVES AND THE WORLD AROUND THEM

FOR MORE OF OUR PRODUCTS
WWW.RODALESTORE.COM
(800) 848-4735

For more information about Picture-Perfect Weight Loss, log on to www.drshapiropictureperfect.com.

To the memory of Ninette Lyon, cook and author,

for inspiring so much of the spirit of this book—

And to her daughter, Anne-Laure Lyon, whose consistent ability

to keep on pursuing her goals is a mark of true courage.

To my sister, Marilyn McLaughlin, who had the courage to fight back

from a difficult cardiac surgery to become a "medical miracle";

To Dr. Craig Miller, professor of cardiovascular surgery, Stanford

University Medical Center, who had the courage not to give up.

And

for my mother, Eleanor Gallner DeWalt,

who gave her children wisdom, love, and the example

of a life well and fully lived.

Their valor is both a lesson and an inspiration.

contents

For more information about Picture-Perfect Weight Loss, log on to www.drshapiropictureperfect.com.

ACKNOWLEDGMENTS

Many people have generously contributed their expertise, their time, and their creativity to the making of this book, and I am pleased to acknowledge them here.

I am grateful as always to the staff at Rodale—to Anne Egan, the superb editor of this book, who showed grace under pressure, extraordinary patience, expertise, and great inventiveness in bringing the project to fruition. Developmental editor Kathy Everleth managed to keep many balls in the air: recipe developers, nutritional analyses, sidebars, and more. Copy editor Kathy Dvorsky trained her supremely watchful eye over every word and every bit of syntax. Christina Gaugler, designer of the book and director of photography, and food stylist Diane Vezza and her assistant, Joan Parkin, did their usual fine job. I thank them as always for making the book look absolutely wonderful and for being so great to work with. I want to express my gratitude also to layout designer Keith Biery and to Frank Moninghoff and Tom Aczel, who did the digital imaging. And of course, I am grateful to deputy editor Mary South.

New to me for this cookbook is an entire kitchen squad. Jackie Newgent, Michele Peters, Miriam Rubin, Mindy Sweetwood, and Marianne Zanzarella were responsible for recipe development, while JoAnn Brader, the redoubtable test kitchen manager, oversaw their work and tested every recipe for accuracy—and, of course, for taste.

Mitch Mandel and his assistant, Matthew Reigner, brought the recipes to life with their photographs; they are also responsible for making me look good in the cover photograph.

Once a book is published, of course, someone has to get the word out and get it sold. Several "someones" were responsible for that, and I want to thank the following Rodale sales and promotion experts: Leslie Schneider, director of trade sales; Janine Slaughter and Sindy Berner of the direct marketing department; Karen Follweiler, promotion art director; and Lori Magilton, promotion account executive.

Special thanks to Rodale senior management, Steve Murphy, Marc Jaffe, Amy Rhodes, and Tammerly Booth, for their consistent support of the Picture-Perfect Weight-Loss message.

The staff at my New York office, this time as every time, adapted themselves to working for an author as well as a doctor with efficiency and good humor. I am grateful to Gerri Pietrangolare, Alexandra Lotito, and Sharon Richter, M.S., R.D.

To Susanna Margolis, I express heartfelt thanks for her continued hard work in crafting the message. I am grateful to my agent, Mel Berger, for getting the book off the ground, and to Cindy Ratzlaff and Mary Lengle of Rodale, Judy Drutz of Dan Klores Communications, and Vanessa Menkes for helping it fly. Special thanks to Anne-Laure Lyon, who again fashion-styled the cover and who this time also contributed the celebrity interviews.

I also want to thank some family members: my nephews Jordan and Ross Shapiro; my brother-in-law, Michael McLaughlin, who was a tower of strength when it was most needed; and Charles DeWalt, who cherished my mother.

Finally, a special thanks as always to Kay von Bergen, who provided her usual valuable support, suggestions, and enthusiasm and tolerated my constantly shifting schedule with grace.

INTRODUCTION

When Dr. Shapiro asked me to interview well-known celebrities for his *Picture Perfect Weight Loss Cookbook*, I jumped at the chance, for cooking is a point of pride with me and one of the great joys of my life. It's also an important part of my background.

First of all, I'm French. That alone says something about my appreciation for cuisine. Beyond that, my mother was a well-known cook and a cookbook writer at a time in France when those professions were still exclusively male precincts. Being in the kitchen, watching my mother, and helping her—she made it all look easy—came naturally to me, and later, I studied cooking under some of the finest chefs in Paris. To this day, the kitchen is a soothing haven for me, whether it's mine or someone else's. I am comforted by the thought of food being prepared, by the smells seeping out of a kitchen, even by the mouthwatering longings those smells evoke—I want some NOW.

Of course, food is vital for survival. But it is also true that food evokes all kinds of personal reactions, and it is those reactions I wanted to explore in the interviews in this book. No two people, it seems to me, have the same attitude toward food or the same experience with it. Food is a private world, and I wanted to ask the people I interviewed to let us in.

Eleven people have done so. All are prominent in the worlds of art, entertainment, and public life. All were generous with their time and thoughtful with their responses. Like all of us, these celebrities are authorities on the subject of their personal likes and dislikes in food. Like all of us, they are happy to share those opinions. I was struck by the amount of time they took to think about such an ordinary subject, one taken so much for granted. Clearly, the subject—an individual's relationship with food—requires a lot of thinking; its very ordinariness surprises people into thought, even as it evokes memories and inspires laughter. I think the responses given—and the tastes described—represent both the diversity and the commonality of our feelings about food and cooking. You'll find these interviews scattered like spices among the recipes.

In addition to the interviews, you'll find among the book's 150-plus recipes 13 recipes created by top chefs from across the country. I know a little something about the lives of chefs; they're by no means easy. Chefs are artists—they must constantly create and constantly better their creations. They are passionate about the ingredients they use for their art, and they will go to the ends of the earth to get the best. Most chefs start their day before dawn. They're off to the fish market, the vegetable market, the fruit seller's, the bakery. An essential item isn't available? It means the chef must be even more resourceful, changing a menu at a moment's notice, digging deeper into an internal well of inventiveness to come up with something new. At the same time, chefs must keep up with the food fashions of the day—decorative nouvelle cuisine, integrative fusion food—but interpret the fashions uniquely.

Yet of course, these chefs also take boundless joy from their work. And the aim of their work is to give joy as well. Certainly, they give joy to people who dine on their creations in restaurants in every region of the country. But they also give joy by sharing their recipes as they have done in this book.

Also sharing their favorite recipes in these pages are several of the many New York City firefighters who have followed Dr. Shapiro's Picture-Perfect Weight-Loss plan to permanent weight loss. These delicious dishes are evidence that firefighters are inventive as well as brave.

All of the recipes in the book, whatever their source, have been created and tested to assure you success every time, while the cooking methods described will help you update your old favorites as well. After all, part of the fun of cooking is experimentation.

The point is to enjoy every aspect of the world of food—creating recipes, preparing ingredients, cooking food, and, of course, eating healthy and delicious meals all your life long. So from my kitchen to yours, I wish you . . .

Bon appétit!

Anne-Laure Lyon

In all Rodale cookbooks, our mission is to provide delicious and nutritious recipes. Our recipes also meet the standards of the Rodale Test Kitchen for dependability, ease, practicality, and, most of all, great taste. To give us your comments, call (800) 848-4735.

COOKING FOR PICTURE-PERFECT WEIGHT LOSS: FROM THE FIREHOUSE TO YOUR HOUSE

A firehouse may seem a funny place to start a cookbook. But the fact is that all firefighters are cooks. They have to be. It's part of the job. Since most firefighters work a 12- or 24-hour shift, they obviously have to eat several meals while at work. And since the job requires being on the spot in the firehouse, ready to move at a moment's notice, there's precious little opportunity for a leisurely restaurant lunch and not much sense in ordering an expensive take-

out dinner that you might not get a chance to eat. That's why part of being a firefighter is taking your turn buying, preparing, and cooking the food for everyone on the shift.

So when a bunch of New York's Bravest asked me to help them achieve Picture-Perfect Weight Loss, it meant that they not only had to embrace a whole new way of eating but also had to undertake a whole new way of cooking. You can, too, and this book will help you do it.

1

Why This Cookbook Is Different: Thin for Life

Picture-Perfect Weight Loss is unlike any "diet" you've ever been on, and this cookbook is unlike any other cookbook you've ever seen. Why? Because Picture-Perfect Weight Loss is not about "dieting"; it's about changing your relationship with food, once and for all. The *Picture Perfect Weight Loss Cookbook* shows you how.

Most diets are about deprivation, avoidance, and eating dull food in restricted portion sizes. Not Picture-Perfect Weight Loss. Thumb through the recipes in the pages that follow. Every taste is represented here: sweet, salty, sour—you name it. Every kind of meal is here—breakfast, lunch, dinner, snack. Every occasion is accommodated, from a lavish dinner party for a dozen guests to a quick lunch that you eat by yourself. Like seafood? It's here. Think of yourself as a meat-and-potatoes person? Your meal is here, too. Want some suggestions for cool eating in the heat of summer or for warm comfort foods on a cold winter's day? Look no further. What about side dishes? Appetizers? Soups? They're all here. All delicious, all healthful. And if you want proof that you don't have to give up desserts to achieve Picture-Perfect Weight Loss, the case is convincingly made in these pages.

Chances are that some of the foods in this cookbook are new to you. Good! Picture-Perfect Weight Loss is about expanding your food options. I hope you'll be inspired to explore even further. An important part of changing your relationship with food is looking beyond your current food "vocabulary" to entire new "languages" of eating.

What all these recipes have in common is that they represent a healthful, low-calorie way for you to enjoy everything you eat, every meal of every day, so that you eat till you're satisfied in a changed relationship with food. They are examples of a way of eating that can keep you thin for life—healthfully and deliciously.

The recipes also emphasize the importance of food. Of course, we all know that food is essential for life. But I mean something more than that—food as an essential aspect of culture. It has been that throughout human history, which is why many of these recipes contain notes about the history or folklore of a food or ingredient.

It's also why the way a food is presented can be so powerful, as the beautiful photographs in the book make clear. They clearly demonstrate that we can and should *enjoy* the food we eat. And that means paying attention not just to filling the stomach but also to the aesthetics of a recipe—to how it looks and smells, to the mingling of textures and tastes, to the way a food or combination of foods appeals to all the senses. Because above all, cooking remains a creative act. That's why I've included recipes in this book from some of the most celebrated, inventive chefs of this generation. And it's why you'll hear from creative artists in other fields—sculpture, dance, painting, theater —who will tell of their own attitudes toward cooking and their personal food passions.

I've also included recipes from some of the scores of firefighters and police officers who have benefited so greatly from Picture-Perfect Weight Loss.

Of course, the most important creativity in cooking is your own. If you're a dedicated cook, the recipes, tips, and nutritional information in these pages should prove a launching pad for your own imagination and inventiveness. In no time, you'll be concocting your own Picture-Perfect Weight-Loss recipes, making the lower-calorie choices expertly in your kitchen.

If you're a dedicated *non*cook, you'll probably want to pay particular attention to the quick-and-easy recipes in this book. Look for the QUICK icon as you browse the pages that follow. They point the way to easy-to-make recipes that can be on the table in 30 minutes or less. In fact, if you make this book your cooking primer, you will soon find that the principles of Picture-Perfect Weight-Loss cooking are second nature—easy and effective, every time.

Changing Your Relationship with Food

The new way of cooking you'll find here is essential for changing your relationship with food. And that's what you're about to do. You're not "going on a diet" that you'll try once and then forget. You're not undertaking some short-term overweight "remedy" that has a beginning, a middle, and an end. Nor is Picture-Perfect Weight Loss a regimen of meals or a prescription of special foods. You don't lose weight following such tactics, and you certainly don't maintain weight loss that way.

Let me say it again: The only way to lose weight and keep it off is to *change your relationship with food*.

Think about it: How would you characterize your current relationship with food? If you're someone who's frequently watching your weight, chances are that any number of the following would apply.

- You fear food, and you crave food.

- You avoid some foods you love, and you force yourself to eat some foods that you don't like.

- You eat like a bird during the day, then eat a blow-out dinner that leaves you feeling overfed, sluggish, guilty, and a failure.

- You diet in January, gain the weight back by June, crash diet before summer, and just "let it go" for the holidays.

Do you see the common thread in all these reactions to food? Food is the enemy! Somewhere along the line, a necessity of life that should also be one of life's great pleasures has become your foe. You're afraid of food. It's your nemesis. You may run a business, control a budget of millions and a staff of hundreds, operate complex machinery, or manage a contemporary household —the kind with multiple people and multiple personal schedules—but when it comes to food, you find that you're up against an opponent you want to beat, but can't. Eating is controlling you, not the other way around.

Picture-Perfect Weight Loss teaches you the other way around. It trains you in what I call Food Awareness. By this I mean awareness not just of how and why you gain weight—and how and why you can lose weight—but of food itself, of the great variety of food options there are in the world, and of the consequences of eating different foods.

Specifically, Picture-Perfect Weight Loss makes you aware of the calorie consequences of food. The reason is simple: Calorie reduction is the key to weight loss. When you take in fewer calories than you expend, through a combination of eating choices and exercise, you will lose weight. Awareness of the calorie consequences of foods equips you to make lower-calorie choices. And awareness of the range of other possibilities for satisfying your appetite empowers you to choose lower-calorie foods that are tasty, satisfying, and filling.

Are you a chocoholic? Life is too short to forswear chocolate forever. In fact, as Picture-Perfect Weight Loss teaches, there are plenty of ways to enjoy chocolate and still lose weight, without beating yourself up for sneaking a piece of candy. There's no more sneaking; you're not "dieting," so you can't "cheat."

Or maybe you're someone who needs a snack in late morning—what the British call *elevenses*. By all means, listen to your body and have the snack. In fact, have something delicious and completely satisfying. Just choose mindfully, making a conscious decision from among a range of snack options—without feeling like a failure or being consumed by guilt.

One more thing: When you eat with awareness, there's no such thing as eating too much or depriving yourself or measuring portions. In fact, since you'll be making lower-calorie choices, you can actually eat more food than you're now eating and still lose weight and keep it off. That's Picture-Perfect Weight Loss, and that's what the *Picture Perfect Weight Loss Cookbook* is all about.

As a doctor, I give a simple prescription for the recipes in this book: Eat your fill. As I'll explain in the next chapter, it's a great way to lose weight. And if you don't believe me, just ask the chefs at the firehouse; they cooked up a loss of 1,854 pounds for their fellow firefighters—deliciously.

Losing Weight and Keeping It Off: What Works

*D*iets don't work. Period. If you've ever been "on a diet," you know what I mean. Have you ever lost weight on a diet? Of course you have. You starved yourself, made a superhuman effort to avoid foods you loved, ate only when the diet book said you should, and carefully measured out the mandated portions of the mandated foods, whether you liked them or not. Two weeks later, you had actually lost weight, maybe even a lot of weight.

And then what happened? How long did it take to gain the weight back? And how many additional pounds did you eventually put on? That's what happens with diets, as many studies and vast research show, and as your experience no doubt confirms.

There are two basic reasons why diets don't work (nor do pills, fasting, food combining, eating according to blood type, or any other fad weight-loss gimmicks). First, diets don't work because they are extracurricular. In other words, they represent a temporary departure from normal life, and once you go back to normal life, you also go back to normal eating and to the weight gain that the normal eating caused.

Second, diets don't work because they're tantamount to deprivation. You deprive yourself of foods you love, of eating when you feel like eating, and of the amount of food you want. Physiologically, all those deprivations are a signal to your body to stop losing weight and start gaining weight.

You don't believe me? Let's look at a few facts.

Making Sense of Metabolism

Obviously, food is essential to life. It's our fuel. It's what produces energy, stimulates growth, repairs tissues and muscles and sinews, and quite literally keeps us alive. The combination of what we eat and what our bodies do with what we eat determines our weight—and both what we eat and what our bodies do with what we eat are determined by genes and environment. Put it this way: We are dealt a particular genetic hand of cards, metabolically speaking, but we can play that hand of cards in different ways.

So what is metabolism? It's a process. Actually, it's a lot of processes. It's the sum total of all the interactions by which the body changes chemicals into the energy needed to live, breathe, and move. Along the way, these interactions, helped by the particular environment in which you live and the things taught to you by upbringing and experience, influence your eating.

Your metabolism is as individual as your fingerprint and just as indelible. Right now, in fact, your metabolism is relaying messages to your cells, blood, intestines, even your brain—messages that shape how you think about food, how different foods taste to you, when and where and how your appetite acts up, and how your body processes the food you eat.

Some bodies are more efficient food processors than others; they take needed energy from food immediately, then store the excess and keep it stored for longer than other bodies. Those bodies are more likely to gain weight than others because they store more calories than they expend. To lose weight, therefore, those people have to take in fewer calories or expend more of them through exercise—preferably both.

But how can you do that if some of your metabolic interactions, egged on by that ad on television and your almost subconscious memory of your mother's cooking, are making you crave certain foods, in certain amounts, at certain times? Isn't the obvious answer to defy appetite, to close your ears to the messages it sends through your body?

No. Absolutely not. Here's the reality about metabolism: When you defy your appetite, it fights back. In fact, the irony is that when you refuse to respond to all those messages that your metabolism keeps sending to your appetite centers about when to eat and what to eat and how much to eat, you actually lower your chances of being able to lose weight. All the scientific evidence culled from years of study confirms what anyone who has tried to lose weight already knows: If you battle your own metabolism, your metabolism wins. An old advertising campaign back in the 1970s warned, "It's not nice to fool Mother Nature." Well, fighting your metabolism is trying to fool Mother Nature, and she responds with an equal and opposite reaction. Those chemical interactions in your body aren't a problem that can be "fixed"; they're part of your genetic code. That's why depriving yourself of foods you like, or going hungry, or living on pills and shakes eventually backfires. In the end, you actually add pounds. The bottom line: You can't change your basic metabolism.

Say No to Deprivation, Yes to New Choices

Just because you can't permanently change your metabolism doesn't mean you're condemned to remain overweight for life. While there's nothing you can do about the genetic hand of cards you've been dealt, there's plenty you can do to play that hand of cards a different way. Simply put, you can empower yourself to deal with your metabolism, and that's exactly what Picture-Perfect Weight Loss is all about.

I'll provide more details on the principles of Picture-Perfect Weight Loss in the next chapter, but there are a few basics you need to understand right at the outset.

You're not going to give up foods you love because there are no bad foods with Picture-Perfect Weight Loss. You're not going to measure portions or eat at set times because there are no "correct" portions or "right times" to eat with

Picture-Perfect Weight Loss. And you're not going to change your life or your lifestyle. Instead, you're going to reduce your calorie intake without feeling deprived and without defying your urge to eat. You can eat as much food as you're eating now—you can even eat more than you're eating now—and still lose weight.

But this doesn't mean that you can just keep on eating as you've been eating. There's a saying I constantly quote to my patients: "If you do what you did, you get what you got." Picture-Perfect Weight Loss helps you stop doing what you did and start doing something else. It helps you change your current relationship with food through knowledge, awareness, and choice, not through deprivation or by avoiding foods you love.

That's the only way to deal with your own personal metabolic hand of cards, and it's a job only you can do. After all, only you are in touch with those highly individual signals your appetite is sending you. Only you are in charge of what you reach for on the table, what you order in the restaurant, what you actually put in your mouth. Each mealtime or snack time offers you a choice—a choice only you can make. Picture-Perfect Weight Loss provides you with the awareness you need to make the healthful and tasty lower-calorie choice. It gives you the tools you need to change your relationship with food fundamentally and forever. Once you've mastered the principles of Picture-Perfect Weight Loss, once they're second nature to you, you will be able to eat when you're hungry, eat foods you enjoy, and eat until you're satisfied while you lose weight and maintain your weight loss for life.

And once you start cooking the Picture-Perfect way, you'll *really* be in charge!

THE PICTURE-PERFECT WEIGHT-LOSS PHILOSOPHY

I have said that Picture-Perfect Weight Loss is not a diet. It's not a food plan or a set of rules. It's really a philosophy that can guide you to a healthy way of eating for losing weight and staying thin for life. Three straightforward principles define the philosophy, and they're your key to changing your relationship with food and achieving Picture-Perfect Weight Loss.

First principle: Calorie reduction is the key to weight loss. Calories measure the energy-producing potential of food—actually, the amount of heat that is released when the body oxidizes the food. Since weight gain comes from storing more energy than you burn up, that makes the calorie count of a food a major player in determining whether it helps you lose weight, gain weight, or break even.

Clocking the fat, sugar, or sodium content of a food may be important to you for a range of reasons, but it often has little to do with your weight. Many low-fat foods are high in calories, and many foods with hefty measures of sugar or sodium are caloric bargains. You can't get a much higher sodium content than in a pickle, for example, but it's a terrifically tasty snack and a very low-calorie one to boot. Or, consider the Tootsie Pop. It's pure sugar, but it has only about 50 calories, and it satisfies your sweet tooth for a while.

Here's one more example: We all know that fat is high in calories, but a handful of olives, which contain a good dose of fat, actually provides you with nutrients you need—namely, essential fatty acids—at a fairly low calorie count. So focusing solely on fat, sugar, or sodium could take you down an entirely wrong path for weight loss.

Instead, to lose weight, you must take in fewer calories than you expend. Picture-Perfect Weight Loss happens when you are comfortable choosing lower-calorie foods that you find tasty. This book will help you prepare delicious low-calorie foods for every season and any occasion.

Second principle: Choice is not deprivation. If you've ever been on a diet, you probably remember how you looked forward to the moment the diet ended so you could reward yourself with your favorite foods. And although you tried to eat "sensibly" from then on, the pounds you may have lost eventually come back. You probably gained even more weight. So it's worth repeating: Deprivation simply does not work; in fact, it backfires. As the National Institutes of Health has concluded, as much as two-thirds of weight lost is gained back within 1 year of a diet, and almost all of it by 5 years. In Picture-Perfect Weight Loss, no food is forbidden and no portion size is prescribed. The best time to eat is when you're hungry, and the weight you lose stays *lost*.

Third principle: You can achieve Picture-Perfect Weight Loss while living your life. Dieting is a process apart from life. It's temporary, irregular, something you do "on the side." In fact, dieting separates you from your life. When you're at lunch or dinner with friends or business associates, and your diet requires you to order special dishes without sauce or dry-broiled, you're calling attention to yourself, reminding everyone else that, as you are painfully aware, you're overweight and unhappy about it.

When you're cooking for your family, serving them steak or pasta or both, while you dejectedly pick at skinless chicken and steamed broccoli, you're setting yourself apart from the people you love best in the world, not to mention that it's a lot of trouble cooking separate meals.

Achieving and maintaining Picture-Perfect Weight Loss is something you do as part of your life—for a lifetime. At client lunches, you'll be ordering as delicious a dish as anyone else, right off the menu. Same with dinner out on special occasions: No more advertising your weight problem with special instructions to the waiter; no more avoiding dessert. And you certainly won't be made to feel guilty because you love to entertain and take pride in your cooking, as the recipes in this book demonstrate. You can live your life according to your tastes, needs, and desires and still make the choices that will lead to Picture-Perfect Weight Loss.

Put it all together, and it looks like this: *You achieve Picture-Perfect Weight Loss by changing your relationship with food, not by changing your life. You change your relationship with food not through deprivation, but by expanding your eating options. Then you choose the option that is lowest in calories, the most nutritious, and the tastiest, and eat till you're satisfied.*

Picture It!

The key to turning the principles of Picture-Perfect Weight Loss into a lifetime habit is food awareness. Once you're aware of the consequences of the food choices you make (the consequences, that is, in terms of your own weight gain or loss), then you're bound to choose in a way that's right for you. Most of the time, you'll make the lower-calorie choice. But when you don't, you'll do so mindfully, aware of the possible effect and prepared to deal with it. And that's always the right choice.

The key to food awareness, in turn, can be found in the saying "A picture is worth a thousand words." That thought is at the heart of my medical practice in New York City, where my staff nutritionists continually create food comparison demonstrations that give patients graphic evidence of the real caloric costs of food.

A typical demonstration shows two related food offerings, one high-calorie and the other, similar in taste or texture, but lower in calories.

In some cases, the two offerings will have the same number of calories, and you'll be able to eat much more of the lower-calorie food to equal the calorie count of the smaller-size high-calorie food. See the following sample demonstration.

Tart for a Start

It would take more than three servings of tart to equal the calorie count of this single cheese omelet. But calories are only part of the story. The omelet, made with two eggs and Cheddar cheese and fried in butter, has five times more fat than the tart. What's more, the omelet contains the "bad" saturated fats that raise levels of LDL cholesterol and may increase the risk of heart disease. Start your day instead with nutrient-rich, fiber-filled vegetables in a tasty tart.

1 cheese omelet
490 calories 38 grams fat

=

**3½ servings Vegetable Tart
with Potato Crust**
490 calories 7 grams fat

Of course, I'm not actually recommending that you eat all the food pictured on the right, although you could; it's simply to demonstrate that with low-calorie foods, you can actually eat considerably more and still take in the same, or even fewer, calories.

In other cases, the two offerings will be equal in portion size but very different in calorie count. Those demonstrations will pit two foods against one another, and you'll see the "vs." sign for "versus" between them. See the sample demonstration below.

Conned by Carne

The portions are similar, the taste is the same, but the chili *without* carne gives you health benefits and a calorie savings that just about boggles the mind. If you love the taste and texture of beef, try adding veggie ground beef to the Five-Bean Chili recipe. You'll get almost no rise in calories for a substantial addition of meat taste.

1 cup chili con carne (no beans)
530 calories 43 grams fat

VS.

**1 serving
Five-Bean Chili**
290 calories 4 grams fat

Again, none of this has anything to do with how much you should eat. Rather, the demonstration shows that you can eat as much of the food on the right as will satisfy your hunger and still save calories. That's the heart and soul of the Picture-Perfect Weight-Loss way of eating.

The food comparison demonstrations are meant to instill awareness about the calorie content of foods. They bring the message to life more vividly than calorie counters that get lost in the bottom of your handbag or charts in a book sitting on a shelf at home. Instead, when you see the difference, you remember it, and you're empowered to make the lower-calorie choice.

How can I be sure of this? Because I've seen the Picture-Perfect method work for thousands of people over more than 2 decades of medical practice. I've seen it work for the tens of thousands of readers of my earlier books, *Dr. Shapiro's Picture Perfect Weight Loss* and *Picture Perfect Weight Loss 30-Day Plan*. That's why food comparison demonstrations are the organizing principle of this cookbook as well. The difference is that here, I'll give you the recipe for the lower-calorie food.

Eat the Pyramid, Fill the Pantry, Avoid the Saboteurs

*T*his chapter presents more graphic representations that will help you achieve Picture-Perfect Weight Loss—my own food pyramid (see page 16) and a helpful guide I call the Anytime List.

You've probably seen food pyramids before. Mine offers an effective way of translating the principles of Picture-Perfect Weight Loss into action. It guides you to lower-calorie food choices and maps the proportionate representation of foods in an overall eating plan. I'm not dictating what foods you should eat, nor how frequently nor how much; instead, I'm suggesting how you can allocate your food choices over time and across a range of meals.

What does the pyramid tell you? Let's take it from the bottom up.

First, it tells you to make fruits and vegetables the foundation of your eating. Just as the pyramid is necessarily widest at the base, let fruits and vegetables be the foods you eat most—most often, most regularly, and most *of*. For purposes of both weight loss and overall health, you really can't do better than filling up on fruits and vegetables. I use the phrase "filling up" advisedly. Because of their high fiber content, fruits and vegetables give you a sense of being satisfied. That's because fiber, instead of being digested and absorbed, takes up space in the intestine for about 14 hours—the time it takes for it to pass through. In addition, fruits and vegetables are filled with vitamins, minerals, and phytochemicals that we need to stay healthy. In fact, research shows that substances in fruits and vegetables actually work to prevent disease. So whether they're fresh, frozen, canned, plain, grilled, marinated, in soup, whole, or chopped up, eat fruits and vegetables frequently and eat them until you're satisfied. Make them the mainstay of your eating.

Next, go for protein. But as often as possible, get your protein from the healthiest sources—beans and other legumes, seafood, and soy products. Although no food is forbidden, it is best that meats, poultry, and dairy play a smaller role in our eating.

The next category in the pyramid comprises grains. Nutrient-dense whole grains such as barley, brown rice, quinoa, and millet are the healthiest choices for starchy side dishes. Always prepare these grains, a great source of fiber, with plenty of vegetables to keep the calories down. Among bread products, choose whole grain or lite versions whenever possible. Whole grain baked goods are loaded with iron, fiber, and B-complex vitamins that are not only good for you but also

Dr. Shapiro's Picture-Perfect Weight-Loss Food Pyramid

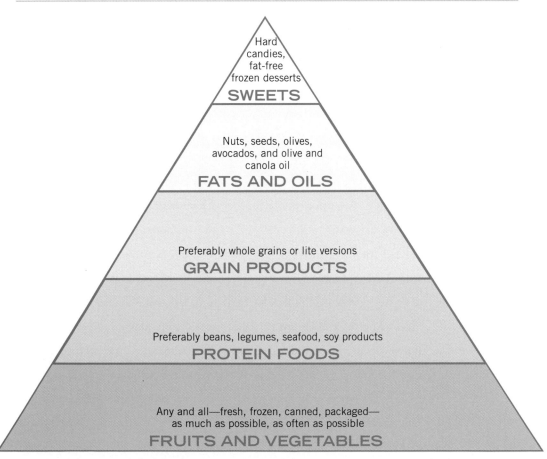

Hard candies, fat-free frozen desserts
SWEETS

Nuts, seeds, olives, avocados, and olive and canola oil
FATS AND OILS

Preferably whole grains or lite versions
GRAIN PRODUCTS

Preferably beans, legumes, seafood, soy products
PROTEIN FOODS

Any and all—fresh, frozen, canned, packaged—as much as possible, as often as possible
FRUITS AND VEGETABLES

satisfying and filling, which makes them helpful in weight control. But such products are also high in carbohydrate calories, so one good alternative is to go for lite breads. Offered by just about every commercial bakery, these lite versions of baked goods come in a range of flavors and forms—rye, wheat, sourdough, oatmeal, even Italian bread—and are true calorie bargains.

Next up on the pyramid are oils. When using oils, choose either olive oil or canola oil wherever possible. They're sources of the so-called "good" fats known as essential fatty acids. Nuts, seeds, olives, and avocados are also good sources of essential fatty acids and are therefore also good fats. Fats in general provide energy and, because they take a long time to digest, help make you feel full. The good fats also help activate both the immune system and the nervous system. But all fats are also a highly concentrated source of calories. For example, a tablespoon of any kind of oil weighs in at about 125 calories. So keep that in mind when you choose among fats or oils.

When you crave a sweet treat, go for hard candies and fat-free frozen desserts. Whatever you do, don't try to avoid sweets. It's unnatural to do so, and as with any force of nature, if you dam it up for too long, it will eventually spill over explosively. Avoid the blowout binge by satisfying your sweet tooth with hard candies, lollipops, fat-free frozen yogurts and sorbets, and fat-free frozen pops and fudge bars. And don't forget to try the delectable dessert recipes in this cookbook.

The Picture-Perfect Weight-Loss Food Pyramid is pretty simple and straightforward. It offers you a wide range of foods, sufficient to satisfy every taste and every appetite. Make the pyramid your guide, and you will be thin for life.

Dr. Shapiro's Anytime List

As you might expect, the foods on the Anytime List can be kept on hand to eat anytime, for any reason, in the amount that satisfies you.

On the Anytime List (see page 18), you'll find soups; sauces, condiments, and marinades; dressings and dips; candy; beverages; and desserts—plus any and all
(continued on page 20)

The Anytime List

Here are the foods you'll want to have on hand to help keep you on track. If you always have them in stock, it'll be a lot easier to make smart choices when hunger hits.

Fruits and Vegetables

- All fruits and vegetables—raw, cooked, fresh, frozen, canned, in soups. Avoid any packaged fruits that have added sugar.

Soups and Broths

Satisfying, easy, versatile. Soups can be a snack, part of a meal, or a cooking ingredient. And soups with vegetables and/or beans offer a nutritional bonus. Stock up!

Sauces, Condiments, and Marinades

Use these to add flavor, moisture, texture, and versatility to every food, every meal.

- Oil-free and/or low-calorie salad dressings
- Fat-free or lite mayonnaise, fat-free sour cream, fat-free yogurt (plain) or lite yogurt with Nu-traSweet
- Mustards: Dijon, Pommery, and other kinds
- Tomato purée, tomato paste, tomato sauce
- Clam juice, lemon or lime juice, tomato juice, V-8 vegetable cocktail
- Butter Buds, Molly McButter
- Cooking sprays in butter, olive-oil, garlic, or lemon flavors, such as Pam
- Vinegars: balsamic, cider, tarragon, wine, or other flavors
- Horseradish: either red or white

- Sauces: A-1, barbecue, chutney, cocktail, duck sauce, ketchup, relish, salsa, soy, tamari, and Worcestershire
- Onion: fresh, juice, flakes, or powder
- Garlic: fresh, juice, flakes, jarred minced, or powder
- Herbs: all, including basil, bay leaves, chives, dill, marjoram, oregano, rosemary, sage, tarragon, thyme
- Spices: all, including allspice, cinnamon, cloves, coriander, cumin, curry, ginger, nutmeg, and paprika
- Extracts: including almond, coconut, maple, peppermint, and vanilla
- Cocoa powder

Dressings and Dips

Fat-free or lite are recommended. The lite versions may be called low-fat, reduced-fat, or low-calorie and are often tastier than the fat-free. Use as toppings or even cooking liquids as well as for dipping and dressing. I recommend keeping several variations of dressings and dips on hand, including at least one creamy version.

Candy

Avoid the "dietetic" variety; it's almost as caloric as the real thing but far less satisfying. And you'll tend to eat more—for more calories. Here are the best bets.

- Any chewing gum or gumballs
- Any hard candy, including candy canes, Hershey's TasteTations, Jolly Ranchers, lollipops

like Tootsie Pops or Blow Pops, sourballs, and Werther's Original Butterscotch

Frozen Desserts

Any fat-free frozen yogurt or nondairy substitute or sorbet is a fine addition to the freezer. Try for the lower-calorie choices among them.

- In soft-serve, stick to varieties that contain up to 25 calories per ounce, as in Skimpy Treat, Columbo fat-free frozen yogurt, ICBY or TCBY, and Tofutti

- In hard-pack, choose items with up to 400 calories per pint, as in all Italian ices, Sharon's Sorbet, Sweet Nothings, and Low-Fat Tofutti

- In Creamsicles, frozen fudge bars, and Popsicles or other bars, opt for those with up to 45 calories per bar, as in Dolly Madison Slender Treat Chocolate Mousse, Tofutti Chocolate Fudge Treats, Weight Watchers Smart Ones Chocolate Mousse and Orange-Vanilla Treats, and Welch's Fruit Juice Bars

- In individually packaged frozen bars, choose ones with between 80 and 120 calories each, as in FrozFruit, Häagen-Dazs orange and vanilla sorbet bars, and Starbucks Coffee Frappuccino and Mocha Frappuccino bars

Beverages

Low-calorie beverages are good to keep on hand to supplement water, but avoid beverages labeled "naturally sweetened" or "fruit juice-sweetened."

- Coffees and teas

- Crystal Light, Diet Mistic, Diet Natural Lemon Nestea, Diet Snapple, and other brands of iced tea

- Diet sodas, including cherry chocolate, chocolate, cola, cream, orange, root beer, and more

- Seltzer, including plain or flavored (check the calorie count if the product is labeled "naturally sweetened")

- Hot cocoa mixes: Stick with ones with 20 to 50 calories per serving, as in Nestlé Carnation Diet and Swiss Miss Diet (avoid cocoa mixes that have 60 calories or more)

- Milk shake mixes: Choose varieties with no more than 80 calories per serving, as in Alba Fit 'n Frosty and Weight Watchers chocolate fudge

fresh fruits and vegetables. Make the foods on the list the staples of your cooking. Stock your pantry, refrigerator, and freezer with them. Then, when you're seized by a craving for sweets in the middle of the night, all these great low-calorie choices will be available to you. When you decide to throw together something warm and comforting for lunch one day, just reach into your pantry. If the foods in there are on the Anytime List, you can be confident that whatever you pull out will be a low-calorie choice.

The list represents varying tastes. Take particular note of the section on sauces, condiments, and marinades. Use these freely to enhance the taste and quality of whatever you're cooking. In fact, creative cooks will find the Anytime List a good launching pad for their inventiveness, while novice cooks should see it as a good, basic beginning.

My physician's prescription for the Anytime List? Take as needed.

Expanding Your Options

As you fill your kitchen with foods from the Anytime List and plan your eating in accord with my food pyramid, take the opportunity to expand your food options. Branch out and go beyond your usual food vocabulary to discover the riches of new food languages. So far from deprivation, that's really what Picture-Perfect Weight Loss equates to: widening your horizons and extending the range of your food options.

Instead of cutting back on foods, Picture-Perfect Weight Loss asks you to try foods that you've never tried before, to find new ways of eating old favorites, to take a fresh look at the old standbys of your daily menu. Burly New York firefighters who once never even noticed the salad bar in the deli now pile their takeout cartons with marinated vegetables, beans, pickles, and stuffed bean curd. Meat eaters have discovered that blackened tuna and veggie Italian meatballs fit the bill just as well. Guys who thought that Chinese food meant egg rolls and spareribs now debate the merits of ginger garlic versus black bean sauce on their lobsters. Or they've expanded their horizons to include Vietnamese, Malaysian, Indonesian, and Japanese cuisines. And men who habitually snacked on dough-nuts and potato chips have discovered the pleasures not just of apples and bananas but of persimmons, clementines, even kiwifruit.

That's the point. And that's what the recipes in this cookbook will do—ex-pand your horizons and help you think beyond those horizons to whole new ways of cooking and eating. It's a delicious way to lose weight and maintain your weight loss for life.

Saboteur Foods

There is one category of food I do recommend you avoid in order to achieve Picture-Perfect Weight Loss. I call them the saboteurs.

The dictionary defines sabotage as "treacherous action to defeat or hinder a cause or an endeavor." That is a perfectly apt definition for what these packaged foods do. They sound like they ought to help you lose weight healthfully—"nat-ural" cereal or yogurt-covered pretzels or sugar-free candy or fat-free cookies—but the truth is that they do nothing for weight loss at all. In fact, because these foods can seriously undermine your efforts to lose weight and keep it off, they can actually add pounds. That's because the saboteur foods tend to do a number on your head as well as on your waistline. Swayed by the claims of "fat-free" and the advertisements for "natural" ingredients, you can all too easily give yourself permission to wolf down the fat-free muffin for breakfast or the natural trail mix for an afternoon snack. Then it's just another tiny step to allowing yourself a second muffin or another handful of trail mix—so healthy!—and before you know it, you've rationalized your way to taking in hundreds of calories.

So let me make it clear: These are high-calorie/empty-calorie foods that only pretend to help you lose weight. Behind your back, they're actually hindering you from achieving your weight-loss goal.

(continued on page 24)

Denise Austin

Denise Austin has been helping America get fit and stay fit since the early 1980s. In 1981, she became co-host to the legendary Jack La Lanne. Three years later, she began regular appearances as the fitness expert on NBC's *Today Show* and started penning a fitness column for the *Washington Post*. Today, she hosts the longest-running and highest-rated fitness show on television, *Denise Austin's Daily Workout*, as well as the number two–rated fitness show, *Fit & Lite*, on Lifetime Television. She is the author of five books, and her 35 exercise videos have sold 13 million copies. Denise has served on the President's Council on Physical Fitness and Sports under Presidents Clinton and George W. Bush.

Is there a food that you cannot under any circumstances resist?

DA: Girl Scout Thin Mint cookies.

What is the comfort food you turn to in times of distress—and why?

DA: Mashed potatoes. My mom would make the best mashed potatoes when I was little.

What is the most unusual combination of food you have ever eaten?

DA: I like strawberry jam inside cottage cheese.

Your favorite ethnic food?

DA: Indian. I love Indian food.

Is supermarket shopping a pleasant or unpleasant experience for you? And do you check food labels?

DA: Yes, it's very pleasant, but I do check labels on new things that I buy.

How does food relate to your career?

DA: It relates big-time because one of the biggest questions I'm asked is what I eat. And when I'm out to dinner with people for the first time, they always want me to order first. I'll order my steak and potatoes, and then they'll feel good and order whatever they want.

Do you like to cook—and why?

DA: I like to cook when I have time because I love to make my friends and family happy with great-tasting food.

What does food mean to you? Does it make you feel good?

DA: Yes, I love food. I'm from a big family, so food is very important to us. Our whole life we gathered around big tables with food. All we did was eat and have everyone come over to our house. Food is a form of energy. I'm not afraid of any foods.

Ever have a particularly laughable situation with food?

DA: The first time I traveled in France, I was about 25 years old and already very much interested in food. I was invited to a three-star restaurant, and I ordered what I thought was some sort of veal. Much to my disgust, the dish that arrived was definitely not veal. To this day I would rather not know what it was, even though I ate it.

What is your favorite smell in the kitchen?

DA: Cinnamon rolls.

What is your favorite seasoning?

DA: Garlic.

As a child, what was your least favorite food?

DA: Asparagus.

What is your least favorite food now?

DA: Liver.

If you were on a desert island, which five food items would you have with you?

DA: A really good breakfast cereal, yogurt, strawberries, coffee ice cream, sourdough bread, and coffee—I have to have my coffee.

Which items do you keep in your refrigerator on a regular basis?

DA: Skim milk, lots of fruits and vegetables, and tuna.

Whom would you most like to have dinner with?

DA: Bono from U2.

I divide the saboteurs into two subcategories: the have-nots and the haves. The have-nots are the packaged foods that are free of all those ingredients you are sure are putting on the pounds; they're sugar-free, fat-free, salt-free, and—my personal favorite—cholesterol-free. Well, potato chips and french fries, to use just two examples, are entirely cholesterol-free, as is any plant food. But both these items are off the charts when it comes to both calories and fats.

The low-fat/no-fat crowd, mostly baked goods, comprises classic saboteurs. You think you're saving calories by the bushel when you grab that fat-free morning muffin or low-fat chocolate wafers for dessert after dinner. But all you're really doing is replacing the fat calories you wouldn't allow yourself to eat with refined carbohydrate calories.

Sugar-free cookies? Check the nutrition label. They may be sweetened with honey or fruit concentrate instead of sugar, but they contain just as many calories as full-sugar cookies. The only real difference is in the taste; the sugar-free cookie is probably less satisfying than a "real" cookie, but since the sugar-free label sounds persuasive, you allow yourself to eat another one, and another, and another. Before you know it, you've taken in far more calories than you would have had you simply eaten a "real" cookie—and had far less enjoyment and satisfaction.

The second subcategory of saboteurs, the haves, are the "healthy naturals" that now abound on supermarket shelves—vegetable, apple, or banana chips; a carob bar, not a chocolate bar; yogurt-covered pretzels, not white chocolate–covered pretzels. These foods bear a "nutritional correctness" seal of approval: They contain ingredients that we believe are natural and good for us. The package probably has simple lettering and maybe a picture of a pastoral scene, or verdant mountains, or a stream running through the woods. It's all designed to make you think this food will restore you to health and goodness and thinness.

So there you are at 4:00 in the afternoon. You crave a chocolate bar, but there's that healthy, natural carob bar right next to it. You assure yourself that the carob bar is better for you, so you might as well have it. In fact, it's so good for you, you might as well buy another for later. But a quick reading of the nutrition label would show you the facts: A carob bar has just as many calories as a chocolate bar and just as much fat.

Where saboteur foods are concerned, in most instances, you're better off having the real thing. The rule of thumb that my staff nutritionists give to my patients is this: If you would not have chosen to eat the "real" food, don't eat the saboteur food. Would you choose the chocolate chip cookie from the vending machine at work when you crave an afternoon pick-me-up? No? Then don't have the sugar-free, fat-free cookie, either; chances are, you're just using it as an excuse—a rationalization—for eating a food you believe is inappropriate. Find another alternative.

Because the low-fat or fat-free cakes and cookies are such classic saboteurs, you won't find many recipes for them in the *Picture Perfect Weight Loss Cookbook*, although I have included recipes for cookies and biscotti for those who love to bake. When you absolutely must have cake, have a cake you love.

For Picture-Perfect Weight Loss, the bottom line is choice. When you crave a chocolate cookie, think first of the caloric consequences. Then consider some lower-calorie chocolate alternatives—a Tootsie Pop, a frozen chocolate yogurt, my Chocolate Mousse recipe on page 248, or a chocolate sorbet bar—*not* a fat-free chocolate cookie, the classic saboteur. And if you must have a chocolate cookie because that's the only thing that will satisfy your appetite, then do so with enjoyment—mindful of the consequences. Remember that the only way to lose pounds is to choose lower-calorie foods that satisfy your cravings whenever possible. Saboteurs undermine your ability to do that, so try to avoid them.

THE NEW WAY OF COOKING: FUNDAMENTALS 101

Whether you're a passionate cook who would happily spend hours cutting, chopping, and stirring, or a noncook who can't wait to get out of the kitchen, the 150-plus recipes in this book get you off to a sound start in cooking a whole new way. But even 150-plus recipes are only a beginning. What happens when you stray from this book to another set of recipes? Or go back to an old favorite that you'd like to adapt to your new way of eating? Or find a recipe in the newspaper or a magazine that simply cries out to be tried? *Is it possible to turn a standard recipe into a Picture-Perfect Weight-Loss recipe? You bet it is, and this chapter will show you how.*

There are three basic ways you can ensure that you are cooking the Picture-Perfect Weight-Loss way.

First, you can adapt the ingredients list in that scrumptious-sounding recipe in the Sunday paper so that it's just as scrumptious but much lower in calories. This chapter will give you some basic low-calorie replacements for typically high-calorie ingredients. Once you get the idea, and once you expand your low-calorie vocabulary, you'll be making your own recipe adaptations with confidence—and with results.

Second, bring the appropriate tools to the task. In a world in which new kitchen implements are being invented by the minute, it's easy—and not necessarily costly—to use the right tools for the job of cooking the Picture-Perfect Weight-Loss way. This chapter will give you some tips on how to fill your ideal kitchen toolbox.

Third, adapt your cooking methods. There's more to life than frying, and this chapter will give you tips that can turn a high-calorie killer into a healthful, low-calorie choice.

Ready? Here's the basic course in cooking a new way, the Picture-Perfect Weight-Loss way.

Ingredients Count

First, for any standard recipe for four, consider these adaptations.

- *In meatless main dishes,* limit the amount of oil used to 2 tablespoons. Since plant foods generally contain far less fat than animal foods, you can afford a little more oil, particularly if it's a healthful monounsaturated like canola or olive oil.

- *In recipes calling for cheese, try any of the soy or veggie cheeses as a first choice.* Many are fat-free, and in those that do contain some fat, it's the "good" kind of un-saturated fat. If the soy choice won't work, try a low-fat cheese, but choose one that contains no more than 70 calories per ounce.

- *Use fat-free salad dressings* to marinate poultry, meat, fish, tofu, and veggie cut-lets before broiling or grilling.

- *Puree cooked vegetables as a base* for silken soups and sauces.

- *Pump up flavor* by increasing herbs, spices, and other seasoning ingredients. Ex-periment with shallots, scallions, fresh ginger, dried mushrooms, grated citrus peel, sun-dried tomatoes, and balsamic vinegar. All add depth of flavor and neg-ligible calories. If these ingredients are new to you, try to incorporate one new seasoning a month into your pantry.

- *Keep naturally fat-free condiments* like mustards and salsas on hand. If you crave mayonnaise, mix the low-fat version with such flavor enhancers as chopped fresh herbs, hot-pepper sauce, chopped pickles, or capers.

(continued on page 32)

Kitchen Matchups

Rosemary goes on chicken, but what complements squash? You like dill on fish, but will it work with dips? There are dozens of common herbs and spices to choose from. The list below will help you make good flavor matches.

Herb/Spice	Characteristics	Common Uses
Allspice	Brown or reddish berries with hints of cinnamon, cloves, and nutmeg	Caribbean soups, marinades, chutneys, curries, puddings, and fruit desserts
Anise seeds	Tiny seeds with a licorice flavor	Seafood, chowders
Basil	Sharp, green leaf with hints of mint, anise, and pepper (varieties include sweet basil, cinnamon basil, lemon basil, ruffled basil, and Thai basil)	Pesto, red sauces, tomato salads, green salads, Italian soups, vinaigrettes, and pasta dishes
Bay leaf	Pale green leaf with a subtle woodsy flavor and brittle texture	Bouquets garnis, poaching liquids, soups, marinades; always remove before serving
Caraway seeds	Small seeds with a licorice scent	Rye bread, roasted poultry, eastern European dishes, root vegetables, and cabbage dishes
Cardamom seeds	Hints of citrus and ginger	Curry dishes, rice puddings, pickles, chutneys, flatbreads, and sweetbreads; can be bought ground or in the pod; to use, break the pods, then crush the seeds
Celery seeds	Subtle celery flavor	Coleslaw, salad dressings, pickles, poultry stuffings, and potato salad
Chervil	Delicate green leaf with hints of parsley, anise, and celery; has the appearance of very fine Italian parsley leaves	Sauces for chicken and fish, egg dishes, and salads; used in fines herbes
Chives	Tender green shoots with faint onion and scallion flavor	Creamy soups, chowders, dips, egg dishes, vinaigrettes, salads, and fines herbes
Cilantro	Pungent flavor; appearance is similar to Italian parsley	Asian, Mexican, and Indian dishes; salsa, rice, beans, curries, and peanut sauces
Cinnamon	Sweet and fragrant	Poultry rubs, pilafs, curries, cakes, muffins, rice puddings, pumpkin soups and pies, winter squash dishes, and mulled drinks

Herb/Spice	Characteristics	Common Uses
Cloves	Intense, burnt-orange scent and fragrant, pungent flavor	Curries and chutneys, rice dishes, sweet-breads, muffins, winter squash soups, mulled drinks
Coriander seeds	Lemony, musky flavor	Thai and Indian curries, Middle Eastern legume dishes, Mexican dishes, and Asian peanut sauces
Cumin seeds	Earthy, rustic flavor	Indian curries, Mexican dishes, black bean soup, hummus, Tex-Mex chili, guacamole, and chutneys
Dill	Refined feathery green strands with distinctive lemony caraway flavor	Vichyssoise, sauces, seafood chowders, cucumber salads, bisques, and yogurt dips
Dill seeds	Similar in flavor to caraway seeds	Gravlax, potato salads, and pickles
Fennel	Feathery fronds similar to fresh dill, with a slight licorice taste	Italian tomato sauces, sausage, fish dishes, pickles, and European desserts
Fennel seeds	Slightly sweet with a licorice-anise taste	Breads, Mediterranean fish stews, borscht, and cabbage dishes
Garlic	Pungent, strongly scented member of the onion family	All savory dishes, including soups, salads, pesto, garlic bread, and stir-fries; Italian, Mexican, Indian, French, and Middle Eastern dishes; roasting makes garlic's flavor milder
Ginger	Slightly sweet, pungent flavor with spicy aroma	Chinese dishes, curries, carrots, sweet potatoes, chicken, fish, meats, cakes, pumpkin pie, and fruit salads; available fresh, ground, and candied; forms are not interchangeable
Horseradish	Very hot and pungent	Sauces for roast beef, chicken, fish, and eggs; salad dressings, cocktail sauce, sandwiches, and borscht; available as a whole root or grated
Lemon balm	Green leaf with citruslike taste and grassy perfume	Fruit jams, jellies, light soups, fruit salads, sorbets, and teas
Lemongrass	Sturdy, pale green-to-white tightly furled stalk with mild lemony flavor	Stir-fries, Asian soups, peanut sauces, soy sauces, and chicken and fish dishes; available fresh and dried

(continued)

Kitchen Matchups (cont.)

Herb/Spice	Characteristics	Common Uses
Lovage	Strong celery taste	Substitute for celery in salads, stuffings, and stews; stalks can be braised as a vegetable
Mace	Very similar to nutmeg but more pungent and intense	Sauces, puddings, and fruity desserts; mace is the outer covering of the nutmeg seed
Marjoram	Small green petals with oregano-like resinous flavor	Tomato sauce, fish, red meat, poultry, grains, marinades, pasta sauces, soups, dressings, and dips; can be used in place of oregano; prevalent in Italian and Greek cuisine
Mint	Forest green to dark green leaves with refreshing, palate-cleansing taste and clean nuance	Fruity salads, lamb and game, light soups, tabbouleh, yogurt sauces, desserts, jellies, and teas; varieties include peppermint, spearmint, lemon mint, pineapple mint, apple mint, and orange mint
Mustard seeds	Powerfully pungent	Pickles, chutneys, and other condiments
Nutmeg	Sweet, fragrant flavor with hints of allspice, cinnamon, and mace	Rice dishes, fruit salads, pancakes, vegetable and broccoli soups, and poultry marinades
Oregano	Dark green petals have resinous pine-needle flavor similar to marjoram	Soups, chili, salads, pasta sauces, Greek salad dressing, marinades, grilled vegetables, sauces for chicken and meat, and pilafs; prevalent in Italian, Mexican, and Greek cooking
Paprika	A dark red powder made from certain dried peppers, it varies from mildly sweet to hot	Spanish and Hungarian stews, chowders, chicken, broiled fish, roasted or mashed potatoes, and Tex-Mex chili
Parsley	Has a refreshing flavor with grassy undertones; Italian flat-leaf parsley has a slightly stronger flavor than curly parsley	Soups, dressings, sauces, dips, marinades, and meats; fish, vegetable, or chicken dishes; anything with potatoes, grains, or pasta
Peppercorns, black	Roundish dried berries with a spicy floral taste	Soups, stews, salads, meat, poultry, fish, vegetables, dressings, and egg dishes
Peppercorns, white	Grayish-white berries with a smooth peppery flavor	Creamy, light-colored soups, sauces, and dressings; interchangeable with black pepper
Poppy seeds	Tiny blue-gray seeds with a slightly sweet, nutlike flavor	Noodle dishes, salad dressings, coleslaw, breads, and rolls

Herb/Spice	Characteristics	Common Uses
Rosemary	Narrow needlelike leaves with a fragrant evergreen scent	Lamb, pork, poultry, potato chowders, summer squash, root vegetables, marinades, and focaccia; sprigs can be used as skewers for grilled vegetables
Saffron	Mild aromatic scent with rich yellow-orange hue	Curries, Spanish and Middle Eastern rice and grain dishes, and Milanese risotto
Sage	Pale green to silvery leaves with earthy, musky flavor	Poultry stuffing, stewed white beans, vegetables, legumes, pasta sauces, and Italian soups; dried sage has a stronger presence than fresh
Savory	Summer savory is mild and grassy; winter savory is spicier	Legume dishes (especially lima beans and lentils), poultry and vegetable entrées
Sesame seeds	Mild, sweet, nutty flavor	Breads, Middle Eastern spreads like hummus, casseroles, salads, cakes; toasting the seeds releases their rich, nutlike flavor
Star anise	Star-shaped brown pod containing eight shiny seeds; similar in flavor to anise seeds but more bitter	Chinese dishes, teas, and baked goods; an ingredient in Chinese five-spice powder
Szechuan pepper	Similar in size to black peppercorns with a mildly hot, pungent flavor	Chinese dishes
Tarragon	Long feathery green leaves with a subtle anise flavor	Sautéed chicken, pasta salads, potato salads, seafood entrées, egg dishes, mustard sauces, and vinaigrettes; used in herbes de Provence and fines herbes
Thyme	Tiny greenish-gray petals with a pungent earthy flavor and strong scent	Potato and fish chowders, squash bisque, vinaigrettes, marinades, roasted vegetables, mushrooms, potatoes, bean dishes, poultry, and wild rice; used in bouquets garnis; varieties include common thyme, French thyme, English thyme, and lemon thyme
Turmeric	Mildly pungent flavor with yellow-orange hue; substitute for saffron for its color	Gives mustard pastes, curries, and rice dishes a brilliant yellow glow
Vanilla bean	Sweet, mellow, aromatic flavor	Cakes, cookies, muffins, fruit desserts, and poached pears

■ *Go for lite bread, rolls, or English muffins in place of bagels,* and spread with fruit jams, fruit butters, or a hummus spread mixed with chopped herbs instead of butter, margarine, or full-fat cream cheese.

■ *For fat-free salad dressings,* use canned fat-free broths, vegetable juices, and fruit juices as a base.

■ *Rub dry spice seasonings* into lean meats, chicken, or fish before broiling or grilling.

■ *Instead of frying fish,* bake or grill fillets in foil packages along with fresh herbs and thinly sliced vegetables of your choice.

■ *Use veggie Canadian bacon, veggie ham, or veggie bacon strips* instead of regular bacon. For smoky flavor with no fat, try chipotle chile peppers (smoked jalapeño chile peppers). These will also add fiery heat. For smoky flavor with no heat, try a drop or two of liquid smoke seasoning (available in the spice or condiment aisle of most supermarkets).

■ *To create a crisp crust* on fish or fowl cutlets without frying, dredge the cutlets alternately in flour, beaten egg white, and seasoned bread crumbs. Coat both sides with nonstick spray, and bake in a preheated pan.

■ *Meat, poultry, and fish recipes* should have no more than 1 tablespoon of added oil. If the recipe calls for more, ask yourself why. Is the oil used to fry? You can brown foods in a nonstick skillet with nonstick spray instead. Is the oil part of a sauce or dressing? If so, consider replacing it with broth, vegetable juice, soy-based or reduced-fat sour cream, or fat-free evaporated milk, depending on what style of sauce it is.

The Low-Calorie Toolbox

Take a look around your kitchen. Chances are you have a lot of the equipment that will make the recipes in this book—and your own Picture-Perfect Weight-Loss cooking—not just easier but a joy to do. If there are some items you don't yet own, put them on your wish list and gradually buy them—but none is essential to a new way of cooking or a new way of eating.

Blender. This practical appliance is indispensable for making creamy smooth purees, soups, and sauces.

Broiling pan. This pan with a rack is great for broiling or roasting pieces of poultry and meat. Just place the food on the rack and allow the fat to drip into the pan for easy removal.

Egg separator. This little gadget neatly separates the whites from the cholesterol-laden yolks.

Fat skimmer. To remove the fat that rises to the top of homemade stock, soup, or stew, use a flat mesh skimmer. Or pour the liquid into a special measuring cup—it's got a spout that reaches to the bottom so you can easily pour off the fat-free portion of the liquid. Alternatively, use a stock made from onion or vegetables—and you won't need a skimmer at all.

Food processor. This handy device can do just about everything a blender can do and more. It cuts, chops, grates, and juliennes vegetables within seconds. Slice onions, make coleslaw, and toss off a perfect low-calorie sauce for poached salmon in seconds.

Hot-air corn popper. Popcorn is a great snack for Picture-Perfect Weight Loss, as readers of my earlier books well know. And today's air poppers allow you to make this crunchy treat without using any oil. To season air-popped corn, squirt it with a shot of no-stick spray, then sprinkle with an herb seasoning or butter-flavored granules.

Microwave oven. This is the ultimate convenience for today's busy health-conscious cook. Foods cook quickly without the need for added fat.

Nonstick saucepans, skillets, and baking pans. Absolutely basic. Cookware with a good-quality, nonstick coating lets you fry, sauté, and bake with minimal oil. To avoid scratching the coating, use only plastic or wooden utensils.

Paper muffin cups. Look, Ma: No grease in the muffin pan!

Skewers. These are great for grilling or broiling chunks of vegetables, fruits, lean meats, and poultry. Just thread the pieces onto the skewers and brush with a juice marinade or your own barbecue sauce during cooking.

(continued on page 36)

Geoffrey Holder

*D*ancer, choreographer, costume designer, set designer, writer, painter whose work can be found in museums and private collections worldwide: Geoffrey Holder is a man so multitalented in the arts that no single field can satisfy his creative energy. A native of Trinidad, Holder is at home everywhere—and everywhere, he is renowned as a gourmet.

GH: Cooking is like painting: It's a matter of throwing things together and making it work. I began to learn how to cook because I wanted to entertain. Being in the arts and the theater, you have to meet many people. In the '70s, I went to live in Paris and stayed in the house of Jacques Sigurd, a movie writer, who introduced me to the city, as did Jeanette Spaniet. I lived around the corner from a marvelous street market. There were sumptuous fresh vegetables, and the fish smelled like the ocean. To me, that's when fish smells wonderful. It is also in Paris that I learned about herbs.

Tell me about a disaster you've had in the kitchen.

GH: None.

Did you ever have a panic in the kitchen?

GH: Never, never, never, never. I am the king of improvisation. A good cook must always improvise.

Did you ever have a fight with Carmen in the kitchen? (Holder is married to the great dancer-choreographer Carmen de Lavallade.)

GH: Our kitchen is small and I take up space and Carmen needs space. It's a matter of who's in the kitchen and who's doing what. We can dance on the same stage, but to be in the same kitchen at the same time, the rhythm goes off.

Do you have an interesting story about an experience in the kitchen?

GH: In Paris, Jacques [Sigurd] threw a party for me. He invited important people from the galleries and from the movies. One of the friends brought along Marlene Dietrich. I had met her once a long time ago doing *House of Flowers* and found her to be a charming woman. She always took care to order coffee and doughnuts for all the young dancers, even going out into the rain to buy them food. To me, that is a star; that is a grand lady. Once backstage, when I tore my trousers, I went downstairs to have them fixed, and who was sewing buttons with the wardrobe ladies? Dietrich. So the night of the party, someone happened to say: "Oh my God, I love you, you're the greatest actress. I saw you in *Blue Angel*." And Dietrich turned back to the man and said, "I hate the movie." Another one said, "Oh, Miss Dietrich, I would love you to be on my television program." She said, "Call my agent." This is very typical behavior in

France. You don't approach a star like that; you allow them their privacy. The evening went on. I served the food and all of a sudden, we missed Dietrich. As I entered the kitchen I found her . . . doing the dishes. The beautiful thing about this is that she upstaged everyone with her grace.

If there were one food you couldn't resist under any circumstance, what would it be?

GH: Oh, I'm not fussy.

What is the most unusual combination of foods that you eat?

GH: There are no unusual combinations. People only *think* of them as unusual.

Some people find chicken and peanut butter unusual.

GH: When you're creative, you can put unusual combinations together. It depends on the culture.

What is your favorite ethnic food?

GH: French.

When you go to the grocery store, do you check labels?

GH: No, I don't buy labels, like I don't buy labels in clothes. I am an eye man—when I see it, I know what I want.

What is your favorite smell in the kitchen?

GH: Cinnamon when it's cooked, or vanilla that comes from baking.

What's your favorite seasoning?

GH: Thyme.

As a child, what was your least favorite food?

GH: Eggs, raw eggs.

What's your least favorite food now?

GH: Still eggs.

What's your favorite food?

GH: Fish.

If you were on a desert island, which five food items would you have?

GH: I always travel with rice, thyme, garlic, salt, and hot sauce.

Which food items do you keep in your refrigerator on a regular basis?

GH: Just herbs.

Whom would you most like to have dinner with, living or dead?

GH: Jean Cocteau. Living I can't say, because I know almost everybody.

An actor?

GH: No.

A dancer?

GH: No.

A painter?

GH: No.

Anyone?

GH: Bill Clinton, my favorite president.

Geoffrey, thank you.

GH: Thank you, darling.

Slow cooker. This is a wonderful appliance for saving time in the kitchen as well as for preparing healthy meals. A slow cooker lets lean meats simmer slowly in their own juices so they become tender. It's also great for preparing long-cooking soups, stews, and legumes.

Steamer. Whether you choose a simple stainless-steel basket, an elaborate multitiered oriental bamboo version, or a self-contained electric model, a steamer cooks vegetables to crisp-tender perfection. You can also use it to cook fish, seafood, and boneless poultry cutlets.

Stovetop grill. Make grilling an indoor, year-round event with one of the many stovetop grill pans available. Electric indoor grills are another great option.

Cook It the Low-Calorie Way

Now you're ready for the next step: cooking techniques for keeping calories to a minimum.

Nonstick cooking pans are the gold standard in today's kitchens. Thanks to this essential item in the Picture-Perfect Weight-Loss kitchen toolbox, just a whisper of cooking spray lets you brown foods with virtually no fat. Look for flavored sprays like garlic or Cajun to expand flavors. Or, make your own sprays by pouring such flavorful oils as olive or toasted sesame into clean plastic spray bottles. And to really bring out the flavor of garlic, onion, and other aromatics, simmer them in a bit of chicken or vegetable broth in a nonstick skillet.

Baking and roasting. These two methods are great for meats, poultry, fish, and such vegetables as squash and potatoes. Cover the food for part of the cooking time to keep it moist. Use a rack for meats and poultry so that they don't sit in pan drippings and soak them up.

Braising. Also known as stewing, braising refers to cooking food in liquid. It's one of the best methods for tenderizing lean cuts of meat and poultry. An advantage to braising is that the fat seeps into the cooking liquid so you can easily skim it off.

Broiling and grilling. These are excellent alternatives to frying. You cook the food directly under or over a heat source and on a rack to allow the fat to drain away. If you're broiling or grilling a fish or soy product, of course, there's no need to drain away fat content because it's the good kind of fat.

Microwaving. Quick and convenient, microwaving is one of the best cooking methods for preserving the nutrients while still keeping the food moist and flavorful. It's ideal for preparing extra-lean foods like fish fillets and boneless white-meat poultry—without adding calories or even a speck of fat.

Oven frying. Cooking in this way lets you mimic the texture of fried food without getting the excess fat and calories frying would impart. All you need to do is dip the food—skinless chicken breasts or fish fillets, for example—into beaten egg whites, then roll it in fine bread crumbs before baking.

Poaching. Generally used with quick-cooking items like fish or boned poultry, poaching is similar to braising.

Sautéing and stir-frying. These are fine alternatives to cooking in butter or oil. Use a nonstick skillet or wok along with cooking spray or a small amount of water, broth, or citrus juice. If you feel the need for a little oil, pour some into the pan, then wipe it out with a paper towel to leave only a thin coat.

Steaming. Steaming lets you cook vegetables, seafood, and some poultry cuts without losing nutrients and without adding calories.

And here are some tips for a fresh approach to some old favorites.

- *Prevent pasta from sticking* without adding oil to the water. Simply save a few tablespoons of the cooking water before draining the pasta. Toss the pasta with the reserved water before adding the sauce and it won't clump.

- *Poultry will stay moister* if it's cooked with the skin on. Remove and discard the skin before serving for a lower-calorie dish. (If you use a soy-based poultry product, this isn't an issue.)

Got the picture? You're ready to start cooking the Picture-Perfect Weight-Loss way.

BREAKFASTS

Setting the Tone for Picture-Perfect Weight Loss Every Morning

You know the line about breakfast being "the most important meal of the day"? My Picture-Perfect Weight-Loss patients would agree. For them, breakfast is more than a meal. It's the place where they set the tone for a day of healthful, low-calorie eating . . . a chance each morning to recommit themselves to the principles of Picture-Perfect Weight Loss and to the kinds of eating I've recommended in my Picture-Perfect Weight-Loss Food Pyramid and Anytime List.

And when it comes to setting the tone and making a commitment, no one is more in charge than the cook. You're the one choosing the ingredients, determining cooking style, experimenting with taste enhancements. You have the power to send the whole family off on a low-calorie path to losing weight and keeping it off.

I have two suggestions that will help you do all this.

First, try to include fruits or vegetables in your breakfast. A sure path to Picture-Perfect Weight Loss—and to overall health and fitness—is to make fruits and vegetables the mainstay of your eating. Breakfast is the perfect place to start, which is why every one of the recipes that follow includes either fruit or vegetables. It's a great way to give a boost to your nutrition for the day, and it's especially great when you can do so as imaginatively and deliciously as in these recipes.

Second, think soy. We all know soy is good for us, but as a vegetable protein with a minimal calorie count, it's particularly good for people trying to lose weight or maintain weight loss. And with people everywhere beginning to catch on to soy's benefits—I'll wager it's the next big health trend—food manufacturers are responding with an ever-widening range of products. Soy-based breakfast products happen to be particularly good, and these recipes make use of that fact.

Ready to head for the kitchen? It's a new morning—time for a fresh start and a delicious breakfast.

Yukon Gold Potato Pancakes with Sausage

Prep time: 20 minutes ■ Cook time: 40 minutes

Topping

8 ounces fat-free sour cream

2 tablespoons minced fresh chives or scallions

   Hot-pepper sauce, to taste (optional)

Pancakes and Sausage

1 package veggie breakfast sausage (8 links)

1 pound Yukon gold or russet potatoes, unpeeled

1 pound sweet potatoes, peeled

1 medium yellow onion

4 large egg whites, lightly beaten, or ½ cup liquid egg substitute

1 teaspoon salt

¼ teaspoon freshly ground black pepper

To make the topping: In a small bowl, combine the sour cream, chives or scallions, and hot-pepper sauce (if using). Chill until ready to serve.

To make the pancakes and sausage: Cook the sausage according to package directions.

Meanwhile, using a grater or food processor, coarsely grate the potatoes, sweet potatoes, and onion. Place in a sieve and thoroughly squeeze all the water over a medium bowl. The potato starch will settle to the bottom of the bowl. Reserve the starch after you have poured off the water. Mix the drained potatoes and onion with the reserved potato starch. Stir in the egg whites, salt, and pepper.

Heat a large nonstick skillet coated with cooking spray over medium heat. For each pancake, spoon about ½ cup of the potato mixture into the pan and flatten with a spatula. Cook for 5 minutes per side, or until golden brown. Keep warm. Repeat with the remaining batter to make 8 pancakes.

Serve the pancakes with the sausage and topping.

Makes 4 servings
Per serving: 380 calories, 4 g fat

Medal-Winning Breakfast

Half a muffin looks like a virtuous, low-calorie breakfast, especially next to this pancake meal fit for a king. But the facts tell a different story. The anemic-looking half-muffin has the same calorie count as the robust serving of pancakes with sausage but carries an even higher fat content. The pancakes are not only more filling—and more satisfying to the tastebuds—but they also offer the health benefits of various vegetables and an ample amount of soy in the veggie sausage. There's no contest between these two breakfasts, so go for the gold!

½ 8-ounce sugar-free muffin
380 calories **9** grams fat

1 serving Yukon Gold Potato Pancakes with Sausage
380 calories 4 grams fat

PUMPKIN PANCAKES WITH PEAR SYRUP

QUICK

Prep time: 10 minutes ■ *Cook time: 20 minutes*

Apples substitute nicely for the pears in the flavorful pancake topper.

Pear Syrup

2 hard ripe pears, cored and cut into
    ½" slices

1 tablespoon minced crystallized
    ginger

½ cup lite maple syrup

Pancakes

1½ cups whole grain pastry flour

2 tablespoons packed brown sugar

1 tablespoon baking powder

2 teaspoons pumpkin pie spice

½ teaspoon salt

½ teaspoon baking soda

1 cup fat-free milk or plain soy milk

1 cup canned pumpkin

½ cup liquid egg substitute

To make the pear syrup: Heat a medium skillet coated with cooking spray over medium heat. Add the pears and ginger and cook, stirring occasionally, for 5 minutes, or until lightly browned and tender. Add the syrup and cook for 1 minute. Keep warm.

To make the pancakes: In a large bowl, combine the flour, brown sugar, baking powder, pumpkin pie spice, salt, and baking soda. In a medium bowl, combine the milk, pumpkin, and egg substitute. Add to the flour mixture, stirring until combined.

Heat a nonstick griddle or large skillet coated with cooking spray over medium heat. Pour the batter by ¼ cupfuls to make 4" pancakes. Cook for 2 minutes, or until the tops of the pancakes look dry and some bubbles form on the surface. Turn the pancakes over and cook for 2 minutes longer, or until browned. Keep warm. Repeat with the remaining batter to make 12 pancakes.

Serve the pancakes with the syrup.

Makes 6 servings
Per serving: 210 calories, 2 g fat

Potatoes: Giving Breakfast a Nutritional Bang

While breakfasting on fruit is a common way to begin the day, adding vegetables to your breakfast is also a great way to give yourself a head start on nutrition. Among vegetables, the potato is one of the great nutrition packages, rich in vitamins and minerals and offering loads of antioxidant power to fight disease and the effects of aging.

An excellent source of potassium, potatoes help boost cardiovascular health by reducing the risk of high blood pressure and stroke. They also contribute to bone strength by helping the kidneys retain calcium. Even a medium-size potato—say, 6 ounces—contains 21 percent of the Daily Value for potassium.

It also contains 22 milligrams of vitamin C—fully 37 percent of the Daily Value. Vitamin C is a powerful antioxidant, so it neutralizes the effects of the so-called free radicals that are by-products of cell metabolism. These free radicals roam through your body's cells, disrupting molecular structure and causing the kind of damage that contributes to many of the problems of aging.

So start your day with a potato—and stay young, strong, and healthy.

Jesse Ziff Cool

Flea St. Café and jZcool Eating and Catering Company, Menlo Park, California; and Cool Café, Stanford University

For nearly 30 years, Jesse Ziff Cool has been dazzling customers with innovative culinary creations prepared from fresh, local organic ingredients. All of her restaurants use as many organic products as possible—about 85 percent. Cool grew up in a loving family that respected the old traditional ways of growing, gathering, and preparing foods, and she passed down these values to her own children and restaurant clients. As down-to-earth as she is talented, Chef Cool embodies the organic philosophy and lifestyle. Her refreshing Raspberry Millet Pancakes are brimming with healthy helpings of grain and fruit.

RASPBERRY MILLET PANCAKES

⅓ cup millet

1 cup water

2 eggs

1½ cups buttermilk

¼ cup pure maple syrup

2 tablespoons vegetable oil

1 teaspoon vanilla extract

1½ cups unbleached whole grain pastry flour

1½ teaspoons baking soda

1 teaspoon ground cinnamon

½ teaspoon salt

1 pint raspberries

1 cup vanilla yogurt

Place the millet in a medium saucepan over medium heat. Cook, shaking the skillet often, for 3 minutes, or until lightly browned and toasted. Add the water and bring to a boil over high heat. Reduce the heat to low, cover, and simmer for 15 minutes, or until the liquid is absorbed. Remove from the heat, but do not remove the cover, and let stand for 15 minutes. Cool to room temperature.

Meanwhile, in a medium bowl, combine the eggs, buttermilk, maple syrup, oil, and vanilla extract.

In a large bowl, combine the flour, baking soda, cinnamon, and salt. Form a well in the center of the flour mixture and stir in the buttermilk mixture just until blended. Add the millet, stirring to blend.

Lightly oil a griddle or large skillet and heat over medium-high heat. Drop the batter by ¼ cups onto the griddle or skillet. When the uncooked side begins to bubble, flip and cook on the other side, about 4 minutes.

To serve, place 2 pancakes on a plate. Top with the raspberries and yogurt.

Makes 8 servings
Per serving: 258 calories, 7 g fat

VEGETABLE TART WITH POTATO CRUST

Prep time: 20 minutes ■ Cook time: 55 minutes

Crust

- 1 pound frozen hash brown potatoes, thawed
- 3 scallions, chopped
- ½ cup liquid egg substitute
- 1 teaspoon finely chopped fresh thyme
- ¼ teaspoon salt

Filling

- 1 small zucchini, chopped
- 1 clove garlic, minced
- 2 slices soy Canadian bacon or veggie bacon strips, chopped
- 2 cups packed spinach leaves, coarsely chopped
- 1 small tomato, cored and chopped
- ¼ teaspoon salt
- ¼ teaspoon freshly ground black pepper
- ¾ cup liquid egg substitute
- ¼ cup (1 ounce) shredded fat-free Cheddar cheese or soy alternative

To make the crust: Preheat the oven to 350°F. Coat a 9" pie plate or tart pan with removable bottom with cooking spray.

In a medium bowl, combine the potatoes, scallions, egg substitute, thyme, and salt. Press the mixture onto the bottom and up the side of the prepared pan. Bake for 30 minutes, or until firm to the touch. Cool on a rack.

To make the filling: Meanwhile, heat a medium nonstick skillet coated with cooking spray over medium heat. Add the zucchini and garlic and cook, stirring, for 2 minutes, or until tender. Add the Canadian bacon, spinach, tomato, salt, and pepper and cook, stirring frequently, for 5 minutes, or until the spinach is wilted and the liquid has evaporated. Remove from the heat and cool. Stir in the egg substitute.

Pour the vegetable mixture into the crust. Sprinkle with the cheese. Bake for 25 minutes, or until the filling is set and the crust is golden brown.

Makes 6 servings
Per serving: 140 calories, 2 g fat

Tart for a Start

It would take more than three servings of tart to equal the calorie count of this single cheese omelet. But calories are only part of the story. The omelet, made with two eggs and Cheddar cheese and fried in butter, has five times more fat than the tart. What's more, the omelet contains the "bad" saturated fats that raise levels of LDL cholesterol and may increase the risk of heart disease. Start your day instead with nutrient-rich, fiber-filled vegetables in a tasty tart.

1 cheese omelet
490 calories **38** grams fat

**3½ servings Vegetable Tart
with Potato Crust**
490 calories **7** grams fat

Montel Williams

Emmy Award winner Montel Williams hosts the daily, hour-long *Montel Williams Show*. He has also established the Montel Williams MS Foundation, aimed at furthering scientific understanding of the disease with which he has been diagnosed. A firm believer that success is measured by what you give back to others, Williams works actively with such charitable organizations as the AFS (American Field Service) Edge program, which offers scholarships for disadvantaged youth to study abroad, the Make-A-Wish Foundation, the Humane Society of the United States, the Joey DiPaolo AIDS Foundation, and the Carol M. Baldwin Breast Cancer Research Fund.

What's the one food you can't resist under any circumstances?

MW: I can resist almost any food if I have to, but I definitely have a weakness for ice cream. I only allow myself that treat very occasionally.

What's your comfort food of choice in times of distress—and why that food?

MW: Having grown up in Baltimore, Maryland, I usually turn to seafood—crab in particular.

What's the most unusual food combination you eat?

MW: Grilled chicken and scrambled eggs.

What is your favorite ethnic food—and why?

MW: I love sushi and eat it often. It's healthy and delicious. But truthfully, I would have to say I really love collard greens.

Do you find it pleasant or unpleasant to shop in a supermarket? Do you check food labels when you shop?

MW: Shopping is pleasant for me. I always make sure not to go to the store hungry, and yes, I am a committed label checker.

Do you like to cook? What do you like about it?

MW: I love to cook. I find it very relaxing. Besides, it's something I've done my whole life.

What does food mean to you? Does it make you feel good?

MW: Food helps me to maintain optimum health—and of course, it makes me feel great.

Do you relate food and your childhood in any way?

MW: Well, when I was 15 years old, I lied about my age and experience to the manager of a local restaurant in Baltimore called The Ship's Café, and I got hired as an assistant to the main chef. After about 2 days, it was pretty obvious that I couldn't cook at the level I had claimed. I attempted to cook seafood Newburg, which is typically baked, in a frying pan. Still, the main chef took me under his wing, and I went on to work for him the entire summer. A week after I left to go back to school, the restaurant burned down. I swear I had nothing to do with it.

What is your favorite kitchen smell?

MW: The smell of food frying in the kitchen is irresistible to me. Fortunately—or unfortunately—I don't indulge in fried foods too often.

What is your favorite seasoning?

MW: Emeril's Cajun or hot spices. I really love hot, spicy food.

As a child, what was your least favorite food?

MW: Peas and Brussels sprouts.

And your least favorite food today?

MW: Peas and Brussels sprouts. Some things never change!

What is your favorite food?

MW: Lean protein.

If you were on a desert island, which five food items would you have?

MW: Chicken, fish, brown rice, collard greens, and yams.

Which food items are regularly in your refrigerator?

MW: Protein.

Whom would you most like to have dinner with?

MW: My children.

ROASTED VEGETABLE QUICHE

Prep time: 25 minutes ■ Cook time: 30 minutes

2   teaspoons extra-virgin olive oil

¾ cup (2 ounces) finely chopped
      shiitake mushrooms

1   medium onion, chopped

1   large parsnip, chopped

1   orange bell pepper, chopped

2   large cloves garlic, minced

1   medium carrot, grated

2   cups finely chopped spinach leaves

1   teaspoon salt

¾ teaspoon ground sage

¼ teaspoon freshly ground black
      pepper

1¼ cups old-fashioned oats, finely
      ground in a blender or food
      processor

3   large egg whites, lightly beaten

Preheat the oven to 425°F. Coat a 9" quiche pan or pie pan with cooking spray.

Heat the oil in a large skillet over medium-high heat. Add the mushrooms, onion, parsnip, and bell pepper and cook, stirring, for 3 minutes. Stir in the garlic, carrot, and spinach and cook for 1 minute. Add the salt, sage, black pepper, oats, and egg whites and stir to combine.

Evenly spread the vegetable mixture in the prepared pan. Bake for 25 minutes, or until browned. Slice into 4 wedges and serve.

Makes 4 servings
Per serving: 200 calories, 4 g fat

Bagel Buster

Add it up: A third of a buttered bagel isn't very satisfying, packs a wallop in calories and fat content, and has no redeeming health benefit. Instead of the bagel's refined-carbohydrate density, go for this light and appetizing Roasted Vegetable Quiche. It's colorful and highly satisfying. And one unusual ingredient—oats—gives the quiche substance and a big nutritional plus with healthful whole grain, fiber, and B vitamins.

⅓ 5-ounce buttered bagel
200 calories **11** grams fat

1 serving Roasted
Vegetable Quiche
200 calories **4** grams fat

SMOKED SALMON HASH

Prep time: 20 minutes ▪ Cook time: 25 minutes

1   pound red-skinned potatoes, finely chopped

1   tablespoon olive oil

5   ribs celery, finely chopped

4   small red, yellow, and/or orange bell peppers, finely chopped

3   scallions, sliced

1½ tablespoons minced fresh dill

1   teaspoon grated lemon peel

½   teaspoon salt

¼   teaspoon freshly ground black pepper

1   plum tomato, finely chopped

¼   pound sliced smoked salmon, diced

Place a steamer basket in a large saucepan with ½" of water. Place the potatoes in the steamer and bring to a boil over high heat. Reduce the heat to medium, cover, and cook for 15 minutes, or until the potatoes are very tender. Drain well.

Heat the oil in a large nonstick skillet over medium heat. Add the celery, bell peppers, and scallions and cook, stirring, for 3 minutes. Add the potatoes, dill, lemon peel, salt, and black pepper. Increase the heat to medium-high and cook, stirring occasionally, for 5 minutes, or until the potatoes begin to brown. Add the tomato and cook for 2 minutes. Stir in the salmon. Press the mixture with the back of a spatula to mash the potatoes slightly before serving.

Makes 4 servings
Per serving: 180 calories, 5 g fat

Hashing Out a Difference

Like hash? Get two servings of delicious Smoked Salmon Hash for less than the calorie price of one plate of corned beef hash—and replace 23 grams of the saturated fat in corned beef with 10 grams of the good fat in the salmon. In fact, anytime you can replace a meat dish with a fish version, you save in calories and fat content and gain a definite bonus of nutritional benefits.

1 serving (6 ounces) corned beef hash
650 calories **23** grams fat

2 servings
Smoked Salmon Hash
360 calories **10** grams fat

Baked Apples

Prep time: 10 minutes ■ Cook time: 45 minutes

Not just for dessert, these warm, wholesome apples are a great way to start the day.

4 large apples, such as Granny Smith or Red Delicious

¼ cup wheat germ

¼ cup whole natural almonds, chopped

3 tablespoons golden raisins

1 cup + 1 tablespoon lite pancake syrup

Preheat the oven to 375°F.

Core each apple, leaving ½" of the bottom intact. Peel each apple one-third of the way down. Using a paring knife, slightly enlarge the opening of each apple by removing a V-shaped piece of apple. Dice the V-shaped pieces.

In a large bowl, combine the diced apple, wheat germ, almonds, raisins, and syrup.

Place the apples in an 8" × 8" baking pan. Spoon the filling into the center of each apple. Add ½ cup water to the baking pan. Bake for 45 to 55 minutes, or until tender.

Makes 4 servings
Per serving: 224 calories, 5 g fat

All About Almonds

The almonds that help make this Baked Apples recipe so special are kernels of the fruit of the almond tree. Native to Asia, almond trees are cultivated in such "Mediterranean"-style climates as California, Australia, South Africa, and—not surprisingly—all around the Mediterranean. The almonds used in this recipe, and indeed in all cooking, are delicately flavored sweet almonds, available universally. Bitter almonds are toxic until and unless heated—the raw nuts contain lethal prussic acid—and their sale is illegal in the United States. Processed bitter almonds, however, are used to flavor extracts, liqueurs, and certain syrups.

BREAKFAST RICE PUDDING

Prep time: 10 minutes ■ Cook time: 20 minutes

This quick pudding is a terrific way to use leftover brown rice. The plums, peach, and blueberries along with the brown rice make this dish a great source of fiber.

3   cups vanilla soy milk

⅓   cup sugar

3   tablespoons cornstarch

¼   teaspoon salt

2   cups cooked brown rice

¼   teaspoon ground cinnamon

2   small plums, pitted and chopped

1   small peach or nectarine, pitted
      and chopped

½   cup blueberries

4   fresh mint sprigs

In a medium saucepan, bring the milk, sugar, cornstarch, and salt to a boil over medium heat. Reduce the heat to low. Add the rice, cover, and simmer, stirring occasionally, for 15 to 20 minutes, or until thickened.

Stir in the cinnamon. Remove from the heat, cover with plastic wrap, and set aside to cool slightly.

In a large bowl, combine the plums, peach or nectarine, and blueberries.

Alternately layer the pudding and fruit mixture in 4 parfait glasses. Repeat layering to use all the pudding and fruit. Garnish with the mint.

Makes 4 servings
Per serving: 297 calories, 5 g fat

The Record on Rice

Rice is the staple food for half of the world's population—primarily the Asian half—and it has been cultivated since at least 5000 B.C. In fact, archaeologists digging in China have uncovered portions of rice estimated at some 8,000 years old, well-preserved in sealed pots buried in dry earth. Today, there are more than 7,000 varieties of rice, grown either in flooded fields or on hills in almost any tropical or subtropical terrain.

Rice is classified by its grain length—long, medium, or short. Long-grain rice includes the aromatic basmati rice of eastern India—light, dry grains that separate easily when cooked. Short-grain rice, also called pearl rice or glutinous rice, becomes moist and viscous when cooked and is preferred by chopstick users and for risottos.

Medium-grain rice splits the difference between long and short: Though fairly fluffy right after being cooked, it begins to clump once it starts to cool.

Rice is also divided into brown and white. Brown rice is the entire grain with only the inedible outer husk removed. It's highly nutritious, is filled with minerals and B-complex vitamins, and packs a real fiber wallop; it also has a distinctive nutlike flavor and chewy texture. In white rice, the husk, bran, and germ of the grain have been removed; if the white rice is converted, the unhulled grain has been soaked, pressure-steamed, and dried before milling, thus gelatinizing the starch in the grain and infusing some of the bran and germ nutrients into the kernel.

APPETIZERS

A Matter of a Taste

recipes

There is something very civilized about appetizers. Whether they are the tidbits served at a cocktail party or the prelude to a meal, they are meant to be "just a taste"—something, as the name suggests, to stimulate the appetite, get the juices flowing, and maybe get the conversation going as well. They're there to please, excite, and entertain you—the opening act that warms you up for the main attraction.

But that doesn't mean that appetizers can't be part of a program of Picture-Perfect Weight Loss. On the contrary. As the recipes in this chapter amply demonstrate, when you're in charge of preparing the appetizers, you can create hors d'oeuvres that are not just exotic and delicious but also low in calories and high in health benefits. The guests at your cocktail bash or dinner party will thank you for both sets of attributes. So will your family. And of course, so will your waistline.

The appetizers here offer a range of tastes and textures—spicy and cool, sweet and tart, soft, chewy, and crunchy. Here are wraps to nibble at and bites to swallow. Things to dip and things to spear. Meat, fish, vegetables, and legumes.

For the weight-conscious, I believe that filling up on appetizers, especially appetizers like these, is a great idea. For while hors d'oeuvres stimulate the appetite, they also smooth over its edge. Result? You don't arrive starved at the meal that follows. It's why some politicians actually sit down and eat before they start an evening of fund-raising parties and dinners. The snack gives them control over their appetite as the evening wears on; it helps put them in charge of what they eat—and of course, politicians thrive on being in charge. Take a tip from their book and take a bite of the appetizers that follow. Bon appétit!

ROASTED RED PEPPER AND BASIL DIP

Prep time: 2 hours ■ *Cook time: 15 minutes* ■ *Chill time: 2 hours*

19 ounces silken tofu

6 large cloves garlic, unpeeled

1 jar (12 ounces) roasted red peppers, drained and patted very dry

½ cup packed fresh basil leaves

3 tablespoons balsamic vinegar

½ teaspoon salt

¼ teaspoon freshly ground black pepper

Drain the tofu and place between double layers of paper towel in a colander over a bowl. Place a small plate on the tofu and then place a 1-pound can on the plate. Refrigerate the tofu for 2 hours.

Meanwhile, in a small nonstick skillet over medium heat, cook the garlic, turning the cloves occasionally, for 12 minutes, or until dark golden brown on most sides and softened. Remove from the heat, let cool, then peel.

In a blender or food processor, combine the tofu, garlic, roasted red peppers, basil, vinegar, salt, and black pepper. Process until smooth. Refrigerate the dip until ready to serve.

Makes 2 cups
Per 2 tablespoons: 30 calories, 1 g fat

Triple Dipping

For weight loss and for health, there's nothing better than vegetables. And dips are a great way to add interest and variety to your vegetable intake. But check out the difference in calorie count and fat content between the cheese dip and one of these flavorful dips: For the same cost in calories and far less fat, you could enjoy three times as much of the pepper and basil dip or the curried yogurt dip—and take in more of what's good for you.

1 serving (2 tablespoons) cheese dip
90 calories **8** grams fat

1 serving (2 tablespoons)
**Roasted Red Pepper
and Basil Dip**
30 calories **1** gram fat

OR

1 serving (2 tablespoons)
Curried Yogurt Dip
(see page 58)
30 calories **1** gram fat

Photo on page 57

CURRIED YOGURT DIP

QUICK

Prep time: 5 minutes

2 cups low-fat plain yogurt or soy
    alternative

1 jar (9 ounces) mango chutney

1½ teaspoons curry powder

¼ teaspoon salt

⅛ teaspoon ground red pepper

In a large serving bowl, combine the yogurt, chutney, curry powder, salt, and pepper until well-blended. Refrigerate the dip until ready to serve.

Makes 2¾ cups
Per 2 tablespoons: 30 calories, 1 g fat

Taste of India

Curry is not a specific spice but rather a blend of many spices. The word was coined during the time of British colonial rule in India, originally to refer to a hot and spicy soup containing a mix of ingredients. Today, any dish that blends traditional Indian spices qualifies as a curry, although the basic ingredients typically include turmeric, cumin, coriander, and cayenne pepper. Curries may also include chiles, cloves, cinnamon, fenugreek, nutmeg, ginger, mace, mustard seed, fennel, poppy seed, allspice, anise, bay leaves, and black or white pepper. Ground nuts, cream, and yogurt are also commonly mixed in with curry.

MUSHROOM AND SUN-DRIED TOMATO PHYLLO TRIANGLES

Prep time: 25 minutes ■ Cook time: 30 minutes

The mushroom mixture can be made up to 1 day in advance and refrigerated until you're ready to use it.

1 tablespoon olive oil

12 ounces mushrooms, chopped

1 large shallot, minced

½ teaspoon salt

¼ teaspoon freshly ground black pepper

3 cloves garlic, minced

¼ cup dry-packed sun-dried tomatoes

¼ cup (2 ounces) goat cheese, crumbled

3 tablespoons chopped fresh oregano or 1 teaspoon dried

8 sheets thawed whole wheat phyllo dough

Heat the oil in a large nonstick skillet over medium-high heat. Add the mushrooms, shallot, salt, and pepper and cook, stirring occasionally, for 12 minutes, or until all of the liquid has evaporated and the mushrooms are golden brown. Add the garlic and cook, stirring constantly, for 1 minute. Remove the mushroom mixture to a medium bowl and let cool.

Meanwhile, in a small bowl, soak the tomatoes in hot water for 10 minutes, or until soft. Drain the tomatoes, pat dry, and finely chop. Add to the mushroom mixture along with the cheese and oregano.

Preheat the oven to 375°F.

Place 1 sheet of phyllo on a work surface and cover the remaining dough with plastic wrap. Coat the phyllo sheet with cooking spray and layer 1 more sheet on top. Coat with cooking spray, then evenly cut the dough crosswise into 6 equal strips (each about 2¾" wide).

Place 1 tablespoon of the mushroom mixture at one end of each strip. Fold one corner of each strip over the filling to make a triangle. Fold the triangle over toward the strip. Continue folding each strip, then place the triangles, seam side down, on an ungreased baking sheet. Repeat to use all the remaining phyllo and filling. Coat the triangles with cooking spray.

Bake for 15 minutes, or until golden brown.

Makes 24 triangles
Per triangle: 64 calories, 2 g fat

STUFFED PORTOBELLO MUSHROOMS

Prep time: 10 minutes ■ *Marinate time: 1 hour* ■ *Cook time: 5 minutes*

6   dry-packed sun-dried tomato halves

¼   cup fat-free Italian salad dressing

¼   cup balsamic vinegar

6   medium portobello mushrooms, stems and gills removed

3   cloves garlic, finely chopped

1   large shallot, finely chopped

½   cup fresh whole wheat bread crumbs

2   tablespoons chopped fresh thyme

⅛   teaspoon freshly ground black pepper

Preheat the broiler or grill.

In a small bowl, soak the tomatoes in hot water for 10 minutes, or until soft. Drain the tomatoes, pat dry, and finely chop.

In a zip-top plastic bag, combine the salad dressing and vinegar. Add the mushrooms to the bag, seal, and marinate, turning occasionally, for 1 hour.

Remove the mushrooms from the marinade, reserving the marinade. Broil or grill the mushrooms 6" from the heat for 4 minutes, or until they just begin to brown. Do not turn off the heat.

Meanwhile, in a medium bowl, combine the tomatoes, garlic, shallot, bread crumbs, thyme, pepper, and 2 tablespoons of the reserved marinade. Add up to 2 tablespoons additional marinade if the mixture seems dry.

Evenly divide the filling among the mushrooms. Broil or grill the mushrooms until tender and the filling is heated through.

Makes 6 mushrooms
Per mushroom: 45 calories, 1 g fat

Fungal Fillers

Picture-Perfect Weight Loss applauds the technique of filling up on appetizers—especially if the appetizers are low-calorie, healthful, and tasty. These Stuffed Portobello Mushrooms fit the bill. Start with the mushrooms themselves, about as healthful a food as you can find, low in calories, with zero fat, and packed with disease-fighting phytochemicals. Then load them up with vegetables for nutrition and herbs for taste. Compared with another famous filler, the egg roll, you'd need nine of the stuffed mushrooms to come close to matching the calorie burden of even one egg roll, while the egg roll's fat content is off the charts.

1 egg roll (6 ounces)
400 calories **18** grams fat

**9 servings Stuffed
Portobello Mushrooms**
400 calories 9 grams fat

Thomas Von Essen

When Tom Von Essen joined the New York Fire Department in 1970, his first assignment was in a busy South Bronx firehouse known as La Casa Elefante. The name was a tip-off to the kind of eating that went on in the firehouse—La Casa's firefighters were so huge they looked like elephants. Von Essen spent 13 years as a firefighter on the line, then another 7 in the firefighters union, eventually winning election as president of the union. He moved from the union's leadership to being appointed Commissioner of the Fire Department of New York City. It's in that role that the nation and the world recognize him—standing at Mayor Giuliani's side each day as we were walked through the trauma and aftermath of 9/11. After 32 years in the department, Von Essen retired from the FDNY on December 31, 2001.

TVE: I've had a million meals in every firehouse throughout the city and enjoyed the cooking of so many people. I always laughed at the Irish guys trying to cook Italian meals because some of them would try to put sugar in their gravy. The fights between the firemen arguing about whose gravy or sauce was better was just a constant source of entertainment throughout all my years in the department. I think in every firehouse, you have the German guy making your basic pork and sauerkraut and potatoes; you have the Irish guy who puts together beef, potatoes, and vegetables; and then there's this creative "artiste," who'll come in and create this Italian extravaganza.

Is there a story or memory that still brings a smile to your face?

TVE: There were two guys that I absolutely adored—excellent firefighters. One was Frank Pampalone; he really cared and was so concerned about getting everything just perfect. He would cook these great Italian meals, pick the stuff up on his way in from Long Island, and go to great trouble to bring all the ingredients. The other guy was Artie Santangelo. Together they were like oil and water. They loved each other but would fight all the time. When Frank put the dishes on the table, Artie would tell him how delicious it was and then he would go in the kitchen, wash everything off—he would wash everything with soap and water because he couldn't stand garlic. He would put it all back on a dish, bring it in, sit down at the table, and tell Frank how delicious it was. It used to drive Frank crazy. At some point he would choke Artie, or at least try to choke him, because it made him so crazy that someone could take away all the flavor, all the work he had done, and tell him how delicious it was. That's one story that really meant a lot to me, and I was always in the middle of it because I enjoyed egging them both on and enjoyed the battle that would ensue between them.

So who's the culinary artist in the family?

TVE: When I got married, my wife was such a good cook, I never even ventured into the kitchen. Even today, after watching her all these years she can put something together in 5 minutes—she's just like her mother. Ten people can arrive 5 minutes before we eat and she can put something together, but I don't have any of that skill.

What is the most unusual combination of foods that you eat?

TVE: Scrambled eggs with bologna. My wife's mother used to make it.

What is your favorite ethnic food and why?

TVE: Jewish-American Chinese food. The Chinese food that the Jewish people in New York City have made popular is what I like. Nothing fancy: shrimp and garlic sauce, fried rice, steak and peppers, and the pancakes.

Is shopping in the supermarket a pleasant or unpleasant experience for you? Do you check the food labels?

TVE: I check dates. Everything should be dated the day that it's made, the day that it leaves the factory. I don't mind going to the market if I have time, which I never really do. When I go, I do check labels and prices.

What is your favorite smell in the kitchen?

TVE: I love how it smells when my wife's frying chicken and shrimp with bread crumbs.

What is your favorite seasoning?

TVE: Garlic.

As a child, what was your least favorite food?

TVE: Chicken à la king.

What is your least favorite food now?

TVE: Fennel and coriander.

What is your favorite food?

TVE: Shrimp with garlic and bread crumbs, linguine.

If you were on a desert island, which five food items would you have?

TVE: Fruit, semolina bread, vegetables, coffee, and garlic.

Which food items do you keep in your refrigerator on a regular basis?

TVE: Orange juice, peanut butter and jelly, yogurt, milk, coffee, cheese, beer, soda, water, and peeled garlic.

Whom would you most like to have dinner with?

TVE: The Pope.

CITRUS TERIYAKI SHRIMP KEBABS

Prep time: 10 minutes ■ Cook time: 5 minutes

12 large shrimp, peeled and deveined

12 chunks (1" each) fresh or canned pineapple (about 1¼ cups)

2 tablespoons bottled teriyaki baste and glaze sauce

2 tablespoons pineapple or orange juice

2 tablespoons sesame seeds, toasted

Preheat the broiler.

Thread 1 shrimp and 1 pineapple chunk on each of 12 small skewers or wooden picks. Arrange the skewers on a rack set in the broiler pan.

In a cup, combine the teriyaki sauce and juice. Generously brush the kebabs with the sauce mixture.

Broil the kebabs, turning once, for 5 minutes, or until the shrimp are opaque. Place the kebabs on a plate and sprinkle with the sesame seeds.

Makes 12 kebabs
Per kebab: 40 calories, 1 g fat

Skewer or Fry?

You do the math: You'd need just over 12 servings of the Citrus Teriyaki Shrimp Kebabs to equal the calorie count of one dish of fried shrimp. And you'd need more than twice that number of kebabs to match the fat content of the fried crustaceans. What's more, frying adds lots of unneeded calories to an otherwise low-calorie food. Skewer and broil the shrimp instead—and enjoy the exciting citrus teriyaki flavoring of this recipe.

12 servings Citrus Teriyaki Shrimp Kebabs
480 calories **12** grams fat

1 serving (7 ounces) fried shrimp
480 calories **28** grams fat

SWEET-AND-SOUR TURKEY MEATBALLS

Prep time: 20 minutes ▪ Cook time: 20 minutes

These bite-size treats will disappear quickly, so you may want to make a double batch. You can form the meatballs ahead of time and freeze them. Just thaw thoroughly before broiling so that they cook evenly.

3	slices whole wheat bread, torn into bite-size pieces (1 cup)
¼	cup fat-free milk or soy milk
1	pound ground turkey breast
3	cloves garlic, minced
¼	teaspoon salt
⅛	teaspoon freshly ground black pepper
½	cup bottled plum sauce
¼	cup pineapple juice
2	tablespoons cider vinegar
½	teaspoon Chinese five-spice powder

Preheat the broiler.

In a medium bowl, combine the bread and milk and let stand for 10 minutes. Add the turkey, garlic, salt, and pepper and stir just until blended Shape the mixture into 24 small meatballs (about 1") and arrange in an 11" × 7" baking pan.

In a medium bowl, combine the plum sauce, pineapple juice, vinegar, and five-spice powder until blended. Pour the sauce over the meatballs.

Broil the meatballs, turning once, for 20 minutes, or until browned, glazed, and no longer pink.

Toss the meatballs in the pan glaze. Serve with wooden picks.

Makes 24 meatballs
Per meatball: 50 calories, 2 g fat

BAKED CRAB WONTONS

Prep time: 20 minutes ▪ Cook time: 15 minutes

These wontons make such an impressive presentation, no one will suspect they're so easy to prepare. Fresh crabmeat works best, but you can substitute the canned variety if it's already in your cupboard.

8	ounces fresh lump crabmeat, picked over
1	scallion, chopped
¼	cup reduced-fat mayonnaise
1	tablespoon Dijon mustard
18	refrigerated wonton wrappers (3¼" square)

Preheat the oven to 375°F.

In a medium bowl, combine the crabmeat, scallion, mayonnaise, and mustard until well-blended. Spoon 1 tablespoon of the crab mixture in the center of each wonton wrapper. Brush the edges with water. Fold each corner over the filling in toward the center and pinch all edges tightly to seal. Place the wontons, seam side up, on an ungreased baking sheet and coat with cooking spray. Repeat with the remaining filling and wrappers to make 18 wontons.

Bake for 12 minutes, or until golden brown and crisp.

Makes 18 wontons
Per wonton: 40 calories, 1 g fat

MEDITERRANEAN WRAPS

Prep time: 10 minutes

These wraps make a terrific take-along lunch. Just skip the slicing step and wrap each roll individually. Your usual sandwich will seem boring by comparison!

1   cup shredded Romaine lettuce

1   medium tomato, seeded and
     chopped

½   medium cucumber, peeled,
     seeded, and chopped

2   tablespoons lemon juice

1   tablespoon chopped fresh dill

⅛   teaspoon salt

⅛   teaspoon freshly ground black
     pepper

8   ounces flavored hummus, such as
     roasted red pepper

4   whole wheat tortillas (8" diameter)

In a medium bowl, combine the lettuce, tomato, cucumber, lemon juice, dill, salt, and pepper.

Evenly spread the hummus on the tortillas, leaving a 1" border. Evenly divide the tomato mixture among the tortillas and spread over the hummus. Roll tightly to enclose the filling. Secure with 2 toothpicks and cut each into 10 slices.

Makes 40 slices
Per slice: 20 calories, 1 g fat

Mediterranean Cuisine

It has long been favored by chefs and nutritionists alike. But what, exactly, constitutes Mediterranean cuisine? At first glance, there seems to be little commonality among the sweet, saffron-flavored foods of northern Africa, the yogurts of the Middle East, the octopus salads and moussakas of Turkey and Greece, Italian sopressatas, and the seafood stews of France and Spain. But certain threads do persist through all these regions, and it's the commonality that makes the differences among them even more enriching. For one thing, vegetables play a major role everywhere in the Mediterranean— things like eggplants, mushrooms, squashes, arti-chokes, and a range of lettuces—as do legumes of every color and size. Olive oil is used instead of butter, and you rarely find complex sauces or cream dishes. For obvious reasons, fish is also central to this cuisine, but beef is not because the land cannot sustain sizable herds. Poultry, lamb, goats, sheep, and small game supplement the vegetables and seafood, and sheep and goats supply yogurt and cheeses. For flavor enhancers, Mediterranean chefs just reach down and pluck some fresh herbs from the dry soil; rosemary, basil, cilantro, parsley, mint, dill, fennel, and oregano grow in profusion and literally scent the air.

Dean Fearing

The Mansion on Turtle Creek, Dallas, Texas

Dean Fearing, executive chef of The Mansion on Turtle Creek in Dallas, Texas, is the author of two books and was named the James Beard Foundation's Best Chef in the Southwest in 1994. Chef Fearing's dishes highlight such seasonal, native Texan ingredients as homegrown peppers, chiles, jicama, cilantro, and tomatillos. His Southwest cuisine also carries the influences of the down-home barbecue of his native eastern Kentucky and his extensive travels. The Tex-Mex dishes here, Pico de Gallo and Guacamole, heady with cilantro and chiles, exemplify Chef Fearing's bold sense of flavor.

PICO DE GALLO

- 1 tomato, ¼" dice
- ½ white onion, ¼" dice
- 2 cloves garlic, minced
- 1 jalapeño, minced (with or without seeds)
- 2 tablespoons cilantro, chopped fine
- 1 tablespoon lime juice
- 1 tablespoon olive oil
  Salt to taste

In a medium bowl, combine all ingredients and let marinate for about 30 minutes.

Makes 10 servings (¼ cup each)
Per serving: 20 calories, 2 g fat

GUACAMOLE

- 2 tablespoons corn oil
- 2 tablespoons fresh lemon juice
- ¾ teaspoon salt
- 3 avocados, peeled, seeded, and cut into ½" dice
- 1 large tomato, diced
- 2 cloves garlic, minced
- 3 serrano chiles, chopped
- 1 small bunch fresh cilantro, chopped
  Fresh lime juice to taste

In a small bowl, combine oil, lemon juice, and salt. Mix thoroughly. Combine with remaining ingredients in a medium bowl until thoroughly mixed. Taste for seasoning, and keep at room temperature until ready to serve.

Makes about 16 servings (¼ cup each)
Per serving: 74 calories, 7 g fat

Jerk Chicken Quesadillas with Cool Fruit Salsa

 QUICK

Prep time: 15 minutes ■ Cook time: 10 minutes

2   cups shredded cooked chicken

2   tablespoons dried Caribbean jerk seasoning

2   cups (8 ounces) shredded reduced-fat Cheddar cheese or soy alternative

4   whole wheat flour tortillas (10" diameter)

1   avocado, pitted, peeled, and chopped

1   can (11 ounces) mandarin oranges, drained

2   tablespoons raspberry wine vinegar

½   teaspoon grated lime peel

⅛   teaspoon salt

Preheat the oven to 375°F.

In a medium bowl, combine the chicken and jerk seasoning and toss until evenly coated. Spread ¼ cup of the cheese over half of each tortilla, then top with ½ cup of the chicken. Top each again with ¼ cup cheese, then fold each tortilla in half. Place the tortillas on a baking sheet and bake for 10 minutes, or until the tortillas are crisp and the cheese is melted.

Meanwhile, in a medium bowl, combine the avocado, oranges, vinegar, lime peel, and salt and toss until evenly coated.

Cut each quesadilla in half. Serve with the fruit salsa.

Makes 8 servings (½ quesadilla)
Per serving: 320 calories, 8 g fat

Who's a Jerk?

Just using reduced-fat cheese, as recommended in the recipe for Jerk Chicken Quesadillas, saves enough calories that you'd have to add a cup of black bean soup to reach the calorie count of the high-fat chicken quesadilla. That's a bonus: The soup is high in fiber and has a host of minerals, and the Jerk Chicken Quesadilla recipe is particularly tasty—filled with the richness of avocado, the tang of citrus, and the heat of Caribbean jerk sauce. Great taste, good health, and enough of a calorie savings to add a delicious, nutritious soup. Which one is the jerk?

1 chicken quesadilla (5¾ ounces)
420 calories **22** grams fat

1 serving Jerk Chicken Quesadillas with Cool Fruit Salsa
320 calories 8 grams fat

+

1 serving Cuban Black Bean Soup (see page 284)
100 calories 3 grams fat

420 calories
11 grams fat

CARAMELIZED ONION AND ROASTED RED PEPPER PIZZA

Prep time: 10 minutes ■ Cook time: 35 minutes

1 tablespoon olive oil

2 large onions, halved and thinly
   sliced

½ teaspoon salt

1 jar (12 ounces) roasted red
   peppers, drained, patted dry,
   and coarsely chopped

2 tablespoons balsamic vinegar

5 whole wheat pitas or flatbreads
   (8" each)

⅓ cup (1½ ounces) freshly shaved
   Parmesan cheese or soy
   alternative

¼ cup loosely packed fresh basil
   leaves, cut into strips

Heat the oil in a large nonstick skillet over medium heat.
Add the onions and salt and cook, stirring occasionally, for
20 minutes, or until very tender and golden brown. Stir in
the peppers and vinegar.

Preheat the oven to 400°F.

Place the pitas or flatbreads on a baking sheet. Evenly divide
the onion mixture among the pitas and sprinkle with the
cheese. Bake for 10 minutes, or until the pitas are crisp. Remove the pizzas from the oven and sprinkle with the basil.
To serve, cut each pizza into quarters.

Makes 20 wedges
Per wedge: 80 calories, 2 g fat

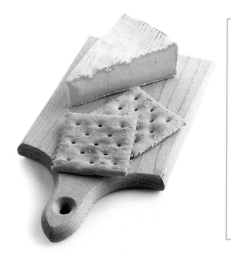

Which Wedge?

Even with two crackers, this slender wedge of Brie doesn't offer as
much to eat as a single wedge of the pizza. And since it brings with
it a huge calorie count, a high content of saturated fats, and the du-
bious health effects of a dairy food, consider the pizza instead. You
could have four wedges for the same cost in calories—and enjoy a
range of tastes into the bargain.

1 wedge (3 ounces)
Brie with two crackers
320 calories **25** grams fat

4 servings Caramelized Onion and Roasted Red Pepper Pizza
320 calories 8 grams fat

Marcus Samuelsson

Aquavit, New York City

Born in Ethiopia, Marcus Samuelsson and his sister were adopted by a Swedish couple. It was in Sweden that he developed his love for cooking. This made for a natural transition to New York's premier Scandinavian restaurant, Aquavit, where he is the youngest chef ever to earn a three-star rating from the *New York Times*. His recipe for gravlax, a Scandinavian classic, blends traditional techniques and ingredients with gorgeous presentation. It's spectacular served with the mustard sauces.

GRAVLAX WITH MUSTARD SAUCE

½ cup kosher salt

1 cup sugar

2 tablespoons cracked white peppercorns

3 pounds fresh salmon fillets (preferably center piece, skin on)

3 bunches fresh dill

Lemon slices

1 tablespoon sweet (honey) mustard

1 teaspoon French (Dijon) mustard

2 teaspoons sugar

1 tablespoon white wine vinegar

Salt and pepper

¾ cup salad oil

¼ cup chopped fresh dill

To make the gravlax: Mix the salt, sugar, and peppercorns. Take a handful and rub it on both sides of the salmon. Place the salmon in a dish and sprinkle the rest of the mix on top. Cover the salmon with dill and let it stand for 6 hours at room temperature. Put in the refrigerator for 24 to 30 hours, depending on how thick the salmon is.

Slice the salmon off the skin in thin slices and place the slices on a platter. Decorate platter with lemon and dill.

To make the mustard sauce: Mix the mustards, sugar, and vinegar and season with pinches of salt and pepper. Mix in the oil while you pour it in a steady stream. When the sauce has a mayonnaise-like consistency, stir in the chopped dill.

Makes 24 servings gravlax, 1 cup sauce
Per serving: 285 calories, 19 g fat

MANGO AND BLACK BEAN BRUSCHETTA

Prep time: 20 minutes ■ *Cook time: 5 minutes*

Traditional Italian bruschetta is rubbed with garlic and drizzled with olive oil. This Latin American variation is topped with a healthy mixture of mango, black beans, and jalapeño plus a splash of lime juice.

2   ripe mangoes, peeled, seeded,
      and chopped

1   can (15 ounces) black beans,
      rinsed and drained

1   medium tomato, seeded and
      chopped

1   shallot, finely chopped

1   jalapeño chile pepper, seeded and
      chopped (wear plastic gloves
      when handling)

3   tablespoons lime juice

¼   teaspoon salt

1   loaf Italian or French bread, cut
      diagonally into ½" slices

1   clove garlic, halved

Preheat the broiler.

In a medium bowl, combine the mangoes, beans, tomato, shallot, chile pepper, lime juice, and salt.

Place the bread slices on a broiler pan and coat with olive-oil cooking spray. Toast the bread under the broiler until golden. Rub the garlic over the toasted bread.

To serve, spoon the mango mixture on the bread.

Makes 32 servings
Per 1 slice bread with 2 tablespoons topping: 59 calories, 1 g fat

Triple Health Wallop

This appetizer serves up three foods that are Picture-Perfect Weight-Loss champions. Mangoes, black beans, and, yes, jalapeños offer lots of nutritional and health benefits at a very low cost in calories. Mangoes, sometimes called the king of fruits, are still somewhat exotic in the United States, which is too bad because they're juicy and sweet and excellent sources of fiber, beta-carotene, vitamins, and minerals. Calorie content? Minimal. Ditto for black beans, which are also a nutritionist's dream food. They're loaded with fiber, vitamins, phytochemicals, and lots of minerals including potassium, magnesium, zinc, copper, and iron. As for the jalapeños, they're an excellent source of antioxidants that may help prevent blood clotting and even cancer. Bottom line? Here's a combination—sweet fruit, chewy legumes, and hot chiles—that offers an exceptional taste sensation and packs a formidable health wallop as well.

Soups

Slurp Your Way to Picture-Perfect Weight Loss

recipes

*S*oup is just about the most powerful weight-loss tool I know, and I recommend it as an absolutely rock-solid aid to Picture-Perfect Weight Loss. Soups bring you maximum nutrition for a minimum of calories. A bowl of soup is literally a meal in itself.

If you don't believe me, ask any of the New York firefighters who are veterans of Picture-Perfect Weight Loss. These are big, burly, powerful men. Men whose jobs require them to carry upwards of 70 pounds of equipment up steep flights of stairs.

There was a time when these men mindlessly chowed down high-calorie, fat-laden lunches and dinners as a matter of course—then wondered why their knees hurt and their lungs ached as they proceeded up stairs. But ask them today what their food of choice is, and they will answer, almost to a man: "Soup." They've learned from experience that filling up on soup is a great way to take in health-advancing vegetables, a low-calorie way to satisfy big appetites, and a fabulous cooking ingredient—remember, all firefighters are cooks. For firefighter graduates of Picture-Perfect Weight Loss, hearty vegetable soup has become the delicious centerpiece of their favorite meals.

The recipes in this chapter make it easy. They exemplify the astonishing range of flavor and consistency that soups can offer. From hot and hearty to cool and delicate, from spicy to tart, from fishy to corny, soup is truly a year-round food that can satisfy any craving, fit any mood, match any appetite. Think of it as a delicious, healthful weight-loss prescription: Take as needed, with refills.

Cold Tomato and Avocado Soup

Prep time: 10 minutes ▪ Cook time: 30 seconds ▪ Chill time: 1 hour

Soup

- 2 pounds ripe tomatoes
- 1 medium European or Kirby cucumber, peeled, halved, and seeded
- 1 large clove garlic, peeled
- ¾ cup chilled tomato juice
- 2 tablespoons lemon juice
- 1 tablespoon extra-virgin olive oil
- ½ teaspoon salt
- ¼ teaspoon freshly ground black pepper

Avocado Topping

- ½ ripe avocado, cut into ¼" chunks
- 1½ tablespoons slivered fresh mint leaves

To make the soup: Bring a medium saucepan of water to a boil over high heat. Place a tomato in the pan and boil for 30 seconds to loosen the skin. Cool under cold running water and slip off the skin. Repeat with the remaining tomatoes.

Core the tomatoes and cut into quarters. With your fingers, scrape out the tomato seeds and discard.

In a food processor or blender, working in batches if necessary, process the tomatoes, cucumber, and garlic until very smooth. Place in a bowl and stir in the tomato juice, lemon juice, oil, salt, and pepper. Cover and chill for at least 1 hour, or until ready to serve.

To make the avocado topping: In a small bowl, gently combine the avocado and mint.

To serve, ladle the soup into 4 serving bowls. Evenly divide the avocado mixture among the bowls.

Makes 4 servings
Per serving: 140 calories, 8 g fat

The Battle of the Fats: Good versus Bad

When it comes to fat content, it isn't just a matter of how much but of what kind. One grilled cheese sandwich (made with two slices of cheese) has the same number of calories as this delicious soup-and-burrito meal, but it contains far more fat of the saturated variety, the kind that can raise cholesterol levels in the bloodstream. By contrast, the fat in the soup comes mostly from the avocado and the olive oil, which are "good" fat, providing essential fatty acids that are key to your health. And the burrito is packed with beans for protein and with other vegetables that provide fiber and a host of nutrients. Between the soup and burrito and the single sandwich, where health and your waistline are concerned, it's no contest.

1 grilled cheese sandwich
490 calories **23** grams fat

**1 serving Cold Tomato
and Avocado Soup**
140 calories **8** grams fat

+

**1 Bean and Bell
Pepper Burrito with
Fresh Salsa (see page 114)**
350 calories **6** grams fat

490 calories **14** grams fat

COLD CUCUMBER AND YOGURT SOUP

Prep time: 1 hour 10 minutes

Cool and creamy, this soup is a refresher in summertime. It's lovely served with tea sandwiches or a fresh fruit salad.

1½ cucumbers, peeled, seeded, and sliced, or 3 medium Kirby cucumbers, peeled and thinly sliced

½ teaspoon salt

1 medium shallot, sliced

1 small clove garlic

8 ice cubes

1 cup fat-free plain yogurt or soy alternative

½ cup buttermilk

2 teaspoons finely chopped fresh dill

Diced tomato, thin cucumber slices, and dill sprigs for garnish (optional)

Place the cucumbers in a colander and sprinkle with the salt. Place the colander in a bowl, cover, and let stand at room temperature for 1 hour to let the cucumbers drain.

In a food processor or blender, combine the cucumbers, shallot, garlic, and ice cubes. Process until very smooth. Pour into a bowl.

Whisk in the yogurt, buttermilk, and dill. Serve immediately or cover and chill until ready to serve. Garnish with the tomato, cucumber slices, and dill sprigs (if using).

Makes 4 servings
Per serving: 56 calories, 1 g fat

The Common Cucumber

We tend to think of the cucumber as a dull, routine sort of vegetable, yet the evidence shows a rather exotic history. The cucumber is native to India and has been cultivated in Asia for some 3,000 years. The Chinese were particularly fond of cucumbers, as were the ancient Romans. It is via the Roman Empire that the cucumber spread across Europe, and it was via European trappers, traders, buffalo hunters, and explorers that the cuke entered North American agriculture. It is believed that the Mandan Indians of the Dakotas found the cucumber to be a natural addition to their cultivation of pumpkins, squashes, and gourds.

CHILLED PUREE OF PEA SOUP WITH MINT

Prep time: 10 minutes ■ Cook time: 2 minutes ■ Chill time: 3 hours

It's the fresh mint that gives this beautiful pea soup its unexpected zippy flavor. If you don't have freshly shelled peas for garnish, you can thaw a handful of the frozen kind instead.

1   package (10 ounces) frozen tiny tender peas

1   bunch watercress, tough stems trimmed, rinsed and dried (about 2 cups)

3   cups water

1½ cups vegetable broth

¼   teaspoon salt

⅛   teaspoon freshly ground black pepper

½   cup 1% milk or soy milk

1   tablespoon finely chopped fresh mint leaves

½   cup shelled fresh peas (optional)

Place the frozen peas and watercress in a medium saucepan. Add the water and bring to a boil over high heat. Boil for 2 minutes. Drain in a colander and rinse briefly under cold running water.

In a food processor or blender, process the pea mixture for 3 minutes, or until very smooth, pouring the vegetable broth through the feed tube or the blender top as you work. Pour the soup into a bowl and stir in the salt and pepper. Cover and chill for 3 hours, or until very cold.

Just before serving, stir in the milk, mint, and fresh peas (if using).

Makes 4 servings
Per serving: 76 calories, 1 g fat

Mint Methodology

There are more than 30 species of the aromatic herb known as mint. It is native to the Mediterranean and western Asia but is now cultivated widely throughout Europe and the United States as well. Its characteristic cool, clean edge derives from the volatile oil menthol, which is a favorite ingredient in folk medicines and alternative therapies. Mint is also a symbol of hospitality, epitomized by Southern gentry on their verandas sipping mint juleps and fanning themselves languidly. Place your bunch of mint stem side down in a glass of water and cover the leaves with a plastic bag. The mint will stay fresh in the refrigerator this way for up to a week—be sure to change the water every 2 days.

COLD SPICED PLUM SOUP

Prep time: 5 minutes ■ *Cook time: 40 minutes* ■ *Chill time: 3 hours*

1½   pounds plums, cut into thin wedges

1½   cups water

½   cup seedless blackberry low-sugar preserves

¼   cup dry red wine

1   cinnamon stick

1   piece (3") orange peel, removed with a vegetable peeler

   Pinch of ground cloves

2   teaspoons cornstarch

1   cup lite vanilla yogurt or soy alternative

In a large saucepan over medium heat, combine the plums, water, preserves, wine, cinnamon stick, orange peel, and cloves. Bring just to a simmer. Reduce the heat to low, cover, and simmer for 6 minutes, or until the plums are tender but the slices are still intact.

In a cup, dissolve the cornstarch in 1 tablespoon water. Stir into the soup and cook, stirring gently, for 1 minute.

Remove the pan from the heat and let stand, covered, to continue cooking, for 30 minutes. Pour the mixture into a bowl, cover with plastic wrap, and refrigerate for at least 3 hours, or until chilled. After the soup has chilled for 1 hour, remove the cinnamon stick and orange peel.

To serve, evenly divide the soup among 4 bowls and top each with ¼ cup of the yogurt.

Makes 4 servings
Per serving: 116 calories, 1 g fat

A Touch of the Exotic

When you crave something a little out of the ordinary, it's all too easy to reach for a handful of high-fat crispy noodles—then another handful, and another, and another. Ladle up some of this Cold Spiced Plum Soup instead. It's refreshing, tangy, and festive, and you can down an entire quart of it before you approach the calorie count of this tiny portion of the noodles, and at one-sixth the fat content.

1 dish (3 ounces) crispy Chinese noodles
464 calories **24** grams fat

4 servings Cold Spiced Plum Soup
464 calories **4** grams fat

Morou Ouattara

Tribe, Washington, D.C.

As a child on the Ivory Coast of Africa, Morou Ouattara watched his mother pull together amazing dinners for as many as 40 on just a few hours' notice. Ouattara didn't understand until later that the magic that she performed with food was fusion cooking—her dishes borrowed freely from the cuisines of the Middle East, Africa, and France. Chef Ouattara's cooking career began in Washington, D.C., where he rose to prominence at Red Sage, Mark Miller's Southwest-inspired restaurant. There he put into practice the lessons learned from his mother. He has since left Red Sage to open Tribe, which will serve African-accented American cuisine. The recipe he shares here puts gazpacho in a whole new light.

YELLOW TOMATO GAZPACHO WITH CELERY ICE

For the Gazpacho

- 4 medium yellow tomatoes, chopped
- 1 medium yellow pepper, chopped
- 1 cup cucumber, chopped
- 1 medium red onion, chopped
- 1 tablespoon parsley, chopped
- 2 tablespoons olive oil
- 1 tablespoon white balsamic vinegar
  Salt to taste
  Sugar to taste

For the Celery Ice

- 1 pound celery, peeled and chopped
- 1 cup water
- ½ cup sugar
- ½ cup fat-free milk

To make the gazpacho: Puree all the vegetables and the parsley together. Add the olive oil and vinegar. Season with salt and sugar to taste. Refrigerate until ready to serve.

To make the celery ice: In a saucepan, bring all the ingredients together to a boil. Remove from the heat, cover, and refrigerate for 1 hour, or until cold.

Puree in a blender and press through a sieve into a shallow metal baking pan. Cover and freeze for 2 to 3 hours, stirring every 30 minutes with a fork or electric mixer to break up lumps, until frozen but still slushy. Serve with the gazpacho.

Makes 8 servings
Per serving: 125 calories, 4 g fat

Harvest Soup

Photo on page 87

Prep time: 15 minutes ■ *Cook time: 35 minutes*

1 tablespoon extra-virgin olive oil

1 medium sweet white onion,
   quartered and thinly sliced

1 large red bell pepper, chopped

1 large yellow bell pepper, chopped

3 cloves garlic, minced

1 teaspoon chopped fresh rosemary
   or ¼ teaspoon dried

¾ teaspoon salt

½ teaspoon freshly ground black
   pepper

2 medium yellow summer squash,
   cut lengthwise into quarters,
   each cut into ¼"-thick slices

3 large tomatoes, peeled, seeded,
   and chopped, or 3 cups
   chopped drained canned Italian
   tomatoes

1½ cups vegetable broth

¼ cup chopped fresh basil leaves

Heat the oil in a Dutch oven over medium heat. Add the onion, bell peppers, garlic, rosemary, salt, and black pepper. Reduce the heat to low, cover, and cook, stirring frequently, for 12 minutes or until the vegetables are tender.

Add the squash. Cover and cook, stirring once, for 5 minutes, or until the squash just starts to get tender.

Increase the heat to medium. Add the tomatoes, cover, and cook, stirring frequently, for 5 minutes, or until the tomatoes start to give up their juices.

Add the broth and stir to mash the vegetables slightly. Cover and cook, stirring and mashing once or twice, for 10 minutes, or until the vegetables are very tender.

Stir in the basil and serve.

Makes 4 servings
Per serving: 135 calories, 5 g fat

Chilled Roasted Red Pepper Soup with Basil and Crab

Prep time: 45 minutes ▨ Cook time: 12 minutes ▨ Chill time: 2 hours

You'll love the combination of sweet and savory in this brightly colored soup. The crabmeat "croutons" are the perfect topper.

1	tablespoon extra-virgin olive oil
½	teaspoon dried marjoram, crumbled
½	teaspoon salt
¼	teaspoon freshly ground black pepper
1	medium sweet white onion, halved and cut into thick slices
3	large red bell peppers, cut into large, flat pieces
1	cup fat-free chicken broth
½	cup water
2	tablespoons chopped fresh basil + extra sprigs for garnish (optional)
1½	teaspoons sherry wine vinegar or balsamic vinegar
4	ounces lump crabmeat, picked over

Preheat the broiler.

In a medium bowl, combine the oil, marjoram, ¼ teaspoon of the salt, and the black pepper. Add the onion and toss to lightly coat. Place the onion on a jelly-roll pan. Add the bell peppers to the bowl. Toss and wipe them along the sides of the bowl to coat with the seasonings. Place the peppers, skin side up, over the onion. (Don't leave much onion exposed, or it will burn.)

Broil the vegetables 5" to 6" from the heat without turning but checking often, moving them around if necessary, for 12 minutes, or until the peppers are charred and tender and the onion is tender. Remove from the broiler and cover with foil to steam the peppers and loosen their skin. Let stand for 30 minutes, or until cooled.

With your fingers, peel the skins from the peppers and discard. Place the vegetables and any juices in a food processor.

Process the vegetables, adding the broth through the feed tube, until the mixture is very smooth. Pour the puree into a bowl. Stir in the water, cover, and chill for at least 2 hours, or until very cold.

To serve, stir the chopped basil, vinegar, and the remaining ¼ teaspoon salt into the soup. Ladle into bowls and top each with some of the crabmeat and a sprig of fresh basil (if using).

Makes 4 servings
Per serving: 109 calories, 4 g fat

CARROT AND GINGER SOUP

Prep time: 15 minutes ■ Cook time: 25 minutes

To make prep time even faster, you can buy a bag of prewashed, presliced carrots in the produce section of your supermarket.

1	pound carrots, sliced
1	medium onion, halved and thinly sliced
1	tablespoon chopped fresh ginger
1½	cups water
1	cup vegetable broth
½	teaspoon salt
⅛	teaspoon freshly ground black pepper
1¼	teaspoons ground cumin
½	cup plain soy milk
2	tablespoons chopped fresh cilantro or parsley

In a large saucepan, combine the carrots, onion, ginger, water, broth, salt, and pepper. Cover and bring to a boil over high heat.

Meanwhile, toast the cumin in a small skillet over medium-low heat, stirring frequently, for 3 minutes, or until fragrant and the cumin begins to change color. Add the cumin to the soup.

Reduce the heat to low, cover, and simmer for 20 minutes, or until the carrots are very tender.

Working in batches, puree the soup in a food processor or blender. Return the soup to the pot and reheat briefly over medium heat, stirring often. Remove from the heat and stir in the milk and cilantro or parsley.

Makes 4 servings
Per serving: 85 calories, 1 g fat

The Roots of Ginger

The story of ginger parallels the history of cross-cultural trade routes and ancient exploration. As far back as the sixth century B.C., the Chinese were using ginger as a fragrant spice in cooking. Arab traders picked up the idea in their travels and brought ginger from eastern Asia to the eastern Mediterranean. From there, Crusaders carried it to Europe, where 16th-century Spanish conquistadores loaded it onto ships headed for the New World. A versatile flavoring, ginger is mild in root form, stronger when candied, and can be bitingly hot in powder form. Closely related to cardamom and turmeric, ginger is also a distant cousin of the banana. It's long been used in folk medicine and seems to help quell surges of nausea. Remember your mother giving you ginger ale when you had an upset stomach as a child?

PUMPKIN, CORN, AND LIME SOUP

Prep time: 10 minutes ■ *Cook time: 35 minutes*

- 2 teaspoons olive oil
- 1 large onion, chopped
- 1 medium red bell pepper, chopped
- 2 cloves garlic, minced
- 2 teaspoons ground cumin
- ½ teaspoon ground cinnamon
- ¼ teaspoon salt
- ¼ teaspoon freshly ground black pepper
- ⅛ teaspoon ground red pepper
- 1 can (16 ounces) plain pumpkin
- 3½ cups vegetable broth
- 1 cup frozen corn kernels
- ½ teaspoon grated lime peel
- 1 tablespoon lime juice

Heat the oil in a Dutch oven over medium heat. Add the onion, bell pepper, and garlic and cook, stirring often, for 12 minutes, or until tender.

Add the cumin, cinnamon, salt, black pepper, and ground red pepper. Cook, stirring, for 30 seconds, or until fragrant.

Stir in the pumpkin and broth. Increase the heat to high and bring to a simmer. Reduce the heat to low, cover, and simmer, stirring occasionally, for 15 minutes, or until the flavors have blended.

Stir in the corn, cover, and cook for 5 minutes.

Remove from the heat and stir in the lime peel and lime juice.

Makes 6 servings
Per serving: 115 calories, 3 g fat

Why the Cheese Stands Alone

It's a special occasion, and you want to serve your guests something special. Instead of the standard cheese log, loaded with saturated fat, consider this colorful, festive array of low-calorie soups. With only a fraction of the fat that the cheese has—and with the good kind of fat—the soups offer nutritional richness and a wealth of taste.

1 cheese log (4 ounces)
420 calories **36** grams fat

1 serving Pumpkin, Corn, and Lime Soup
115 calories 3 grams fat

+

1 serving White Bean, Garlic, and Arugula Soup (see page 95)
170 calories 8 grams fat

+

1 serving Harvest Soup (see page 83)
135 calories 5 grams fat

420 calories 16 grams fat

Firefighter John Regazzi

John Regazzi joined the fire department in 1979, and except for "1 year downtown" has spent his entire career with Engine Company 53, Ladder Company 43 in Manhattan's Spanish Harlem. Regazzi cooks a lot in the firehouse, but home is where he tries out his "experiments." His Hearty Lentil Soup was a highly successful experiment that has been a hit with both the family and fellow firefighters. Regazzi devised the recipe soon after he began his Picture-Perfect Weight-Loss program, on which he dropped 32 pounds in some 6 months. The inspiration for the soup? "Lentils are good for you, and I like potatoes, so I just tried to blend it all together in the food processor." It is, says Regazzi, "a meal unto itself." And it's a "particularly good winter meal because it's pretty hearty." It's also an excellent firehouse meal, he adds, "because you can leave it on the stove all day." You can do the same at home. Try it on a cold winter day, maybe accompanied, as Regazzi recommends, by "a good crusty bread."

HEARTY LENTIL SOUP

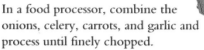

2 medium onions, quartered

3 ribs celery, cut into 3" pieces

3 carrots, cut into 3" pieces

2 cloves garlic

1 can (14 ounces) chicken broth

1 can (14 ounces) vegetable broth

2 cups water

1 pound dry lentils, rinsed

1 box (10 ounces) frozen chopped spinach, thawed

1 large sweet potato or russet potato, peeled and cut into small pieces

2 cubes chicken bouillon

2 tablespoons balsamic vinegar

In a food processor, combine the onions, celery, carrots, and garlic and process until finely chopped.

Heat a large saucepan, coated with cooking spray, over high heat. Add the onion mixture and cook, stirring constantly, for 2 minutes. Add the chicken broth, vegetable broth, water, lentils, spinach, potato, and bouillon. Bring to a boil. Reduce the heat to low, cover, and simmer for 1 hour, or until the lentils and vegetables are soft, adding water as needed. Stir in the vinegar.

Makes 6 servings
Per serving: 360 calories, 2 g fat

GREAT NORTHERN BEAN SOUP WITH SAGE

Prep time: 15 minutes ■ Cook time: 1 hour 45 minutes ■ Stand time: overnight

To save time, quick-soak the beans: In a large saucepan, cover sorted and rinsed beans with 4 times the volume of water (about 4 cups water for each cup of beans). Bring to a boil, reduce the heat to medium-low, and simmer about 10 minutes. Cover, remove from the heat, and let stand about 1 hour.

1½ cups great Northern beans, sorted and rinsed

1 tablespoon olive oil

2 medium carrots, chopped

1 large onion, chopped

1 medium leek, white and some green, halved, well-rinsed, and thinly sliced

5 cloves garlic, minced

⅓ cup chopped fresh sage leaves

1 bay leaf

4½ cups cold water

2 medium zucchini, halved lengthwise and cut into thin half-moon slices

1 teaspoon salt

½ teaspoon freshly ground black pepper

Place the beans in a large bowl and add cold water to cover by 2". Cover and let stand overnight. Drain the beans.

Heat the oil in a Dutch oven over medium heat. Add the carrots, onion, leek, and garlic and cook, stirring often, for 8 minutes, or until tender. If the pan gets dry, add a little water, 1 tablespoon at a time.

Stir in the sage, bay leaf, beans, and water. Increase the heat to high and bring to a boil.

Reduce the heat to low, cover, and simmer for 1 to 1½ hours, or until the beans are very tender.

Remove 2 cups of the beans with some of the broth and place in a food processor or blender. Puree until smooth. Return to the pot along with the zucchini, salt, and pepper. Cover and simmer for 5 minutes, or until the zucchini is tender. Remove and discard the bay leaf before serving.

Makes 4 servings
Per serving: 310 calories, 5 g fat

Leek Lore

You may already know that leeks are the national symbol of Wales. In fact, Welsh warriors wore leeks on their helmets as identifying marks to distinguish them from their enemies. The more successful the warriors were, the more they were convinced that the leeks helped them win their battles. Certainly, leeks can be strong; they are part of the same family as onions and garlic and look like giant scallions. A good source of vitamins, minerals, and calcium, the leek is an excellent low-calorie ingredient in dishes ranging from cold vichyssoise to a hot mixed-vegetable grill. Leek leaves are the barometer of their freshness and "health": Look for moist, crisp leaves and straight, narrow stems.

Photo on page 215

CURRIED YELLOW SPLIT PEA SOUP

Prep time: 20 minutes ■ Cook time: 3 hours 15 minutes

- 1   tablespoon olive oil
- 1   large onion, chopped
- 3   cloves garlic, minced
- 2¼ teaspoons curry powder
- ½   teaspoon freshly ground black pepper
- 7½ cups water
- 1¼ cups yellow split peas, picked over and rinsed
- 1   large bunch Swiss chard, chopped (4 packed cups chopped)
- 8   ounces thin-skinned potatoes, scrubbed and cut into ½" chunks
- 2   medium green apples, cored and cut into ¼" pieces
- 1¼ teaspoons salt

Heat the oil in a Dutch oven over medium heat. Add the onion and garlic and cook, stirring frequently, for 6 minutes, or until tender. Add the curry powder and pepper and cook, stirring constantly, for 30 seconds.

Stir in the water and split peas and bring to a boil over high heat. Reduce the heat to low, cover, and simmer for 2½ hours, or until the split peas are very tender and have dissolved.

Stir in the Swiss chard, potatoes, apples, and salt. Cover and simmer, stirring occasionally, for 35 minutes, or until the potatoes are tender.

Makes 6 servings
Per serving: 235 calories, 3 g fat

Polishing the Apple

An apple a day really can keep the doctor away. Apples aren't just great sources of vitamins, minerals, and fiber; they're also packed with disease-fighting phytochemicals, nonnutritive substances that are particularly effective in fighting disease. In the plants from which they come, phytochemicals toughen the plant's cell structure against natural deterioration and the stressful effects of harsh sunlight, pollution, or viral invasions. In effect, they do the same thing in us, and apples, with all their crunchiness and good taste, are potent packages of these phytochemicals. They contain a high level of antioxidants called flavonoids, and they contain a particularly high level of a flavonoid called quercetin. Long known as an inflammation fighter, quercetin also gives apples a beneficial impact on lung function. Research in Britain has found a higher lung capacity—138 milliliters higher—in people who eat apples. So breathe deeply—and keep eating apples.

Cory Schreiber

Wildwood Restaurant, Portland, Oregon

Named Best Chef in the Northwest by the James Beard Foundation in 1998, Cory Schreiber, a Portland, Oregon, native, has shaken up that city's culinary scene. From a family that's been in the oyster business since the mid-1800s, Chef Schreiber has a philosophy of "cooking from the source." His sources are the vast resources of the Pacific Northwest. At his restaurant, Wildwood, the food is "straightforward and simple," allowing the natural flavor and beauty of the ingredients to shine through. This luscious soup, which is best made with spring's fresh asparagus, is just one example of his careful, tasteful cooking.

LEEK AND ENGLISH PEA SOUP WITH ASPARAGUS AND CURLY PASTA

2	tablespoons extra-virgin olive oil
4	leeks (white part only), washed and cut into long, thin strips
2	cloves garlic, thinly sliced
½	teaspoon salt
½	teaspoon ground white pepper
4	cups vegetable broth
1½	cups cooked fusilli or corkscrew pasta
12	ounces English peas, shelled, or 10 ounces frozen peas
4	ounces asparagus, trimmed and cut into ½-inch-long pieces
4–5	leaves fresh sorrel or basil, finely shredded

In a 3-quart saucepan, heat 1 tablespoon of the olive oil over medium heat. Add the leeks, garlic, salt, and pepper. Sauté for 4 to 5 minutes, stirring to prevent the vegetables from browning. Stir in the vegetable broth. Bring to a boil and cook for 8 minutes. Mix in the pasta, peas, and asparagus, reduce heat, and simmer for 3 to 4 minutes, or until bright green and just tender. Swirl in the remaining 1 tablespoon of olive oil.

To serve, ladle into soup bowls and garnish with the sorrel or basil.

Makes 4 servings
Per serving: 290 calories, 9 g fat

GINGERED LENTIL SOUP WITH BROWN RICE AND SWEET POTATOES

Prep time: 20 minutes ■ *Cook time: 1 hour 35 minutes*

2 tablespoons olive oil

2 medium carrots, chopped

1 large onion, chopped

2 tablespoons finely chopped fresh ginger

4 cloves garlic, minced

1½ teaspoons ground cumin

½ teaspoon freshly ground black pepper

⅛ teaspoon ground allspice

8 cups water

1 cup brown lentils, picked over and rinsed

½ cup brown rice

12 ounces sweet potatoes, peeled and cut into ½" chunks

¾ teaspoon salt

1 cup thawed frozen chopped spinach, squeezed dry

Heat the oil in a Dutch oven over medium heat. Add the carrots and onion and cook, stirring frequently, for 6 minutes, or until tender. Add the ginger, garlic, cumin, pepper, and allspice and cook, stirring, for 1 minute.

Add the water, lentils, and rice and bring to a boil over high heat. Reduce the heat to low, cover, and simmer for 1 hour, or until the lentils and rice are tender.

Stir in the sweet potatoes and salt, cover, and simmer for 20 minutes, or until the sweet potatoes are tender. Stir in the spinach and cook for 5 minutes.

Makes 6 servings
Per serving: 300 calories, 6 g fat

Soup to Soup

Soups are central to Picture-Perfect Weight Loss. They're filling, loaded with nutrients, can serve as an appetizer or a meal, and are great calorie bargains, with very few exceptions. For example, this thick, rich Gingered Lentil Soup with Brown Rice and Sweet Potatoes is a meal in itself. The classic French onion soup, by contrast, is typically only an appetizer. Yet what really makes the difference is the calories from saturated fat. With 3 ounces melted Gruyère cheese a *de rigueur* component of the onion soup, you're adding hundreds of these calories that neither your waistline nor your arteries will thank you for.

1 serving French onion soup
480 calories **31** grams fat

1 serving Gingered Lentil
Soup with Brown Rice
and Sweet Potatoes
300 calories **6** grams fat

CORN, TOMATO, AND GREEN CHILE SOUP

Prep time: 20 minutes ■ *Cook time: 25 minutes*

For a tangy flourish, serve this south-of-the-border soup with wedges of lime and fat-free baked tortilla chips.

2   teaspoons olive oil

2   ribs celery, chopped

1   green bell pepper, chopped

1   large onion, chopped

1   teaspoon chili powder

½   teaspoon salt

½   teaspoon freshly ground black
      pepper

1   can (14½ ounces) diced tomatoes
      with green chiles, drained

1   can (14½ ounces) diced tomatoes,
      drained

      Corn kernels from 2 to 3 medium
      ears or 1–1½ cups frozen corn
      kernels

1   cup vegetable broth

½   cup water

2   tablespoons snipped fresh chives
      (optional)

Heat the oil in a Dutch oven over medium heat. Add the celery, bell pepper, and onion and cook, stirring frequently, for 4 minutes, or until tender. Stir in the chili powder, salt, and black pepper.

Add both cans of tomatoes and bring to a boil. Reduce the heat to low, cover, and simmer for 10 minutes.

Stir in the corn, broth, and water. Bring to a boil over high heat. Reduce the heat to low, cover, and simmer for 5 minutes, or until the corn is tender-crisp.

Sprinkle with the chives (if using).

Makes 4 servings
Per serving: 152 calories, 3 g fat

The Gift of Maize

Corn figures prominently in American history. What Europeans still call maize derives from a Native American word—*mahiz*—and "Indian corn," as the first New England colonists called it, is a native American food. It is also a wonderfully versatile and useful gift, as the colonists learned from their Indian neighbors: The husks serve as food "wrappers," the silk for medicinal tea, the kernels for food, and the stalks for fodder. In addition, corn is the foundation of such by-products as bourbon, corn flour, cornmeal, corn oil, cornstarch, corn syrup, corn whiskey, and laundry starch. Americans find themselves particularly grateful for corn when summer rolls around and they can munch it on the cob.

WHITE BEAN, GARLIC, AND ARUGULA SOUP

Prep time: 15 minutes ■ *Cook time: 25 minutes*

Photo on page 87

1 tablespoon + 1 teaspoon extra-virgin olive oil

1 large sweet white onion, halved and thinly sliced

8 cloves garlic, thinly sliced

2 teaspoons chopped fresh thyme leaves or ½ teaspoon dried

¼ teaspoon salt

¼ teaspoon freshly ground black pepper

2½ cups chicken broth

1 can (14–19 ounces) cannellini beans, rinsed and drained

1 cup water

2 bunches arugula or watercress, tough stems removed, rinsed and dried (about 4 cups), or 4 cups baby or flat-leaf spinach

¼ cup (1 ounce) freshly shaved Parmesan cheese

Heat 1 tablespoon of the oil in a Dutch oven over medium-high heat. Add the onion, garlic, thyme, salt, and pepper and cook, stirring frequently, for 10 minutes, or until the onion is tender. Toward the end of the cooking time and as the pan gets dry, add ¼ cup of the broth, 1 tablespoon at a time, stirring after each addition, to brown the onion.

Stir in the beans, water, and the remaining 2¼ cups broth and bring to a boil over high heat. Reduce the heat to low, cover, and simmer for 10 minutes, or until the flavors have blended. Remove from the heat.

Heat the remaining 1 teaspoon oil in a large nonstick skillet over medium-high heat. Add the argula, watercress, or spinach and cook, tossing frequently, for 2 minutes, or until wilted. Remove from the heat.

Stir the wilted greens into the soup. Sprinkle with the Parmesan.

Makes 4 servings
Per serving: 170 calories, 8 g fat

Give Arugula a Try

Italians love arugula, but to American palates, it has often proven too assertive. Certainly, this salad green has a peppery, mustardish flavor—there's nothing bland about it. But it is a lively addition to any salad, to soups, and to sautéed vegetable dishes. And it's a health powerhouse, filled with iron, beta-carotene, and other vitamins. Give it a try, but keep in mind that arugula is very perishable and will not last more than 2 days or so in the refrigerator. Be sure also to wash arugula thoroughly; it tends to hold a lot of grit.

Shrimp and Bok Choy Soup with Pineapple

Prep time: 20 minutes ■ *Cook time: 20 minutes*

Shao-hsing is an inexpensive cooking wine that's available in Asian markets and in the international aisle of larger supermarkets.

12	ounces large shrimp, peeled and deveined, tails left on
3	tablespoons shao-hsing cooking wine or dry sherry
2	tablespoons reduced-sodium soy sauce
2	cloves garlic, minced
1	tablespoon minced fresh ginger
2	teaspoons cornstarch
½	teaspoon toasted sesame oil
¼	teaspoon ground white pepper
2	cups water
1¾	cups vegetable broth
4	cups thinly sliced baby or regular bok choy or Napa cabbage
2	large carrots, diagonally sliced
1	large onion, halved and thinly sliced lengthwise
1	cup ½" pieces cut fresh pineapple or juice-packed canned pineapple tidbits, drained
1	scallion, chopped

Place the shrimp in a medium bowl. Add 1 tablespoon of the wine or sherry, 1 tablespoon of the soy sauce, half of the garlic, 1 teaspoon of the ginger, the cornstarch, sesame oil, and white pepper. Toss to combine, cover, and let stand for 20 minutes.

Meanwhile, in a Dutch oven, combine the water, broth, and the remaining 2 tablespoons wine or sherry, 1 tablespoon soy sauce, garlic, and 2 teaspoons ginger. Cover and bring to a boil over high heat. Reduce the heat to low and simmer for 5 minutes to blend the flavors.

Stir in the bok choy, carrots, and onion. Cover and simmer for 10 minutes, or until the vegetables are tender.

Add the shrimp and cook, stirring, for 3 minutes, or until the shrimp are opaque.

Stir in the pineapple and scallion and remove from the heat. Serve immediately.

Makes 4 servings
Per serving: 167 calories, 2 g fat

Fresh from the Tropics

An incredible array of tropical and other unusual fruits is now available at supermarkets and specialty stores. Some of these fruits, like kiwifruit, have been widely embraced; others are waiting to catch on. Here are some up-and-comers.

Asian pear. It looks like an apple but tastes like a pear, only crisper. It's best eaten chilled. Or, sauté it to release more of the pear flavor.

Atemoya. Also called custard apple, this artichoke-shaped fruit has a creamy white, custardy interior. It also has a sweet taste, something between a pineapple and a mango.

Carambola. With waxy skin and deep ribs, it resembles a long, yellow pepper. When sliced, it looks like yellow stars, hence the nickname "star fruit." It can be used as a garnish or to add pizzazz to fruit salads with an apple-grape-citrus taste.

Guava. Pebbly green on the outside and pink on the inside, guava is great in salads. It can also be pureed and made into delicious tutti-frutti yogurt by combining it with fat-free plain yogurt, freezing it until firm, and then running it through the food processor.

Kiwifruit. This fuzzy, egg-shaped fruit is one of the most familiar of the unusual tropical fruits. Kiwifruit tastes like a cross between strawberry and pineapple.

Litchi. This comes encased in a barklike brown shell that peels off, revealing a pearly white fruit with a grapelike appearance and perfumey taste.

Mango. As sweet as it is fragrant, the mango is as close to paradise as you can get without getting on a plane. It looks rather like a large misshapen pear, ranging in color from green (unripe) to orange-red.

Papaya. On the outside, it almost looks like a yellow or orange avocado. On the inside, however, is a beautiful orange-pink flesh with edible peppery black seeds. The seeds can be used to give crunch to a salad. The flesh is good in salsas or fruit salads. It also makes a good meat tenderizer.

Passion fruit. Despite the heady name, passion fruit is ready to eat only when it's purple, shriveled, and ugly. Inside you'll find a gelatinous mass of crunchy seeds and juice. The taste is a delightful combination of citrus, honey, and floral.

Persimmon. This is a smooth orange fruit that comes in two varieties. Hachiya persimmons are acorn shaped and must be quite soft to be eaten. They have a smooth, creamy texture. Smaller, tomato-shaped Fuyus can be eaten when still firm, even crisp.

Pineapple. This fruit, with its bumpy skin and long, sheathlike leaves, is best picked ripe, as it won't get sweet if picked before it's ready. Look for crisp, green leaves without yellowed or browned tips. Fresh pineapple contains an enzyme that prevents gelatin from setting properly. The enzyme is destroyed by heat, so using the canned variety or cooking fresh pineapple will solve the problem.

Tamarillo. Also called tree tomato, it actually looks more like a plum with either golden yellow or scarlet skin and has a slightly tart taste. It must be peeled with a vegetable peeler or blanched before using. To serve, slice and drizzle it with honey and a dusting of nutmeg.

Whoopi Goldberg

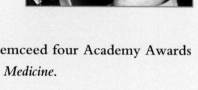

Whoopi Goldberg has won universal acclaim for her work in film, television, and theater and for her humanitarian efforts. Twice nominated for Oscars and Golden Globes, she won one each for *Ghost*.

With hand-, foot-, and braid-prints engraved at Grauman's Chinese Theater, Goldberg is part of Hollywood royalty. She has appeared on television's *Star Trek: The Next Generation* and *Baghdad Café*, hosted her own late-night talk show, co-hosted eight *Comic Relief* specials, and emceed four Academy Awards telecasts. She executive-produces the Lifetime series *Strong Medicine*.

What's the one food that you cannot resist under any circumstances?

WG: None whatsoever. I have no relationship to food.

What is the comfort food that you turn to in times of distress?

WG: Potato chips.

What food makes you laugh?

WG: Anything that is cleverly presented, because I think it's wonderful that people would take the time to make little slivers of carrots curly.

What is the most unusual combination of food that you eat?

WG: It's not really weird, it's very simple. I like dry cereal. . . . I don't like soggy, so I can put combinations of things, dried fruit and coconut and a nut here and there. I do not understand people who soak their cookies in milk. I am quite content with my dry cereal for breakfast.

What is your favorite ethnic food?

WG: Fried chicken.

What does food mean to you and does it make you feel good?

WG: I have to eat. Survival.

Is there any relationship between food and your childhood?

WG: No. Except that I eat probably more meat than I ate as a kid, but it's like a binge—maybe like a 2-week run, where I will eat steak this and steak that, and then I will most probably not eat meat for another 6 months. That's how I relate it to my childhood. My mother was a miracle worker—she was always able to provide for us. There were lots of vegetables—you could always find vegetables. She knew about tamari, cumin. And there was a lot of fish. Even if you were not interested in the food, you were always full.

What is your favorite smell in the kitchen?

WG: Corn.

What's your favorite seasoning?

WG: Paprika.

As a child, what was your least favorite food?

WG: It's the same as it is right now: eggs. I don't eat them. I don't like them, I don't like the smell, I don't like how they look. I don't like them.

What is your favorite food?

WG: It depends on the day.

So give me a good day and a bad day.

WG: On a bad day, when it's cold, I want chicken noodle soup. On a good day, when it's really warm, all I want is a slice of pizza.

Which food items do you keep in your refrigerator on a regular basis?

WG: Water and iced tea.

When shopping at the supermarket, is it a pleasant or unpleasant experience for you, and do you also check the food labels?

WG: It's a duty. And no, I don't.

Here's a question I made up just for you. If there were a food you could create, how would it look?

WG: It would look like an art deco piece of furniture; it would have great lines and wonderful rich color and offer sumptuousness to the eye. It would consist partially of popcorn and potato chips, with a hint of pork chop, and probably with one or two madeleines. And its colors would be gold and brown, beechwood, a little mahogany because I like well-done pork chops. That's what it would look like, that's what it would be made of. And you would just want to touch it.

If you could have dinner with anyone in the world, who would it be?

WG: The Roman emperor Claudius. He was very, very smart in terms of survival, in terms of how to survive in a world where everyone around you is being killed just because the emperor who precedes you doesn't like something. He was handicapped and he stammered so that people assumed he was slow, and he let them think that. But I would just love to know what he was thinking.

How about someone who's alive?

WG: Kofi Annan, the head of the U.N.

Fish Soup Marseilles

Prep time: 15 minutes ▮ Cook time: 35 minutes

2 tablespoons extra-virgin olive oil

1 medium leek, white and some green, halved, well-rinsed, and cut into 1" pieces

1 large red bell pepper, chopped

½ medium bulb fennel, trimmed, cored, and chopped

¼ cup dry white wine

4 cloves garlic, minced

½ teaspoon grated orange peel

⅛ teaspoon freshly ground black pepper

⅛ teaspoon crushed red-pepper flakes

2 cups fat-free chicken broth

1 can (14½ ounces) diced tomatoes, drained

1 cup water

12 ounces skinned cod, halibut, or bass fillets, cut into 1½" pieces, bones removed

Heat the oil in a Dutch oven over high heat. Stir in the leek, bell pepper, and fennel. Add the wine and bring to a boil. Reduce the heat to low, cover, and cook, stirring frequently, for 12 minutes, or until the vegetables are tender.

Add the garlic, orange peel, black pepper, and red-pepper flakes and cook, uncovered, stirring, for 1 minute, or until fragrant.

Add the broth, tomatoes, and water and bring to a boil over high heat. Reduce the heat to low, cover, and simmer for 10 minutes, or until the flavors have blended.

Add the fish. Cover and cook, stirring gently 2 or 3 times, for 3 minutes, or until the fish just flakes. Remove from the heat and serve immediately.

Makes 4 servings
Per serving: 250 calories, 8 g fat

Mediterranean Matchup

France's Provence region has given the world great fish soups, but for those interested in weight loss, some make more sense than others. Bisques typically start out with a pork fat base and use butter and cream as prime ingredients. The result is a high amount of the bad kind of fat. The calorie difference between a lobster bisque and this even heartier Fish Soup Marseilles, which addresses a similar taste, is great enough that you can treat yourself to delicious French bread as well.

1 serving (1⅓ cups) lobster bisque
410 calories **18** grams fat

**1 serving Fish Soup
Marseilles**
250 calories 8 grams fat

+

**2 slices French bread
(1 ounce each)**
160 calories 1 gram fat

410 calories 9 grams fat

The Bean Scene

Beans have moved beyond basic. While healthy cooks haven't abandoned the old standbys like lentils and navy beans, they're also experimenting with exotic "designer" beans like flageolet and anasazi beans. Here are cooking times and suggestions for some of the more common beans, and also for some that you may not have tried yet.

Bean	Characteristics	Stove-Top Cooking Time	Pressure-Cooking Time	Recommended Uses
Adzuki (also called azuki)	Small, oval; burgundy color; nutty flavor	1–1½ hours	15–20 minutes	Asian desserts and red rice
Anasazi	Kidney-shaped; mottled with purple and white	1½ hours	10–12 minutes	Stews, chili, and soups
Black (also called turtle bean)	Medium, oval; gray to jet black; earthy flavor	1½ hours	15 minutes	Mexican, Brazilian, and Cuban dishes
Black-eyed pea (also called cowpea)	Oblong; the color of creamy coffee, with a dark eye on the ridge; mealy texture; slight sweetness	1½ hours	10 minutes	Often used for hoppin' John and for southern soups and salads
Chickpea (also called garbanzo and ceci bean)	Beige; acorn-shaped with a tiny peak; nutty flavor; chewy texture	2–3 hours	Not recommended	Used in hummus, falafels, and other Middle Eastern, Spanish, and Indian dishes
Cranberry (also called Roman bean and tongue of fire)	Mild; kidney-shaped; cranberry mottle that turns pink when cooked	1½ hours	12–15 minutes	Goes well with stews and Italian soups
Fava (also called broad bean)	Small, round or kidney-shaped; light brown	1½ hours	Not recommended	Commonly used in Middle Eastern, Italian, and South American stews and purees

Bean	Characteristics	Stove-Top Cooking Time	Pressure-Cooking Time	Recommended Uses
Flageolet	Pale green, kidney-shaped gourmet French bean	1–1½ hours	10–15 minutes	Stews, soups, and side dishes
Great Northern	Ivory white; kidney-shaped; mild flavor	1½ hours	15–20 minutes	Use interchange-ably with navy and cannellini beans; good for baked beans, cassoulet, and European soups
Lentil	Thin, oval; mild, earthy flavor; common colors are green, red, yellow, and brown	30–45 minutes	Not recommended	Indian, Middle Eastern, and North African side dishes, soups, and salads
Lima (also called butter bean)	Small, creamy white; mild flavor; soft, mealy texture	1½–2 hours	Not recommended	Soups, stews, and garlicky sauces
Pigeon pea (also called Congo pea)	Pale, brownish; tiny eye on the ridge; earthy flavor; soft, mealy texture	1–1½ hours	8–10 minutes	Caribbean and Hispanic soups and rice dishes
Pinto	Oval; pink and brown speckles	1½–2 hours	15–20 minutes	Refried beans, chili, and burritos
Red kidney	Large, kidney-shaped; pale to dark red; full-flavored; chewy texture	1½–2 hours	20 minutes	Chili, soups, salads, Louisiana beans and rice, and Jamaican red pea soup
White cannellini (also called white kidney or haricot blanc)	Creamy white; kidney-shaped; smooth, firm texture; nutty flavor	1½–2 hours	20 minutes	Minestrone, salads, stews, and side dishes

CREOLE-STYLE RED BEAN SOUP WITH SHRIMP

Prep time: 15 minutes ■ *Cook time: 25 minutes*

1	tablespoon olive oil
6	scallions, thinly sliced
1	medium green bell pepper, chopped
1	medium rib celery, chopped
2	cups vegetable broth
1	can (14–19 ounces) red kidney beans
1	can (14 ounces) Italian tomatoes, chopped
½	teaspoon dried marjoram, crushed
½	teaspoon freshly ground black pepper
12	ounces medium shrimp, thawed if frozen, peeled and deveined, tails left on

Heat the oil in a Dutch oven over medium heat. Add the scallions, bell pepper, and celery and cook, stirring frequently, for 4 minutes, or until the vegetables are tender, adding some of the broth, 1 tablespoon at a time, if the pan gets dry.

Stir in the beans (with juice), tomatoes (with juice), marjoram, black pepper, and the remaining broth. Bring to a boil over high heat. Reduce the heat to low, cover, and simmer, stirring occasionally, for 15 minutes, or until the flavors have blended.

Add the shrimp and cook, uncovered, stirring frequently, for 2 minutes, or until the shrimp are opaque.

Makes 4 servings
Per serving: 210 calories, 5 g fat

Shrimp for Dinner

Hungry for shrimp? Have a small cup of shrimp fried rice and take in 26 grams of the bad kind of fat. Or, down two bowls of this soup with shrimp. The latter is a satisfying main course that gives you the added nutritional power of varied vegetables, the good kind of fat, and exceptional Creole-style taste.

1 cup shrimp fried rice
420 calories **26** grams fat

**2 servings Creole-Style Red
Bean Soup with Shrimp**
420 calories **10** grams fat

VEGETARIAN DISHES

They're Not Just for
Vegetarians Anymore

There are almost as many gradations of vegetarian as there are notes on a musical scale. Among the variations on the basic theme are lactovegetarians (who supplement plant foods with dairy products), ovolactovegetarians (who eat eggs as well as dairy), pescatarians (who add fish to the mix), and strict vegans (who touch no animal products whatsoever). The recipes in this chapter, however, will stick to the fundamentals: They're meatless, but some use modest amounts of dairy products.

What's the point? Well, a vegetarian diet can be both healthy and economical. Studies show that even a diet that focuses predominantly if not exclusively on plant-based foods can reduce the risk of cancer, heart disease, and stroke. Vegetarians do tend to have lower blood pressure, are less prone to hypertension, and have fewer intestinal disorders than meat eaters do. And here's an important consideration for weight-conscious readers: You very rarely see an overweight vegetarian—probably because of the high fiber intake.

I am not advocating that you adopt a vegetarian diet. On the contrary: One of the cardinal principles of Picture-Perfect Weight Loss is that *no food is forbidden*. Meats of every variety, a great range of dairy products, and rivers, lakes, and oceans full of fish and seafood are part of the dazzling panoply of foods available to us—the choice is yours.

What I suggest, however, is that you take another look at the role vegetables play in your eating. Today, we consume meat in ever-bigger portions, while vegetables have been relegated to the status of side dishes. For your health, your waistline, and—not incidentally—your pocketbook, think about reversing those proportions, about making vegetables the centerpiece of your meal. The recipes that follow can help.

STIR-FRIED INDIAN SPICED CAULIFLOWER

Prep time: 15 minutes ■ *Cook time: 20 minutes*

This dish makes a nice, light vegetarian meal. Or, try pairing it with your favorite spicy meat dish.

1   tablespoon extra-virgin olive oil

3   carrots, sliced diagonally

2   ribs celery, finely chopped

1   small onion, finely chopped

¾   teaspoon cumin seeds, crushed

3   tablespoons minced fresh ginger

1   tablespoon ground coriander

1   teaspoon salt

¼   teaspoon ground red pepper

1   head cauliflower, cut into florets

1   can (15½ ounces) chickpeas,
       rinsed and drained

     Dash of lemon juice (optional)

Heat the oil in a large nonstick skillet over medium-high heat. Add the carrots, celery, and onion and cook, stirring constantly, for 5 minutes. Add the cumin seeds, ginger, coriander, salt, and pepper and cook, stirring constantly, for 2 minutes.

Add the cauliflower. Reduce the heat to medium-low and cook, stirring occasionally, for 10 minutes, or until the cauliflower begins to brown.

Add the chickpeas and cook, stirring, for 3 minutes, or until the chickpeas are heated through. Drizzle with the lemon juice (if using).

Makes 4 servings
Per serving: 193 calories, 6 g fat

Cauliflower and Cancer

Much maligned—maybe because the idea of a white vegetable does not seem very appetizing—cauliflower is actually a hotbed of disease-fighting nutrition. Rich in vitamin C, folate, and potassium, cauliflower is also high in fiber and low in calories. Above all, it is packed with cancer-fighting phyto-chemicals called bioflavonoids and indoles. Researchers believe these phytos can help retard or stop the formation of some cancers. All in all, it makes cauliflower the ideal Picture-Perfect Weight-Loss food: filling, low in calories, high in nutrients, and a disease fighter to boot.

Firefighter Tom Kontizas

Tom Kontizas retired after 18 years as a firefighter in Queens—10 years working Engine 312 in Astoria and 8 years in the 14th division in Corona. He climbed a lot of stairs in 18 years, but he also ate a lot of heavy firehouse meals—until he became a poster boy for Picture-Perfect Weight Loss by changing his way of eating and dropping 40 pounds. His Vegetarian Sauté was a firehouse favorite—"the guys loved it," Kontizas says, and it's still served both there and in the Kontizas home. The inspiration for his creation? "I open the refrigerator and use whatever I find. You could say I tighten the refrigerator's belt." It works for people, too—and it's a health powerhouse into the bargain.

VEGETARIAN SAUTÉ

2 tablespoons olive oil

2 cloves garlic, chopped

1 teaspoon ground cumin

1 teaspoon coriander

1 large eggplant, chopped

1 green zucchini, chopped

1 yellow squash, chopped

1 red bell pepper, chopped

1 cup shiitake mushrooms, sliced

1 can (14 ounces) chickpeas, drained

½ teaspoon salt

Heat the oil in a large skillet over medium-high heat. Add the garlic, cumin, and coriander and cook, stirring, for 2 minutes, or until the garlic begins to brown. Add the eggplant, zucchini, squash, pepper, and mushrooms, and cook, stirring frequently, for 8 minutes or until the vegetables are tender. Stir in the chickpeas and salt and cook 2 minutes to heat through.

Makes 4 servings
Per serving: 240 calories, 8 g fat

PUREED VEGGIE TERRINE

Prep time: 40 minutes ■ *Cook time: 2½ hours*

1 small head cauliflower, cut into florets with tender stems sliced (1 pound)

1 pound carrots, sliced

2–3 bunches broccoli, cut into florets with tender stems sliced (1 pound)

1 cup plain soy milk

1 tablespoon lemon juice

3 egg whites, divided

1½ teaspoons salt

¼ teaspoon garlic powder

¼ teaspoon ground ginger

⅛ teaspoon ground nutmeg

Place a steamer basket in a large saucepan with ½" of water. Place the cauliflower in the steamer and bring to a boil over high heat. Reduce the heat to medium, cover, and cook for 15 minutes, or until the cauliflower is very tender. Drain well and place in a medium bowl. Repeat to steam the carrots, then the broccoli. Place in separate bowls.

In a small bowl, combine ¾ cup of the milk and the lemon juice. Add ¼ cup of the milk mixture, 1 egg white, and ½ teaspoon of the salt to each bowl of vegetables. Add the garlic powder to the cauliflower. Add the ginger to the carrots. Add the nutmeg to the broccoli.

Preheat the oven to 300°F. Coat a 9" × 5" nonstick loaf pan with olive oil cooking spray.

In a food processor or blender, separately puree each vegetable mixture, beginning with the cauliflower mixture and ending with the broccoli mixture. Add more soy milk, if needed, to puree each mixture to a mashed-potato consistency. Place each pureed mixture back in its respective bowl.

Evenly layer the vegetable purees in the prepared loaf pan, beginning with the carrot, then the cauliflower, and ending with the broccoli. Coat a piece of waxed paper with cooking spray and place, sprayed side down, on top of the terrine. Place the loaf pan in a larger pan and add enough water to come halfway up the sides of the loaf pan.

Bake for 1¾ hours, or until the terrine is set. Remove from the oven and cool on a rack for 20 minutes.

Remove the waxed paper. Run a knife around the edges and invert the terrine onto a platter. Serve hot or at room temperature.

Makes 6 servings
Per serving: 94 calories, 1 g fat

Appetizing Bargain

An appetizer is just a prelude, so it makes sense to keep the calorie count low as you take the edge off your appetite. But even a single slice of the pâté *en croûte* costs you a king's ransom in calories and adds enough saturated fat to burden your cardiovascular system. Try this terrine instead. Even multiple slices won't break the bank calorically or send your LDL cholesterol soaring.

1 slice (3½ ounces) pâté *en croûte*
470 calories **32** grams fat

**5 slices Pureed
Veggie Terrine**
470 calories **5** grams fat

Hearty Vegetables

Unlike their warm-weather counterparts, winter vegetables tend to keep well. But since they may already have spent time in transit and on the grocer's shelf, try to use them within a reasonable period. That applies especially to those vegetables that require refrigeration; use them within a week.

The following storage and preparation tips will help you preserve the fresh flavors and nutrients of your vegetables.

Vegetable	Storage and Preparation
Beets	Cut off tops 2" above root (save greens, if desired, to steam, sauté, or eat raw); refrigerate in plastic bags. Scrub and boil whole in water to cover until easily pierced with a skewer; drain, cool, and slip off skin. Alternatively, bake or microwave until tender.
Bok choy (pak choi)	Refrigerate in plastic bags. To use, cut off the bottom of the bunch; wash well. Remove the leafy tops and shred or chop them; cut stems into slices. Stir-fry, sauté, or microwave both parts until tender.
Broccoli	Refrigerate in plastic bags. Soak in cold water for 10 minutes to remove insects, especially if grown without pesticides. Remove tough outer leaves and cut tough ends off stalks. Slice or split stalks for quicker cooking. If desired, separate florets from stalks. Cook until just tender. Good methods: steam; stir-fry; cook, uncovered, in a large pot of water; microwave.
Broccoli rabe (broccoli raab, rapini)	Refrigerate in plastic bags. To use, rinse; trim off tough stem ends; if necessary, remove strings from large stalks as with celery. Cut stalks into small sections; shred or otherwise cut leaves; leave florets whole. Steam, stir-fry, or boil in a small amount of water until tender.
Brussels sprouts	Refrigerate in plastic bags. Trim the bottoms and peel away discolored outer leaves. Halve large sprouts lengthwise; otherwise, cook whole (cut an X in the bottom for more even cooking). Cook until easily pierced with a sharp knife. Good methods: steam; cook, covered, in a small amount of water; cook, uncovered, in a large pot of water; microwave.
Cabbage: green, red, savoy, Chinese	Remove and discard tough or ragged outer leaves. Refrigerate in plastic bags. Halve or quarter and cut out inner core. Shred, slice, or cut into wedges. Use raw or steam, sauté, or microwave until just tender.
Carrots	Cut off any green tops; refrigerate in plastic bags. Either scrub with a vegetable brush or peel. Cut as desired. Serve raw or cook until just tender. Good methods: steam; cook, covered, in a small amount of water; cook, uncovered, in a large pot of water; stir-fry; roast; microwave.
Cauliflower	Remove and discard leaves; refrigerate in plastic bags. Break or cut florets from woody core of head; discard the core. Serve raw or cook until just tender. Good methods: steam; cook, covered, in a small amount of water; cook, uncovered, in a large pot of water; stir-fry; microwave.
Celery	Refrigerate in plastic bags. Break ribs from the bunch and wash. If desired, remove leaves; trim tough ends from ribs. Slice as desired; serve raw, sauté, or cook, covered, in a small amount of water.

Vegetable	Storage and Preparation
Fennel (Florence fennel, sweet anise)	Remove coarse or ragged outer layers; trim off stalks and feathery tops. Refrigerate in plastic bags. May be eaten raw. Halve or quarter for oven or stove-top braising. Cut as desired to steam or cook, covered, in a small amount of water.
Jicama	Buy firm, dry tubers with unblemished brown skin. Refrigerate in plastic bags. Peel just before using. Eat raw or cut as desired and steam or cook, covered, in a small amount of water until just tender but still crunchy.
Kale	Refrigerate in plastic bags. Wash just before using. Remove thick stems; tear or cut the leaves as desired. Eat raw, stir-fry, or cook or microwave until just wilted in only the water that clings to the leaves from washing.
Kohlrabi: green or purple	Choose small, firm bulbs less than 3" in diameter. Refrigerate in plastic bags. Peel; save crisp, tender greens for salads. Steam or cook bulbs, covered, in a small amount of simmering water until tender.
Leeks	Refrigerate in plastic bags. To use, remove damaged outer leaves, trim off tough green tops, trim root end. Halve lengthwise and wash under cold running water, fanning the layers to remove sandy grit from between them. Cut as desired. Braise, sauté, stir-fry, or microwave until tender.
Onions	Store in net bags in a cool, dry, dark place. Peel and slice or chop as desired. Eat raw or bake, braise, stir-fry, sauté, steam, or microwave until tender.
Parsnips	Refrigerate in plastic bags. Wash well, peel, and cut off ends. Cut as desired; if inner core is woody, remove it. Bake, braise, microwave, or cook, covered, in a small amount of water until tender.
Potatoes	Store in a cool, dry, dark place; do not refrigerate. Scrub well and remove any sprouts. Bake, steam, or microwave whole and unpeeled. Or peel, cut as desired, and cook until easily pierced with a fork: boil, steam, sauté, or microwave.
Radishes: red, icicle, daikon, black	Refrigerate in plastic bags or in a bowl of water. Scrub and trim tops and roots. Peel if desired. Cut or slice as desired. Eat raw or cook, covered, in a small amount of water until tender.
Sweet potatoes	Store in a cool, dry, dark place. Scrub and bake whole until easily pierced with a sharp knife. Or peel, cut as desired, and boil until tender.
Turnips	Cut off roots and greens. Refrigerate in plastic bags. Scrub; peel thinly, if desired. Leave whole or cut as desired and boil until tender.
Winter squash	Store in a cool, dry place. Scrub and cut in half lengthwise; remove seeds and stringy pulp. If size warrants, cut into smaller pieces. Bake, steam, or microwave large pieces until tender. If desired, cut raw flesh into cubes (peel if desired); steam, microwave, bake, or boil.

BEAN AND BELL PEPPER BURRITOS WITH FRESH SALSA

Prep time: 15 minutes ■ *Cook time: 8 minutes*

Photo on page 77

1   teaspoon extra-virgin olive oil

1   large red bell pepper, cut into thin strips

1   large green bell pepper, cut into thin strips

1   medium onion, sliced

¼   teaspoon salt

1   teaspoon lime juice

4   whole wheat tortillas or lavashes (12" in diameter), warmed

1   can (16 ounces) fat-free refried beans, warmed

1   cup cooked brown rice

½   California avocado, sliced

3   cups shredded fresh spinach

2   tablespoons chopped fresh cilantro

1   cup salsa

Heat the oil in a large skillet over medium-high heat. Add the bell peppers, onion, and salt and cook, stirring frequently, for 8 minutes. Drizzle with the lime juice.

Onto each tortilla or lavash, spread ⅓ cup refried beans and ¼ cup rice. Evenly divide the pepper-onion mixture, avocado, spinach, and cilantro among the tortillas. Tightly roll each up into a burrito. Serve each burrito with ¼ cup salsa.

Makes 4 burritos
Per burrito: 350 calories, 6 g fat

Flatbread Facts

Mexican tortilla . . . Armenian lavash . . . Moroccan khubz . . . Indian naan. . . . All are flatbreads, the world's oldest form of bread. Flatbreads can be made from every kind of grain—wheat, rye, corn, oats, millet, sorghum, rice, and more—or from tubers or legumes. Some flatbreads are unleavened, others leavened. They can be thick for slicing, soft for wrapping, hard as crackers, thin as crepes. They are variously baked in ovens, fried, grilled, steamed, or cooked beneath the sands of the desert, as in the southern reaches of Tunisia and Algeria. In many cases, as with Armenian lavash and Finnish rye rings, the bread is stored in dried form, then sprinkled with water to make it supple for eating. In fact, Finnish rye rings were traditionally hung on the rafters throughout the winter and pulled down as needed. In a place where winters are long, what better way to make your grain supply last?

Tender Vegetables

The bounty of the warm months is highly perishable and at its flavor and nutrient peak when fresh. Use the storage and preparation tips below to reap the very best from your produce.

Vegetable	Storage and Preparation
Artichokes	Refrigerate in plastic bags and use within a week. Trim leaf tips with scissors; boil whole in a large pot of water until a leaf pulls out easily.
Asparagus	Refrigerate in plastic bags. Use within 3 days. To use, break off or peel tough stem ends. Steam or cook, covered, in simmering water.
Beans: green, yellow wax, Italian, purple	Refrigerate in plastic bags and use within 3 days. Rinse, snap off ends, and remove strings, if any. Leave whole, julienne, or cut into 1" pieces. Steam or cook, covered, in a small amount of simmering water.
Corn	Refrigerate in husks; use within 1 day. To use, remove silk and husks; cook whole cobs, covered, in simmering water. Or grill or bake unhusked ears with the silks removed. Or cut kernels from ears and cook, covered, in a small amount of simmering water.
Eggplant	Refrigerate in plastic bags and use within a few days. Rinse; peel if skin is tough. Slice as desired and cook, covered, in a small amount of simmering water, or steam, bake, or broil.
Mushrooms	Refrigerate in paper bags and use within 3 days. Wipe with damp paper towels before using. Leave whole or slice. Use raw or sauté.
Okra	Choose small pods. Refrigerate in plastic bags and use within 3 days. Rinse and cut off stems. Best sautéed whole; otherwise, slice and cook, covered, in a small amount of simmering water.
Peas: snow, sugar snap	Refrigerate in plastic bags and use within 3 days. Rinse, snap off ends, and remove strings, if any. Cook, covered, in a small amount of simmering water.
Peas: sweet green	Refrigerate in plastic bags and use within 2 days. Shell and cook, covered, in a small amount of simmering water.
Peppers: green, red, yellow, orange, purple	Refrigerate in plastic bags and use within a week. Wash, pat dry. Slice as desired; eat raw or sauté. To stuff, halve or leave whole; remove seeds and inner membranes; parboil in water to cover; drain, fill, and bake.
Summer squash: zucchini, yellow, pattypan	Refrigerate in plastic bags and use within 4 days. Wash and pat dry just before using; cut off stem and blossom end. Slice as desired. Cook or microwave, covered, in a small amount of simmering water, or steam or stir-fry.
Tomatoes	Store at room temperature and use within 1 week. Wash and slice as desired. Use raw or cook as recipe directs (if desired, peel before chopping).

ROASTED RED PEPPER SANDWICHES WITH BASIL SPREAD

Prep time: 45 minutes

Basil Spread

- 8 ounces firm tofu
- 2 tablespoons white balsamic vinegar
- 2 tablespoons reduced-fat mayonnaise
- 1 clove garlic
- ½ teaspoon mustard powder
- ¼ cup chopped fresh basil

Sandwiches

- ½ pound loaf ciabatta or whole grain bread, split lengthwise
- ½ California avocado, sliced
- 1 jar (16 ounces) roasted red bell peppers, drained and sliced
- 1 small bunch arugula

To make the basil spread: Drain the tofu and place between double layers of paper towel in a colander over a bowl. Place a small plate on the tofu and then place a 1-pound can on the plate. Let stand for 30 minutes.

In a food processor or blender, process the tofu, vinegar, mayonnaise, garlic, and mustard powder until smooth. Add the basil and process until combined.

To make the sandwiches: Spread the basil spread evenly on the cut sides of the bread halves. Layer the avocado, peppers, and arugula on one of the bread halves. Firmly top with the other half. Slice into 4 sandwiches.

Makes 4 servings
Per serving: 290 calories, 10 g fat

Weight-Loss Wonder

The plain, bland chicken thigh looks like just the sort of thing you would eat if you were on a diet—a small amount of rather flavorless food. Yet for the same number of calories, you could enjoy this appetizing sandwich and fill up, not just on a range of tastes and textures but on a real health treasure. The sandwich's 10 grams of fat come mostly from the avocado—they're the "good" kind of fat, as opposed to the saturated fat in the chicken. What's more, the sandwich's basil spread is tofu-based, so you take in soy protein. And the roasted red bell pepper even chips in with disease-fighting phytochemicals.

1 chicken thigh (4½ ounces)
290 calories **19** grams fat

**1 Roasted Red Pepper
Sandwich with Basil Spread**
290 calories 10 grams fat

Roasted Garlic Pizza with Arugula and Sun-Dried Tomatoes

Prep time: 15 minutes ■ *Cook time: 30 minutes*

Roasted Garlic

10	large cloves garlic
1	tablespoon extra-virgin olive oil

Pizza

12	sun-dried tomato halves
1	pound frozen whole wheat or white bread dough or pizza dough, thawed
1½	cups shredded arugula
¼	teaspoon freshly ground black pepper
⅛	teaspoon salt
¼	cup chopped fresh basil and/or Italian parsley
½	cup (2 ounces) shredded reduced-fat mozzarella cheese or soy alternative
¼	cup (2 ounces) finely crumbled goat cheese

To make the roasted garlic: Preheat the oven to 425°F.

Place the garlic in a small baking dish and toss with the oil. Cover and bake for 15 minutes, or until the cloves are tender and just beginning to lightly brown. Remove from the oven. Cool the garlic slightly and slice. Separately reserve the oil and the garlic for pizza preparation. (This step can be done up to 2 days in advance.)

To make the pizza: Coat a pizza pan or a 10" × 15" baking pan with cooking spray.

In a small bowl, soak the tomatoes in hot water for 10 minutes, or until soft. Drain the tomatoes, pat dry, and slice.

Spread the dough evenly in the prepared pan. Brush the dough with the reserved oil. Prick the dough several times with a fork so that the oil seeps in. In order, top the dough with the reserved garlic, sun-dried tomatoes, arugula, pepper, salt, basil and/or parsley, mozzarella cheese, and goat cheese.

Bake for 15 minutes, or until the crust is golden brown. Remove the pizza from the pan and place on a cutting board. Cut the pizza into 8 slices and serve.

Makes 8 servings
Per serving: 325 calories, 8 g fat

Pizza Power

Like pizza? Who doesn't? But some standard styles can be caloric disasters. Try this colorful red, white, and green alternative that's fun to make and a hit with the tastebuds. If you really crave the taste of pepperoni, you could get an even greater calorie bargain by substituting veggie pepperoni for the goat cheese. It tastes great, and at less than 20 calories for four slices, you could really slather it on and still come out ahead calorically. With or without the veggie pepperoni, the two slices of pizza pack more taste and health power than the single slice with meat.

1 slice pepperoni pizza
650 calories 28 grams fat

2 slices Roasted Garlic Pizza with Arugula and Sun-Dried Tomatoes
650 calories 16 grams fat

Gary Mennie

Canoe, Atlanta, Georgia

Gary Mennie is executive chef at Canoe, a restaurant nestled on the shores of the Chattahoochee river in Atlanta, Georgia. Canoe is known for its inventive, seasonal American cuisine served in a gracious Southern setting. Chef Mennie designs his ever-changing menu around what's fresh, what's in season, and what's grown or produced in the area. He created this Vegetable Paella using a summer's cornucopia of vegetables and fragrant herbs.

VEGETABLE PAELLA

3   cups assorted vegetables, such as trimmed whole baby zucchini, quartered pattypan squash, quartered sunburst squash, halved and trimmed baby artichokes, whole baby carrots, and French (long, slender) green beans, stems removed

1   tablespoon olive oil

1   red onion, cut into ¼" wedges

1   fennel bulb, trimmed and cut into ¼" wedges

1   red bell pepper, cut into ¼" dice

2   garlic cloves, minced

1½ cups basmati rice

4   cups vegetable stock or broth

    Pinch of saffron

½   cup whole cherry tomatoes, stemmed

2   teaspoons fresh thyme, minced

2   teaspoons fresh oregano, minced

2   teaspoons fresh rosemary, minced

1   bay leaf

    Salt and pepper (optional)

Blanch the baby vegetables until crisp-tender. Drain and cool under cold running water.

In a large, deep, heavy skillet, warm the oil over medium heat. Add the onion, fennel, bell pepper, and garlic and cook, stirring often, until tender.

Stir in the rice until coated with the oil. Add the vegetable stock and the saffron. Bring to a boil. Reduce the heat, cover, and simmer for 10 minutes.

Add the blanched vegetables, cherry tomatoes, and herbs; cover and cook for 20 minutes, or until the vegetables are tender and the stock has been absorbed by the rice.

Remove from the heat and let rest, covered, for 5 to 7 minutes. Season to taste with the salt and pepper (if using). Remove and discard the bay leaf before serving.

Makes 8 servings
Per serving: 198 calories, 2 g fat

GRILLED BARBECUE TOFU KEBABS

Prep time: 45 minutes ■ Marinate time: 1 hour ■ Cook time: 45 minutes

If you use wooden skewers for this recipe, soak them in water for 30 minutes first so they don't burn.

1   package (12.3 ounces) extra-firm tofu

1   large clove garlic, minced

1   tablespoon minced fresh ginger

⅓   cup barbecue sauce

1   can (20 ounces) pineapple chunks in juice

16   whole button mushrooms (about 10 ounces)

10   scallions, cut into 2" lengths

2   red bell peppers, cut into 24 chunks

2   green bell peppers, cut into 24 chunks

¾   cup brown rice

Drain the tofu and place between double layers of paper towel in a colander over a bowl. Place a small plate on the tofu and then place the 20-ounce can pineapple chunks on the plate and let stand for 30 minutes. Cut the tofu into 24 cubes.

In a large bowl, combine the garlic, ginger, and barbecue sauce. Add the tofu, pineapple (with juice), mushrooms, scallions, and bell peppers. Marinate for 1 hour.

Meanwhile, prepare the rice according to package directions.

Coat a grill rack or broiler-pan rack with cooking spray. Preheat the grill or broiler.

Thread 8 (12") skewers alternately with the tofu, pineapple, mushrooms, scallions, red peppers, and green peppers. Reserve the marinade.

Grill or broil the skewers for 3 minutes per side, brushing frequently with the marinade.

Serve the kebabs with the rice.

Makes 4 servings
Per serving: 369 calories, 5 g fat

Tips on Tofu

Tofu is the cheeselike soybean curd, and like all soy products, it is a premier vegetable source of protein. It's also packed with iron, B vitamins, calcium, and other minerals and is extremely low in calories and fat. As a cooking ingredient, tofu takes on the flavors of whatever it's being cooked with.

Tofu is highly perishable, so you are probably better off buying the vacuum-packed version. Look for it in either the dairy or deli section of the market and be sure to check the freshness date. Once opened, the tofu should last a week, but it may help to cover it with fresh water each day. If you do buy unpackaged tofu "out of the tub," give it a good sniff; don't buy anything with the slightest hint of sourness.

INDONESIAN TEMPEH AND BROCCOLI STIR-FRY

Prep time: 20 minutes ■ Cook time: 40 minutes

1   cup brown rice

⅓   cup stir-fry sauce

⅓   cup vegetable broth

1   teaspoon toasted sesame oil

8   ounces tempeh, chopped into
      1" pieces

1   medium white onion, chopped into
      large bite-size pieces

4   cloves garlic, minced

1   tablespoon minced fresh ginger or
      1 teaspoon ground

4   cups broccoli florets

3   medium carrots, cut into thin strips

3   scallions, greens only, chopped

¼   cup (1 ounce) finely chopped
      roasted peanuts

Prepare the rice according to package directions.

Meanwhile, in a small bowl, combine the stir-fry sauce and broth; set aside.

Heat a nonstick wok or large skillet coated with cooking spray over medium-high heat. Add the oil and cook the tempeh and onion, stirring constantly, for 5 minutes, or until the tempeh starts to brown. Add the garlic and ginger and cook for 1 minute. Add the broccoli, carrots, and scallions and cook, stirring constantly, for 2 minutes.

Add the reserved sauce mixture to the skillet and stir to combine. Continue to cook, stirring, for 2 minutes, or until the vegetables are tender-crisp.

To serve, place the rice on a serving plate. Top with the tempeh mixture and sprinkle with the nuts.

Makes 6 servings
Per serving: 290 calories, 10 g fat

Far Eastern Fare

It's not just that the Indonesian Tempeh and Broccoli Stir-Fry gives you far more food. And it isn't just that it lets you take in fewer grams of fat. The real difference is in the type of fat. The stir-fry's 10 grams come from soy, sesame oil, and peanuts and offer substantial health benefits, whereas the 15 grams of fat from that small portion of beef is the highly saturated "bad" kind of fat.

1 small skewer (3 ounces beef) beef satay
290 calories **15** grams fat

1 serving Indonesian
Tempeh and Broccoli
Stir-Fry
290 calories **10** grams fat

FIVE-BEAN CHILI

Prep time: 15 minutes ▪ *Cook time: 25 minutes*

1 tablespoon extra-virgin olive oil

2 large onions, chopped

1 jalapeño chile pepper, with seeds, chopped (optional); wear plastic gloves when handling

1 large butternut squash, peeled, seeded, and chopped

4 medium parsnips, peeled and chopped

3½ cups vegetable broth

5 cans (15½ ounces each) beans, rinsed and drained (choose a variety of 5 beans, such as black, kidney, garbanzo, cannellini, and pinto beans)

1 can (28 ounces) diced tomatoes with garlic

1 tablespoon chili powder

1 teaspoon ground cumin

2 tablespoons chopped fresh cilantro

Heat the oil in a large saucepot over medium-high heat. Add the onions and cook, stirring frequently, for 2 minutes. Add the chile pepper (if using), squash, and parsnips and cook, stirring frequently, for 3 minutes.

Add the broth, beans, tomatoes (with juice), chili powder, and cumin and bring to a boil over high heat. Reduce the heat to low and simmer, uncovered, for 20 minutes, or until the parsnips and squash are tender. Stir in the cilantro.

Makes 10 servings
Per serving: 290 calories, 4 g fat

Conned by Carne

The portions are similar, the taste is the same, but the chili *without* carne gives you health benefits and a calorie savings that just about boggles the mind. If you love the taste and texture of beef, try adding veggie ground beef to the Five-Bean Chili recipe. You'll get almost no rise in calories for a substantial addition of meat taste.

1 cup chili con carne (no beans)
530 calories **43** grams fat

1 serving
Five-Bean Chili
290 calories **4** grams fat

Rafal Olbinski

Rafal Olbinski was born in Poland 2 years after the end of World War II and studied architecture. While he was on a visit to the United States, his native country became embroiled in bitter political turmoil, and Olbinski decided to stay in New York City for a while and look for work. He got an assignment designing and illustrating a cover for *Time* magazine. One assignment led to another, and the association with *Time* led to a highly successful career in cover design for *Business Week*, *Der Spiegel*, *Newsweek*, *Atlantic Monthly*, and the *New York Times Magazine*. But cover art is only a part of Olbinski's oeuvre, and his paintings and designs are recognized all over Europe, especially in Poland, and throughout America. He has also become a noted stage designer—most notably perhaps for the projected-image sets for the Philadelphia Opera's production of Mozart's *Don Giovanni*.

Is there any personal cooking experience that you remember distinctly?

RO: When I was about 6 years old, my sister and I tried to surprise my mother by preparing a meal. We decided on crêpes and I was really into it, not necessarily preparing them but flipping them over in the air. I got so good at this, I could flip them twice, but not every try was successful. When my mother arrived, the crepes were either on the ceiling or the floor, but at least a couple were perfect.

While traveling for your work, have you had any extraordinary culinary experiences?

RO: In Japan I was tested—it was almost a macho test. I was invited to an expensive restaurant in Lagoya and was served octopus.

That doesn't sound too scary.

RO: They served us miniature octopus on the plate, but soon I saw the arms moving and realized they were still alive. Trying to catch them with my chopsticks was a horrifying experience, as well as watching everyone looking at me to see if I could chew them, which I did.

That took a lot of courage.

RO: Yes, I proved myself to be a very brave man. Their respect for me grew enormously.

What's the longest meal you've ever had?

RO: A few years ago when my wife and I went to Italy, some good friends met us at the plane to take us to dinner. We landed around 5 P.M. local time. Their welcoming dinner lasted until 6 A.M. By the end of the meal, we could hardly see straight but were extremely happy.

Are there any foods you cannot resist under any circumstances?

RO: Oysters and crème brûlée.

Have you ever had them at the same time?

RO: No, but that sounds very interesting.

What is the most unusual combination of foods that you eat?

RO: Raw salmon and kiwi.

Yummy. What's your favorite smell in the kitchen?

RO: The smell of fresh-cooked bread or garlic.

What is your favorite seasoning?

RO: *Sazón con azafrán* (seasoning with saffron).

As a child, what was your least favorite food?

RO: Porridge.

What's your least favorite food now?

RO: Pizza.

If you were on a desert island, which five food items would you have?

RO: Baguette, cheese, wine, garlic, and prosciutto.

If you could have dinner with anyone in the world, who would it be?

RO: Mona Lisa.

Soy Story

Soy still strikes many Americans as belonging to the cultures and cuisines of the Far East. The Japanese, in particular, put the soybean and soy products front and center in their diet, eating more of them than anybody else—an average of 23 pounds per person per year. It may not be coincidental that the Japanese also enjoy the longest life expectancy of any single population, that Japanese women suffer breast cancer only a quarter as much as American women, or that colon cancer among the Japanese is one-third what it is among Americans.

Coincidence or not, what is not in dispute is that soy is a complete protein—the only vegetable that can make that claim—and a rich source of disease-fighting phytochemicals. And since it figures in some of the world's most delicious cuisines—Chinese, Japanese, Thai, Indonesian, and the like—it must be a pretty useful cooking ingredient as well.

Here's a primer on some basic soy foods.

Soy milk is the liquid obtained when soybeans are boiled. Supermarkets stock a range of brands and a range of flavors—plain, vanilla, chocolate, and more. Use it in cereals, soups, beverages, sauces, desserts, or in any way you would use cow's milk. Starbucks keeps it on hand for those who request soy milk in their cappuccinos or caffé lattes.

Tofu, also known as bean curd or bean cake, is the curd formed by coagulating soy milk with a mineral salt. In other words, it's made much the same way cheese is made from cow's milk. A staple of Asian cuisines, tofu's versatility as a cooking ingredient is its propensity to take on the flavor of whatever it is cooked with or marinated in. You'll find tofu in the produce, dairy, or even deli section of your supermarket, sold in extra-firm, firm, soft, and silken varieties. The softer varieties blend wonderfully into dips, sauces, creamy soups, and desserts. The firmer varieties are good for cubing or slicing for use in barbecues, stir-fries, kebabs, and the like. A new innovation is baked tofu, which has a dense, meaty texture and comes already flavored: Teriyaki, tomato-basil, and Thai peanut are just some of the flavors available. You can eat these right from the package.

Edamame are fresh green soybeans. When boiled and salted in their pods, they are a popular bar snack in Japan and have become the latest hip food trend in the United States. They're available fresh or frozen, in or out of the pod. Use them in salads, soups, and cooked vegetable dishes.

Tempeh, a mainstay of traditional Indonesian cuisine, is the fermented cake of whole soybeans. It has a meaty texture and a slightly pungent aftertaste. You can find it in flavored forms or as the basis of veggie "burgers," "steaks," "bacon strips," or other meat analogues.

Miso is the salty paste of fermented soybeans, derived from a fermentation process that typically starts with a grain—often rice, sometimes wheat or barley. If this sounds unappetizing, the taste is in fact delicious. Miso is perhaps best known as a soup base in Japanese cooking, where it is widely used. It's also great in sauces and dips, where it looks something like peanut butter, its color ranging from pale gold to deep brown. The taste is often described as fruity-winey; the darker the miso color, the stronger the taste.

In addition to these products, soy is the basis of most of the meatless, veggie versions of sausages, burgers, bacon, and deli slices like ham, pepperoni, bologna, and salami.

ROASTED VEGETABLE STEW

Prep time: 35 minutes ■ Cook time: 1 hour 15 minutes

If you prefer, you can grill or oven-char the mixed vegetables instead of roasting them, and prepare them up to a day in advance. For variety, you can use different mixes of vegetables, such as mushrooms, green bell pepper, and fennel.

12 ounces firm silken tofu

4 cups chopped mixed vegetables, such as carrots, bell peppers, zucchini, and onion

½ teaspoon salt

¼ teaspoon freshly ground black pepper

1 tablespoon extra-virgin olive oil

2 large cloves garlic, minced

1⅓ cups brown rice

3½ cups vegetable broth

1 can (14½ ounces) diced tomatoes

2 cups chopped escarole or Swiss chard

¾ teaspoon paprika

1 can (15½ ounces) cannellini or lima beans, rinsed and drained

½ cup fresh or thawed frozen peas

1 scallion, white and green parts, finely chopped (¼ cup)

Preheat the oven to 400°F. Coat a roasting pan with olive oil cooking spray.

Drain the tofu and place between double layers of paper towel in a colander over a bowl. Place a small plate on the tofu and then place a 1-pound can on the plate. Let stand for 30 minutes. Chop the tofu.

Meanwhile, place the mixed vegetables in the prepared roasting pan. Coat with olive oil cooking spray and sprinkle with the salt and pepper. Roast the vegetables, stirring occasionally, for 30 minutes, or until tender.

Heat the oil in a large saucepan over medium-high heat. Add the tofu and garlic and cook, stirring frequently, for 4 minutes, or until the tofu is golden. Add the rice and stir to coat with oil. Add the broth, tomatoes (with juice), escarole or chard, and paprika and bring to a boil over high heat. Reduce the heat to medium-low, cover, and simmer for 35 minutes.

Stir the roasted vegetables, beans, peas, and scallion into the rice mixture. Cover and cook for 8 minutes, or until nearly all the liquid is absorbed and the rice is tender.

Remove from the heat and let stand, covered, for 5 minutes.

Makes 8 servings
Per serving: 293 calories, 5 g fat

ROASTED EGGPLANT PARMIGIANA STACKS

Prep time: 20 minutes ■ *Cook time: 45 minutes*

½ cup whole wheat flour

½ teaspoon garlic salt

½ teaspoon freshly ground black
    pepper

½ cup liquid egg substitute or 4 egg
    whites, lightly beaten

1 cup seasoned dry Italian-style
    bread crumbs

1 large (1½ pound) eggplant, peeled
    and cut into 8 slices

1 zucchini, cut into 16 slices

1⅓ cups fat-free marinara sauce

1 jar (12 ounces) roasted yellow or
    red bell peppers, sliced

½ cup (2 ounces) shredded lite
    mozzarella cheese or soy
    alternative

¼ cup chopped fresh basil leaves

Preheat the oven to 400°F. Coat 2 baking sheets with cooking spray.

On a piece of waxed paper, combine the flour, garlic salt, and black pepper. Place the egg substitute or egg whites in a shallow bowl. Place the bread crumbs on another piece of waxed paper. Dredge the eggplant and zucchini in the flour, coat with the egg, then dredge in the bread crumbs. Place on the prepared baking sheets. Bake for 40 minutes, turning once.

Meanwhile, place the sauce in a medium saucepan and bring to a simmer over low heat.

Working on one of the baking pans, layer 4 of the eggplant slices with 2 slices zucchini, some of the roasted peppers, and another slice of eggplant. Repeat layering with the remaining zucchini and roasted peppers. Top with the cheese.

Set the oven to broil.

Broil the stacks about 4" from the heat for 1½ minutes, or until the cheese is melted.

To serve, evenly divide the marinara sauce among 4 plates. Top each with an eggplant stack and garnish with the basil.

Makes 4 servings
Per serving: 350 calories, 7 g fat

Fat Italian-Style

This small portion (15) of tortellini with ½ cup cream sauce is all refined starch and saturated fats. Its calorie count is way over the top, and its health benefits are nil. You can capture the real essence of Italian cuisine with one serving of this delicious eggplant dish for half the calories and gain the health benefits of vegetable fiber and whole wheat flour in the bargain.

1 serving tortellini in cream sauce
700 calories **31** grams fat

1 serving Roasted Eggplant Parmigiana Stacks
350 calories **7** grams fat

Asian Pasta with Snow Peas and Peppers

Prep time: 10 minutes ■ Cook time: 10 minutes

Sauce

- ¾ cup rice wine vinegar
- ⅓ cup reduced-sodium soy sauce
- 3 tablespoons plum sauce
- 3 scallions, white and green parts, finely chopped

Pasta

- 1 pound whole wheat angel hair pasta
- 2 teaspoons toasted sesame oil
- 1 large red bell pepper, thinly sliced
- 1 large yellow bell pepper, thinly sliced
- 2 cups snow peas, trimmed

To make the sauce: In a small bowl, combine the vinegar, soy sauce, plum sauce, and scallions. Set aside.

To make the pasta: Prepare the pasta according to package directions. Place in a large bowl.

Meanwhile, heat the oil in a medium skillet over medium-high heat. Add the peppers and snow peas and cook, stirring frequently, for 5 minutes, or until tender-crisp.

Toss the vegetables with the pasta. Add the reserved sauce mixture and toss to thoroughly coat. Serve warm or refrigerate to serve cold.

Makes 8 servings
Per serving: 295 calories, 2 g fat

Asian Addition

Twice as much food for about the same calories: It doesn't take an abacus to determine what a bargain that is. When you crave the taste of the Orient, remember that there are lots of options for getting that taste healthfully and at a low calorie count.

½ serving (about 4 ounces)
General Tso's chicken
320 calories **17** grams fat

 VS.

**1 serving Asian Pasta with
Snow Peas and Peppers**
295 calories **2** grams fat

FISH, POULTRY, AND MEAT

Making Choices

We've been eating fish, meat, and poultry since our ancestors first managed to grasp or spear a fish, outrun or outsmart an animal on the hoof, or capture and domesticate fowl. In fact, much of the history of cooking is about inventing new ways to prepare, season, and cook different species of fish, meat, and poultry.

Of course, all of these foods contain a range of vitamins and are rich in protein, which is a fundamental component of cell structure and essential for the growth and repair of tissue. That's why I've put protein foods just above the base of my Picture-Perfect Weight-Loss Food Pyramid (see page 16), one step away from the fruits and vegetables that I hope you'll make the centerpiece of your overall eating plan. But I've also recommended that you get the bulk of your protein from beans, legumes, soy products, and seafood.

The reason? For one thing, meat and poultry can be high in calories, and making lower-calorie choices is at the heart of Picture-Perfect Weight Loss. What's more, both meat and poultry tend to have high amounts of saturated fat and cholesterol, depending on how they're prepared.

Do I think you should give up meat and poultry? Absolutely not. What I do suggest is that you put other protein foods first—and eat meat and poultry after legumes, fish, and soy.

recipes

And when you do want meat and poultry, look to the recipes in this chapter. They succeed admirably in fulfilling the age-old search for new and delicious ways to prepare, season, and cook traditional dishes, and almost all of them tastily add the health benefits of vegetables and fruit. The same for the fish dishes, which offer an astonishing array of tastes—plus the health benefits (except for pregnant women) of lower cholesterol, high protein, and the omega-3 fatty acids the American Heart Association heartily recommends.

BROILED SOLE FILLETS WITH TOMATO-HERB SALAD

QUICK

Prep time: 10 minutes ■ Cook time: 5 minutes

Tomato and basil always go well together, and they're just the right match for delicately flavored fillet of sole. This beautiful, healthy dinner comes together in mere minutes.

½ cup coarsely chopped fresh basil leaves

¼ cup coarsely chopped flat-leaf parsley

2 tablespoons snipped fresh chives

3 cups red and/or yellow cherry tomatoes, halved

½ teaspoon grated lemon peel

2 tablespoons lemon juice

½ teaspoon salt

4 sole fillets (6 ounces each)

1 teaspoon olive oil

Preheat the broiler. Coat a broiler-pan rack with olive-oil cooking spray.

In a medium bowl, combine the basil, parsley, and chives. Remove ¼ cup of the herb mixture and set aside.

To the herb mixture in the bowl, add the cherry tomatoes, lemon peel, 1 tablespoon of the lemon juice, and ¼ teaspoon of the salt. Toss to combine.

Sprinkle the fish with the reserved ¼ cup herbs and the remaining 1 tablespoon lemon juice and ¼ teaspoon salt. Arrange the fish on the prepared rack and drizzle evenly with the oil.

Broil the fish 3" to 4" from the heat for 4 to 5 minutes, or until the fish flakes easily. Remove from the heat. Serve with the tomato salad.

Makes 4 servings
Per serving: 193 calories, 4 g fat

Tomatoes: Back Home to Stay

Among vegetables, only potatoes and lettuce are today more widely consumed by Americans than tomatoes. (Yes, botanically speaking, the tomato is a fruit, but in 1893, the U.S. Supreme Court ruled it a vegetable for tariff purposes.) One of only a few foods native to the Western Hemisphere, tomatoes originated in South America and were first cultivated by the Aztecs of Central America. Spanish conquerors brought the tomato to Europe, where it found the going rough: Many Europeans thought of the tomato as an orna-

mental fruit at best, a poison at worst. But the Spaniards and Italians eventually made the tomato a staple of their cuisines, and although the English who brought it "home" to America thought of it as a medicine rather than a food, none other than Thomas Jefferson was proud to serve it at his dinner table in Monticello. Today, the tomato is a gardening favorite, appearing in more than 85 percent of backyard gardens and, we may assume, adorning an awful lot of salads and sandwiches.

SPICED TUNA SLICES WITH ENDIVE AND AVOCADO SALAD   QUICK

Prep time: 15 minutes ■ Cook time: 1 minute

Serve this lovely dish as a light meal, or as an extra-special appetizer at your next dinner party. For an elegant touch, toss some sliced fresh mango into the salad.

1½ pounds sushi-grade tuna steak, cut crosswise into 12 thick slices

3 tablespoons fresh lime juice

1½ teaspoons chili powder

½ teaspoon salt

½ teaspoon freshly ground black pepper

½ teaspoon grated lime peel

2 teaspoons extra-virgin olive oil

2 heads Belgian endive, cut on an angle into thin slices

2 cups arugula or spinach

½ head radicchio, cored and coarsely shredded

½ small red onion, thinly sliced (about ⅓ cup)

¼ cup fresh cilantro leaves

½ medium avocado, peeled and cut into thin slices

Preheat the broiler. Coat a baking pan with olive-oil cooking spray.

Place the tuna on a cutting board. Sprinkle with 1 tablespoon of the lime juice.

In a cup, combine the chili powder and ¼ teaspoon each of the salt and pepper. Sprinkle over the tuna and place in a single layer in the prepared pan. Set aside while making the salad.

In a large bowl, combine the lime peel, oil, the remaining 2 tablespoons lime juice, and the remaining ¼ teaspoon each salt and pepper. Add the endive, arugula or spinach, radicchio, onion, and cilantro. Do not toss.

Broil the tuna 3" to 4" from the heat for 1 to 3 minutes, without turning, or until the fish is medium-rare. Remove from the heat.

Toss the salad gently and spoon onto plates. Top each with some of the tuna and the avocado.

Makes 4 servings
Per serving: 300 calories, 8 g fat

Avocado: Small Wonders

The avocado, native to the tropics and subtropics, is known for its lush, buttery texture and mild, faintly nutlike flavor. It is also an important source of the good kind of fat, of vitamin C, thiamin, and riboflavin, and of cholesterol-lowering sterols. Once known as alligator pear, avocado comes in varieties ranging from round to pear-shaped, smooth-skinned to pebbly-textured. Florida was the site of the first U.S. avocado trees back in the 1830s, but today, almost 80 percent of the nation's avocado crop comes from California. The two most widely marketed avocado varieties are the pebbly-textured, almost-black Hass, and the green, smooth-skinned Fuerte. To ripen them, place them in a paper bag and set them aside at room temperature for a few days. Ripe avocados last for several days in the refrigerator, but once cut and exposed to the air, avocado tends to discolor rapidly. The solution? Add cubed or sliced avocado to a dish at the last moment.

Taste the Difference

Are you at sea when it comes to choosing fish that'll tickle your tastebuds? Flounder no more. Here are some tips to guide your selection.

Bass. Varieties in this category include striped bass, groupers, black sea bass, and the highly trendy Chilean sea bass. Generally, bass works well for nearly any cooking method, including poaching, broiling, baking, and sautéing.

Catfish. If farm-raised, catfish has a delicate to mild flavor with a slightly sweet taste. Wild catfish usually has a richer flavor that may not be to everyone's liking.

Cod. Delicate in flavor, cod has medium-firm flesh. Atlantic cod, harvested in waters from Virginia to the Arctic, tends to be a bit sweeter than Pacific cod. Salted dried cod, or *baccalà*, is used in a range of cuisines from the Mediterranean to the Caribbean and has become a highly popular dish.

Flounder and sole. These two fish are sweet and delicate. Because they don't have a "fishy" flavor, they appeal to people who claim they don't like fish. Their similarities make them interchangeable in many recipes.

Grouper. Both the red and the black species are delicate to mild in flavor. Because its meat is firm and doesn't easily break apart during cooking, this fish is excellent for chowders, stews, and grilling.

Haddock. Like cod and flounder, haddock has a delicate flavor. Serve it poached, steamed, or grilled with either a mild sauce or a sprinkling of lemon juice and salt-free seasoning.

Halibut. This fish has a delicate, sweet flavor. Because it's a fine-grained, medium-firm fish, it's ideal for kebabs and stir-fries.

Mahi mahi. Also known as dolphinfish (no relation to Flipper), mahi mahi ranks among the most popular finfish these days. That's due in part to its flavorful, moderately fatty, medium-firm flesh. Along with swordfish, king mackerel, and tilefish, mahi mahi is not recommended for pregnant women.

Monkfish. Nicknamed "poor man's lobster," monkfish has the mild flavor and firm flesh characteristic of its namesake. For best results, don't overcook it or you'll lose that texture.

Orange roughy. Orange roughy has delicate flesh, similar to flounder, and a mild flavor that's perhaps a shade stronger than flounder. Native to New Zealand, it has become a favorite in this country.

Red snapper. This fish is lean and moist with a delicate flavor. Fish harvested at 2 to 4 pounds have metallic pink skin. But as they grow larger, their skin darkens; hence the name red snapper.

Salmon. Depending upon the species, salmon can range from mild to full-flavored. Atlantic salmon tends to be the lightest in flavor, followed by coho, chum, pink, chinook or king, and sockeye.

Swordfish. Usually sold in steak form, swordfish has a full flavor; its firm texture is similar to tuna. It's ideal for kebabs. Keep in mind that swordfish is at the top of the list of fish that should be off the list for pregnant women.

Tuna. Tuna ranges from mild to rich in flavor and from dusky white to dark red in color. As you might expect, lighter-colored pieces have the milder flavor.

Baked Haddock with Tomatoes and Cinnamon

QUICK

Prep time: 10 minutes ■ Cook time: 10 minutes

1   medium onion, halved and thinly sliced

4   haddock or bass fillets (6 ounces each), skinned

1   tablespoon lemon juice

1   tablespoon tomato paste

2   teaspoons honey

1   teaspoon extra-virgin olive oil

    Pinch of ground cinnamon

½   teaspoon salt

¼   teaspoon freshly ground black pepper

1   ripe medium tomato, thinly sliced

2   cups cooked brown rice, quinoa, barley, or whole wheat couscous

Preheat the oven to 400°F. Coat an 11" × 8½" baking dish with olive-oil cooking spray. Place the onion in the prepared baking dish. Top with the fish.

In a bowl, combine the lemon juice, tomato paste, honey, oil, cinnamon, salt, and pepper. Add the tomato and toss to coat with the sauce. Arrange the tomato over the fish.

Bake for 10 minutes, or until the fish is opaque and flakes easily. Serve over the cooked rice, quinoa, barley, or couscous.

Makes 4 servings
Per serving: 195 calories, 2 g fat

Greek Glory

When you want to capture the glory of Greek cuisine, there's a high-calorie, high-fat way, and then there's another way. This baked haddock recipe offers the other way—rich in health benefits and a uniquely Mediterranean taste treat.

1 serving (6 ounces) moussaka
520 calories **20** grams fat

**1 serving Baked
Haddock with Tomatoes
and Cinnamon**
195 calories 2 grams fat

SPICED FISH AND VEGETABLE HOT POT

Prep time: 15 minutes ■ Cook time: 25 minutes

Typically made with a hearty meat, this hot pot is a healthier version loaded with nutritious vegetables and low-fat fish.

2½ cups vegetable broth

2 cloves garlic, minced

1¼ teaspoons ground cumin

¾ teaspoon ground ginger

½ teaspoon salt

¼ teaspoon freshly ground black pepper

1 small butternut squash, peeled, seeded, and chopped

2 cups small cauliflower florets

6 scallions, cut into 2" pieces

2 large carrots, sliced

1 can chickpeas, rinsed and drained

12 ounces skinned cod, scrod, halibut, or sole fillets, cut into 2" pieces

¼ cup chopped fresh cilantro

In a Dutch oven, combine the broth, garlic, cumin, ginger, salt, and pepper. Bring to a boil over high heat. Reduce the heat to low, cover, and simmer for 5 minutes to blend the flavors.

Stir in the squash, cauliflower, scallions, carrots, and chickpeas. Raise the heat and bring to a boil. Reduce the heat to low, cover, and simmer for 15 minutes, or until the vegetables are tender.

Add the fish to the pot. Cover and cook, stirring gently once or twice, for 2 to 3 minutes, or until the fish just flakes. Stir in the cilantro.

Makes 4 servings
Per serving: 273 calories, 3 g fat

Spicing It Up: Cumin

Cumin is the dried fruit of a plant in the parsley family, and it offers both aroma and a nutlike flavor to foods. No wonder it is favored in Middle Eastern, Asian, and Mediterranean cooking, used to make curries and chili powders. Cumin seeds come in three colors. Amber is the most widely available, while you may have to search Asian markets to find the white and black varieties. White cumin is a lot like the ubiquitous amber, but black cumin seed has a more peppery taste.

Firefighter Jim Rozas

Jim Rozas has been with Engine 211 in Brooklyn's Williamsburg section since he joined the fire department in 1993. By 2002, he had decided it was time he took off some weight, so he joined up with some fellow firefighters embarking on the Picture-Perfect Weight-Loss program. Rozas took to the new way of eating easily and enthusiastically, dropping 38 pounds in the first 10 weeks. A fish lover, he adapted his Baked Fish Fillet recipe from one his father had devised when *he* was on a diet and "got on a fish kick." Rozas *père*, also a firefighter, created the dish for salmon, but Rozas says "you can use any fillet." He made the dish with sea bass for the crew at Engine 211, and "the guys tore it up." The trick, he says, is to broil the fish "at the very end to brown the mayo and bread crumbs." For accompaniment, Rozas favors a three-bean salad with red onion and lite vinaigrette dressing and maybe a baked potato. Healthy and absolutely Picture-Perfect.

BAKED FISH FILLET

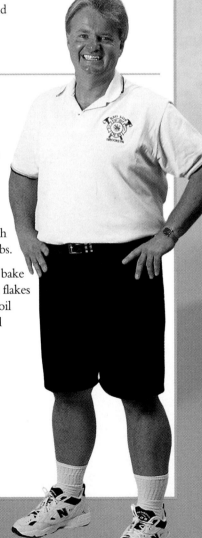

6   fish fillets (such as cod, red snapper, or flounder), 6 ounces each

2   tablespoons lemon juice

1   teaspoon salt

1   teaspoon freshly ground black pepper

½   teaspoon garlic powder (optional)

6   tablespoons lite mayonnaise

6   tablespoons plain or seasoned bread crumbs

Preheat the oven to 400°F. Coat a broiler-pan rack with cooking spray.

Drizzle the fish with the lemon juice and sprinkle with the salt, pepper, and garlic powder (if using). Evenly spread 1 tablespoon of the mayonnaise over each fillet and sprinkle each with 1 tablespoon of the bread crumbs.

Place on the prepared rack and bake for 10 minutes, or until the fish flakes easily. Set the oven to broil. Broil the fillets for 2 minutes, or until lightly browned.

Makes 6 servings
Per serving: 220 calories, 7 g fat

Steamed Fish with Asian Chili Sauce

Prep time: 10 minutes ■ *Cook time: 15 minutes*

2 tablespoons orange juice

1 tablespoon chili garlic sauce

1 tablespoon soy sauce

4 halibut, cod, or salmon fillets, skinned (6 ounces each)

1 pound thin asparagus, cut into 2" pieces

1 medium yellow summer squash, cut into thin diagonal slices

6 scallions, cut into thin diagonal slices

Preheat the oven to 425°F. Tear off 4 pieces of parchment paper or foil, 16" × 12" each.

In a cup, combine the orange juice, chili sauce, and soy sauce.

Fold each piece of paper or foil crosswise like a book, then open up. Coat one half of each sheet with olive-oil cooking spray. Place a piece of fish on the sprayed halves and spoon 1½ teaspoons of the chili sauce mixture over each fillet. Top the fish with some asparagus, squash, and scallions. Spoon another 1½ teaspoons chili sauce mixture over the vegetables in each packet and fold the other side of the paper or foil over the fish. Crimp the edges tightly to seal. Place the fish packets on a jelly-roll pan.

Bake for 15 minutes, or until the fish flakes easily.

Makes 4 servings
Per serving: 250 calories, 4 g fat

Protein Plus

A "dieter" might regard this anemic-looking sandwich as an efficient, if tasteless, way to take in needed protein. Instead, try either this rich-tasting steamed fish recipe or this easy, absolutely delicious salmon dish, and add the fiber benefits of vegetables to your protein—in a generous serving.

**½ white-meat chicken sandwich
(3½ ounces chicken), no mayo
250 calories 5 grams fat**

 VS.

**1 serving Steamed Fish
with Asian Chili Sauce**
250 calories **4** grams fat

OR

**1 serving Grilled Peppery
Salmon with Garlic Greens
(see page 146)**
310 calories **10** grams fat

Photo on page 145

GRILLED PEPPERY SALMON WITH GARLIC GREENS

Prep time: 10 minutes ■ Cook time: 15 minutes

Salmon

1½	teaspoons coarsely ground black pepper
½	teaspoon salt
4	salmon fillets with skin (6 ounces each)

Greens

2	teaspoons olive oil
6	cloves garlic, thinly sliced
¼	teaspoon salt
¼	teaspoon crushed red-pepper flakes
16	cups torn assorted tender greens, such as escarole, arugula, stemmed watercress, stemmed Swiss chard, and/or spinach

To make the salmon: Coat the grill rack or broiler-pan rack with olive-oil cooking spray. Preheat the grill to medium or preheat the broiler.

Sprinkle the salmon with the salt and pepper. Cover loosely and let stand while cooking the greens.

Grill or broil the salmon, skin side down, about 4" from the heat, for 12 minutes, or until the fish is opaque.

To make the greens: Meanwhile, heat the oil in a heavy Dutch oven over medium heat. Add the garlic, salt, and red-pepper flakes and cook, stirring, for 3 minutes, or until the garlic is fragrant and golden.

Add the greens, working in batches if necessary, and cook, stirring, for 3 minutes, or until the greens are wilted.

Remove the salmon skin before eating. Serve the salmon with the greens.

Makes 6 servings
Per serving: 310 calories, 10 g fat

The Goods on Garlic

Is garlic really as good for you as people say? Will it lower blood pressure? Build strength? Prevent colds? Maybe—but more evidence is needed. The first really scientific look at the issue was by the great 19th-century chemist Louis Pasteur, who demonstrated the antiseptic properties of garlic—properties that proved lifesaving on the battlefields of World Wars I and II. More concentrated research in the late 20th century has shown that the allicin in garlic can indeed lower cholesterol and blood pressure levels and may protect against blood clotting. And studies in animals indicate that garlic may lower the risk of colon and other cancers, although no one is saying how much garlic you'd need to obtain those benefits. But garlic does appear to help in fighting infections, and it certainly adds flavor to a range of dishes from many cuisines.

ROASTED SALMON WITH ORANGE AND SOY

Prep time: 5 minutes ■ *Marinate time: 1 hour* ■ *Cook time: 20 minutes*

For a simple yet elegant meal, serve this delicate salmon over a bed of couscous or noodles, accompanied by steamed thin asparagus. If you don't have salmon, cod or Chilean sea bass will also work nicely.

¼ cup orange juice

¼ cup reduced-sodium soy sauce

2 tablespoons chopped fresh parsley

2 cloves garlic, minced

¼ teaspoon dried oregano, crushed

¼ teaspoon freshly ground black pepper

4 salmon fillets, skinned (6 ounces each), preferably thick, center-cut pieces

In a zip-top plastic bag, combine the orange juice, soy sauce, parsley, garlic, oregano, and pepper. Add the salmon, seal the bag, and turn to coat evenly. Marinate in the refrigerator for 1 hour.

Preheat the oven to 450°F.

Remove the salmon from the marinade and place in an 11" × 8" baking dish. Spoon about 1 tablespoon of the marinade over each piece of salmon. Discard the remaining marinade.

Bake for 18 minutes, or until the fish is opaque, basting 2 or 3 times with the pan juices.

Makes 4 servings
Per serving: 253 calories, 11 g fat

Michel Nischan

Heartbeat at the W Hotel, New York City

Michel Nischan, executive chef of the highly regarded Heartbeat restaurant in Manhattan's chic W New York Hotel, is one busy man. He is a board member of Chef's Collaborative, a group that promotes sustainable agriculture and artisanal products, and a key organizer for the New American Farming Initiative. This roasted cod recipe is an inspired, light, pure symphony of tastes. Heartbeat avoids butter and heavy dairy products because Chef Nischan feels that they mask the natural flavors of food. He has a deep respect for the bounty of the earth, and his menu at Heartbeat reflects a philosophy of balance, well-being, and harmony.

PAN-ROASTED COD WITH CELERY AND HEIRLOOM POTATOES

1 quart low-sodium chicken broth, reduced to 1½ cups

4 6-ounce cod fillets

Salt and freshly ground black pepper

2 teaspoons grapeseed or canola oil

2 cups assorted heirloom potatoes, parboiled until fork-tender and cut in half

6 shiitake mushrooms, stemmed and thinly sliced

3 shallots, peeled and thinly sliced

1 cup bias-sliced celery

1 tablespoon freshly picked thyme leaves

⅔ cup organic vegetable broth

Preheat the oven to 450°F.

Put the chicken broth in a saucepan and heat until simmering over medium heat.

Season each cod fillet with salt and pepper and rub them lightly with oil. Heat an ovenproof, medium sauté pan over medium-high heat and when hot, sear the fillets until well-browned on one side. Turn the fillets over and then transfer the fillets to the oven and roast for about 5 minutes, or until cooked through and opaque.

Transfer the fillets to a warm platter, cover with foil to keep warm, and set aside.

Set the pan over medium heat and sauté the potatoes, mushrooms, and shallots for about 3 minutes, or until the shallots and mushrooms just begin to wilt. Add the celery and sauté for an additional 30 seconds. Add the chicken broth and thyme leaves, bring to a simmer, and remove from the heat. Stir in the ⅔ cup vegetable broth and season to taste with salt and pepper.

Spoon the broth and vegetables into 4 warm shallow bowls and top each with a cod fillet. Serve immediately.

Makes 4 servings
Per serving: 234 calories, 4 g fat

BAKED BASS WITH ROMESCO SAUCE

Prep time: 5 minutes ■ *Cook time: 5 minutes*

Romesco, a classic sauce from Spain, is just the right choice for fish. Spoon it over each serving, or decorate the edges of each plate with dots of sauce.

2   small cloves garlic

½   teaspoon salt

4   tablespoons orange juice

¾   teaspoon paprika

¼   teaspoon dried oregano, crumbled

¼   teaspoon freshly ground black
    pepper

4   striped bass or red snapper fillets (6
    ounces each), skinned

1   strip (2") orange peel, removed with
    a vegetable peeler

½   cup roasted jarred red peppers,
    seeded if necessary and patted
    dry

1   tablespoon slivered almonds,
    toasted

½   tablespoon tomato paste

½   teaspoon honey

Preheat the broiler. Coat a baking pan with olive-oil cooking spray.

On a cutting board, coarsely chop 1 clove of the garlic. Sprinkle with ¼ teaspoon of the salt and mash to a smooth paste with the flat side of a chef's knife. Scrape into a cup and stir in 2 tablespoons of the orange juice, ¼ teaspoon of the paprika, the oregano, and black pepper.

Place the fish in the prepared pan. Spoon the spice mixture on top and set the fish aside.

In a food processor, combine the orange peel, roasted peppers, almonds, tomato paste, honey, and the remaining 1 clove garlic, ¼ teaspoon salt, 2 tablespoons orange juice, and ½ teaspoon paprika. Process, scraping down the sides often, until the sauce is completely smooth.

Bake the fish for 5 minutes, or until the fish flakes easily. Serve the fish with the sauce.

Makes 4 servings
Per serving: 211 calories, 6 g fat

Broiled Halibut with Spicy Tartar Sauce

QUICK

Prep time: 10 minutes ■ Cook time: 5 minutes

Tartar Sauce

- ⅓ cup fat-free mayonnaise
- 1½ tablespoons finely chopped dill pickles
- 1½ teaspoons finely chopped fresh dill
- 1½ teaspoons grainy mustard
- ¼ teaspoon grated lime peel
- 1½ teaspoons lime juice
- ¼ teaspoon green Tabasco sauce

Fish

- 4 halibut, scrod, or other white fish fillets, skinned (6 ounces each)
- ¼ teaspoon salt
- ¼ teaspoon freshly ground black pepper
- 2 tablespoons plain dry bread crumbs

To make the tartar sauce: In a medium bowl, combine the mayonnaise, pickles, dill, mustard, lime peel, lime juice, and Tabasco sauce until blended.

To make the fish: Preheat the broiler. Coat the broiler-pan rack with olive-oil cooking spray.

Place the fish on the prepared rack. Sprinkle with the salt and pepper and spread with 1 teaspoon of the sauce. Dust with the crumbs. Completely coat the fish with olive-oil cooking spray.

Broil the fish 8" from the heat, watching carefully so that the crumbs don't burn, for 5 minutes, or until the fish flakes easily.

Serve with the tartar sauce.

Makes 4 servings
Per serving: 220 calories, 5 g fat

What a Difference a Spice Makes!

Condiments and spices turn this halibut with tartar sauce into a taste delight while keeping the calorie count low and the fat content minimal. Contrast it with the plain fried fish pictured on the left—calorically high and a fat-content gut-buster. In fact, the broiled halibut with tartar sauce is such a bargain you would have to add this hefty serving of Oven Potato Medley before you could match the fried fish for calories alone.

1 serving (5 ounces) fried fish fillet
375 calories **19** grams fat

1 serving Broiled Halibut
with Spicy Tartar Sauce
220 calories 5 grams fat

+

1 serving Oven Potato
Medley (see page 212)
155 calories 0 grams fat

375 calories 5 grams fat

STEAMED SCALLOPS WITH VEGETABLES

Prep time: 15 minutes ■ Cook time: 15 minutes

If you prefer, buy the smaller bay scallops instead of sea scallops. If bays aren't available, you could also cut the sea scallops in half.

2   teaspoons olive oil

2   cloves garlic, minced

1¼ teaspoons chopped fresh thyme
    leaves or ¼ teaspoon dried,
    crushed

2   ribs celery, cut into thin diagonal
    slices

2   medium parsnips, cut into thin
    diagonal slices

2   medium carrots, cut into thin
    diagonal slices

1   large leek, white and some green,
    halved lengthwise, well-rinsed,
    and sliced ¼" thick

½   teaspoon salt

¼   teaspoon freshly ground black
    pepper

1½ pounds sea scallops, tough muscle
    on side removed, rinsed and
    patted dry

2   tablespoons dry white wine or
    vermouth

Heat the oil in a heavy Dutch oven, over medium heat. Add the garlic and thyme and cook, stirring, for 2 minutes. Add the celery, parsnips, carrots, leek, ¼ teaspoon of the salt, and ⅛ teaspoon of the pepper and cook, stirring, for 2 minutes.

Reduce the heat to low, cover, and cook, stirring occasionally, for 5 minutes, or until the vegetables are tender-crisp. If the pan gets dry, add 1 tablespoon of water.

Season the scallops with the remaining ¼ teaspoon salt and ⅛ teaspoon pepper. Place the scallops on the vegetables in the pot and sprinkle with the wine.

Cover and cook, turning the scallops twice, for 3 minutes, or until the scallops are opaque.

Makes 4 servings
Per serving: 284 calories, 4 g fat

Pick a Peck of Parsnips

The parsnip is a member of the parsley family and prized for the distinctive taste and texture of its fleshy white root. Cultivated since ancient times, parsnips are found on roadsides and in open places throughout Europe, temperate Asia, and across the British Isles. It was British colonists who introduced the parsnip to North America in the early 17th century, since which time it has been widely cultivated and extensively naturalized. Parsnips are usually served as a cooked vegetable; in both flavor and texture, they fall midway between the carrot and the potato.

BROILED SCALLOPS WITH RED PEPPERS AND OREGANO

Prep time: 20 minutes ▓ Cook time: 25 minutes

A simple salad of fresh mixed greens dressed with a light vinaigrette is a nice accompaniment to this pretty dish.

2 large red bell peppers

2 tablespoons chopped flat-leaf parsley

1 tablespoon balsamic vinegar

1 tablespoon water

½ teaspoon dried oregano, crushed, or 1 tablespoon chopped fresh oregano

2 small cloves garlic, minced

¼ teaspoon salt

¼ teaspoon freshly ground black pepper

1¼ pounds sea scallops, tough muscles at sides removed, rinsed and patted dry

Preheat the broiler. Line a baking sheet with foil.

Place the bell peppers on the prepared baking sheet. Broil 3" from the heat, turning the peppers every 5 minutes, for 20 minutes, or until the skin is blistered and charred. Remove to a paper bag and allow to cool for 10 minutes. Peel and discard the blackened skin. Remove and discard the stems and seeds. Cut the peppers into ½" strips, reserving any pepper juices.

Place the pepper strips and any juices in a medium serving bowl. Add 1 tablespoon of the parsley, the vinegar, water, ¼ teaspoon of the dried oregano (or 1½ teaspoons fresh), 1 clove garlic, and ⅛ teaspoon each of the salt and black pepper. Stir to blend.

Coat a broiler-pan rack with olive-oil cooking spray.

In a medium bowl, combine the scallops, the remaining 1 tablespoon parsley, ¼ teaspoon dried oregano (or 1½ teaspoons fresh), garlic clove, and ⅛ teaspoon each salt and black pepper. Arrange the scallops in a single layer on the prepared rack.

Broil 3" to 4" from the heat for 3 minutes, or until the scallops are opaque.

Add the scallops to the bell pepper mixture and toss gently. Serve warm or at room temperature.

Makes 4 servings
Per serving: 154 calories, 2 g fat

Lidia Matticchio Bastianich

*L*idia Matticchio Bastianich was born in Istria, a peninsula long contested by both Yugoslavia and Italy—today it's in Croatia—and has lived in New York since 1958. She is the creator and star of two top-rated television shows, *Lidia's Italian American Kitchen* and, on PBS, *Lidia's Italian Table*. An acclaimed chef and restauranteur, she is widely regarded as the "First Lady" of Italian cuisine and restaurants in the United States. She received the 2002 James Beard Outstanding Chef Award. In Manhattan, she is the owner of the award-winning Felidia as well as Esca and Becco. She also owns Lidia's in Kansas City, Missouri, and in Pittsburgh. Bastianich was one of the five top television chefs featured in the millennium cooking special *An American Feast*, hosted by Julia Child, which aired in December 2000 in every television market in the United States.

If there was one food that you could not resist under any circumstances what would it be?

LB: Pasta.

What is the comfort food that you turn to in times of distress—and why that food?

LB: Pasta and soups. They are warm and caressing and make you feel good from the inside out.

What is the most unusual combination of food that you eat?

LB: Bread and anchovies. I just take a piece of bread and a few anchovies out of a can and make a sandwich. It has a lot of complexity and flavor and is very satisfying.

What is your favorite ethnic food and why?

LB: Thai food. I like the intensity of the flavors and the overall spiciness. It stimulates my mind and my palate.

Is supermarket shopping a pleasant or unpleasant experience for you—and when you're there, do you check the food labels?

LB: If it's a good supermarket, I love it. I'm amazed and I'm excited to see the specialties, especially in the vegetable and herb departments. And if it's a bad supermarket, it can really be depressing to see all the cellophane. Nothing looks real or alive. I do check labels.

How does food relate to you and your career?

LB: It's essential. It's almost like air. I need to be around it; it gives me all kinds of fulfillment—personal, professional, gustatory, emotional. It's my medium of communication.

How old were you when you started cooking?

LB: Ever since I can remember. I was perched up on a little stool because I was so small while making gnocchi and pasta with my grandmother.

Do you cook at home?

LB: Very much. I have two children and four grandchildren, and my mother lives with me. My table at home is always full. During the weekends that I'm not traveling, I always hear "What's for dinner, Mom? What's for lunch, Grandma?"

Do interesting things happen when you cook?

LB: I was filming one of my television series, and I was making a cake, and instead of sugar I put in salt in great amounts and didn't realize. The whole crew would always wait for me to finish whatever was being cooked that day, and then they would dive in. That day the crew began nibbling the cake, and they were looking at each other but nobody said a word because they didn't want to upset me until I finally tasted it and realized the error.

What does food mean to you? Does it make you feel good?

LB: Food for me is the essence of life. It nurtures us, but it also feeds our emotions. It is social; it is why why the world turns, in a sense. It really makes everything happen. I go back and think about my grandparents: From the moment they got up in the morning till the moment they went to sleep, everything they did was for the ultimate goal of procuring food for the family.

This must have been done with great pride.

LB: Yes, absolutely.

Is there any relation between food and your childhood?

LB: I think that my involvement in food at an early age formulated the basis and passion that later became a career.

What is your favorite smell in the kitchen?

LB: Caramelization of chicken and onions.

What is your favorite seasoning?

LB: All fresh herbs.

As a child, what was your least favorite food?

LB: Chicory.

If you were on a desert island, which five food items would you have?

LB: Oil, pasta, broccoli rabe, bread, and wine.

Which food items do you keep in your refrigerator on a regular basis?

LB: Cheese, celery, carrots, anchovies, butter, mineral water, beer, capers, olives, eggs.

Whom would you most like to have dinner with?

LB: M.F.K. Fisher. She was a great food writer and essayist.

SCALLOPS WITH PENNE, BROCCOLI RABE, AND TOMATO SAUCE

QUICK

Prep time: 10 minutes ■ Cook time: 20 minutes

If the scallops you purchase for this recipe are large, you can slice them in half lengthwise. Or, look for the smaller bay scallops at the fish market if you prefer.

1 medium head broccoli rabe, tough stems removed, cut into ½" pieces

8 ounces penne pasta

1 small onion, chopped

3 cloves garlic, minced

1 can (28 ounces) crushed tomatoes

2 tablespoons dry white wine or vegetable broth

½ teaspoon salt

¼ teaspoon freshly ground black pepper

1 pound sea scallops, tough muscles at sides removed, rinsed and patted dry

½ cup slivered fresh basil leaves

Bring a large pot of water to a boil over high heat. Add the broccoli rabe and return to a boil. Cook for 3 minutes, or until tender. With a slotted spoon, remove to a colander and rinse briefly under cold water to stop the cooking. Drain again and place in a large bowl. Do not discard the cooking water.

Return the water in the pot to a boil. Add the pasta and cook according to package directions. Drain and place in the bowl with the broccoli rabe.

Meanwhile, heat a large nonstick skillet coated with olive-oil cooking spray over medium heat. Add the onion and garlic and cook, stirring often, for 3 minutes, or until tender. Stir in the tomatoes, wine or broth, salt, and pepper and bring to a boil. Reduce the heat to low, cover, and simmer, stirring occasionally, for 8 minutes, or until fairly thick.

Add the scallops to the tomato sauce. Cook, stirring often, for 3 minutes, or until the scallops are opaque. Pour the sauce over the penne and broccoli rabe and toss to coat. Sprinkle with the basil.

Makes 4 servings
Per serving: 379 calories, 3 g fat

MUSSELS IN SCALLION BROTH

Prep time: 15 minutes ■ Cook time: 10 minutes

¼ cup vegetable broth

1 bunch scallions, thinly sliced

5 cloves garlic, minced

½ cup dry white wine

64 medium mussels (about 3 pounds), scrubbed and debearded

⅓ cup chopped flat-leaf parsley

Place the broth, scallions, and garlic in a Dutch oven and bring to a boil over high heat. Reduce the heat to medium, cover, and simmer for 3 minutes, or until the scallions are wilted. Add the wine and increase the heat to high.

Add the mussels. Cover and cook, shaking the pot and stirring frequently, for 5 minutes, or until the mussels open. Remove from the heat and discard any unopened shells. Sprinkle with the parsley.

Makes 4 servings
Per serving: 150 calories, 2 g fat

Mussel Muscle

Here are two classics of Mediterranean seafood, but what a difference! This meager portion of fried calamari costs a full 270 calories. The frying process brings its fat content up to 12 highly saturated grams, virtually wiping away the health benefits that seafood typically presents. Instead, go for this zesty bowl of Mussels in Scallion Broth. It's highly tasty, entirely filling, and adds the power of protein from the mussels and nutrients from the scallions, garlic, and parsley. And it's so low in calories that you can sop up the juices with a thick whole grain roll; that will bring you to the same 270 calories as the fried calamari, but it won't even approach the fat content.

4 ounces fried calamari
270 calories **12** grams fat

**1 serving Mussels
in Scallion Broth**
150 calories **2** grams fat

+

1 whole grain roll
120 calories **1** gram fat

270 calories **3** grams fat

CHILI SHRIMP WITH FRUITY RELISH

Prep time: 20 minutes ■ *Cook time: 5 minutes*

Relish

1   medium mango, peeled and cut into ¼" pieces

1   cup diced fresh or juice-packed canned pineapple (¼" pieces)

1   medium tart green apple, diced

2   tablespoons chopped red onion

¾   teaspoon chili powder

¼   teaspoon grated lime peel

1   teaspoon lime juice

   Pinch of salt

Shrimp

1½   pounds large shrimp, peeled and deveined, tails left on

1½   teaspoons chili powder

1   teaspoon ground cumin

¾   teaspoon salt

½   teaspoon paprika

¼   teaspoon coarsely cracked black pepper

1   teaspoon olive oil

To make the relish: In a medium bowl, combine the mango, pineapple, apple, onion, chili powder, lime peel, lime juice, and salt. Cover while preparing the shrimp.

To make the shrimp: Meanwhile, preheat the broiler. Coat the broiler-pan rack with olive-oil cooking spray.

In a medium bowl, combine the shrimp, chili powder, cumin, salt, paprika, pepper, and oil. Toss to coat well.

Place the shrimp on the prepared rack in a single layer. Broil 4" to 6" from the heat for 5 minutes, or until the shrimp are opaque.

Serve the shrimp with the relish.

Makes 4 servings
Per serving: 190 calories, 3 g fat

With Relish

There's little to relish in this pallid, flavorless chicken leg. Yet it contains 190 calories and 11 grams of saturated fat—a high price to pay for a small amount of unsatisfying food. For the same calorie count and 3 grams of "good" fat, try this healthy serving of zesty chili shrimp. You'll relish both the taste and the health benefits.

1 chicken drumstick (3½ ounces)
190 calories **11** grams fat

**1 serving Chili Shrimp
with Fruity Relish**
190 calories 3 grams fat

GRILLED CURRIED SHRIMP AND VEGETABLE KEBABS WITH CUCUMBER RAITA

Prep time: 20 minutes ■ *Cook time: 15 minutes*

Kebabs

½ cup fresh cilantro sprigs

3 tablespoons lemon juice

2 tablespoons water

3 cloves garlic

1 tablespoon prepared red curry paste

2 teaspoons olive oil

¼ teaspoon salt

1¼ pounds large shrimp, peeled and deveined, tails left on

8 button mushrooms

3 red bell peppers, cut into 1½" pieces

3 medium onions, cut into wedges and wedges separated into pieces

1 medium zucchini, cut into ¼"-thick half-moon slices

Raita

1 cup fat-free plain yogurt or soy alternative

¼ cup grated cucumber

1 tablespoon chopped fresh cilantro

1 clove garlic, minced

⅛ teaspoon salt

To make the kebabs: In a food processor, combine the cilantro, lemon juice, water, garlic, curry paste, oil, and salt. Process until smooth. Divide the mixture between 2 medium bowls.

Add the shrimp to one bowl and toss to coat. Add the mushrooms, peppers, onions, and zucchini to the other bowl and toss to coat.

Coat a grill rack or broiler-pan rack with olive-oil cooking spray. Preheat the grill to medium or preheat the broiler.

Thread the shrimp onto 4 metal skewers. On each of 4 additional skewers, alternately thread the mushrooms, bell peppers, onions, and zucchini.

Place the vegetable skewers on the rack and cook for 7 minutes per side, turning once, or until tender and lightly charred. While the vegetables are cooking, place the shrimp skewers on the rack and cook for 5 minutes, turning once, or until opaque.

To make the raita: In a small bowl, stir the yogurt, cucumber, cilantro, garlic, and salt.

Serve 1 shrimp skewer and 1 vegetable skewer per person, along with the raita.

Makes 4 servings
Per serving: 260 calories, 4 g fat

Tuna Meltdown

Sure, you like the mix of food textures and tastes in a tuna melt. But consider the cost in calories and saturated fat of even the most diminutive wedge. Here's a recipe for an alternative mix of textures and tastes—spicy shrimp, grilled vegetables, and cool raita—that is far healthier and lower in calories.

¼ **tuna melt**
260 calories 16 grams fat

1 serving Grilled Curried Shrimp and Vegetable Kebabs with Cucumber Raita
260 calories 4 grams fat

SPANISH-STYLE SEAFOOD STEW

Prep time: 15 minutes ■ Cook time: 20 minutes

- 2 Italian frying peppers or Cubanelle peppers, or 1 green bell pepper, cut into thin strips
- 1 yellow bell pepper, cut into thin strips
- 1 onion, halved and cut into ½"-thick slices
- ¾ cup vegetable broth
- 4 cloves garlic, minced
- 1 large tomato, coarsely chopped
- 1¼ teaspoons paprika
- ¼ teaspoon salt
- ¼ teaspoon freshly ground black pepper
- ⅓ cup dry white wine
- 1 dozen littleneck clams, scrubbed
- 12 ounces large shrimp, peeled and deveined, tails left on
- 1 skinned cod, hake, halibut, or scrod fillet (10 ounces), cut into 2" chunks
- ½ cup chopped flat-leaf parsley

Heat a large skillet coated with olive-oil cooking spray over medium heat. Add the frying peppers, bell pepper, and onion and cook, stirring frequently, for 7 minutes, or until tender. If the pan gets dry, add a little of the broth, 1 tablespoon at a time.

Stir in the garlic, tomato, paprika, salt, and black pepper, and cook, stirring, for 1 minute.

Stir in the remaining broth and the wine and bring to a boil. Reduce the heat to low, cover, and simmer for 5 minutes, or until the flavors are blended.

Stir in the clams. Cover and cook for 2 minutes. Add the shrimp and fish and stir gently. Cover and cook, stirring once, for 4 minutes, or until the shrimp are opaque, the fish flakes easily, and the clams have opened. Discard any unopened shells. Sprinkle with the parsley.

Makes 4 servings
Per serving: 225 calories, 2 g fat

Stew by Stew

It is possible to prepare seafood in such a way that it is high in calories. This crab imperial is a case in point: The very basis of the recipe is butter. Instead, stick to something like this imaginative Spanish-Style Seafood Stew and get a much more generous serving of food.

1 cup crab imperial
450 calories **22** grams fat **VS.**

**1 serving Spanish-Style
Seafood Stew**
225 calories **2** grams fat

SHRIMP WITH GREEN BEANS, CARROTS, AND GINGER

Prep time: 20 minutes ■ *Cook time: 15 minutes*

Soy sauce, garlic, and ginger combine for a distinctively Asian flavor. If you prefer a milder taste, reduce the amounts slightly to your liking.

1¼ pounds large shrimp, peeled and deveined, tails left on

3 tablespoons reduced-sodium soy sauce

¼ teaspoon ground white pepper

12 ounces fresh green beans, ends trimmed, cut in half

2 large carrots, cut into julienne strips

1½ teaspoons olive oil

¼ cup julienne-cut peeled fresh ginger

4 cloves garlic, peeled and thinly sliced

1 cup vegetable broth

2 teaspoons cornstarch

1 tablespoon water

¼ cup chopped fresh cilantro

¼ cup slivered fresh basil

In a medium bowl, combine the shrimp, 1 tablespoon of the soy sauce, and the pepper. Set aside.

Bring ½" water to a boil in a large nonstick skillet. Add the green beans and return to a boil. Cook for 3 minutes. Stir in the carrots and cook for 3 minutes, or until the vegetables are tender. Drain in a colander and rinse briefly under cold water to stop the cooking. Rinse and dry the skillet.

In the same skillet, heat the oil over medium–high heat. Add the ginger and garlic and cook, stirring, for 2 minutes, or until fragrant and just starting to brown. Stir in the broth and the remaining 2 tablespoons soy sauce and bring to a boil.

Add the shrimp. Reduce the heat to low, cover, and cook for 3 minutes, or until the shrimp are opaque.

In a cup, dissolve the cornstarch in the water. Add to the skillet along with the vegetables and cook, stirring constantly, for 1 minute, or until the broth is thickened and bubbly and the vegetables are heated. Remove from the heat and stir in the cilantro and basil.

Makes 4 servings
Per serving: 184 calories, 3 g fat

Firefighter Martin Tighe

Martin Tighe was a New York City police officer for 5 years before joining the fire department in 1990. He served 2 years in Manhattan, then joined up with Engine 88 in the Bronx and has been there ever since. Tighe, who lost 21 pounds in the first 2 months of his Picture-Perfect Weight-Loss program, cooks in the firehouse when it's his turn, "unless someone else has a better idea." You can't get much better than his recipe for Shrimp and Sun-Dried Tomatoes. It's a recipe he concocted by combining elements from two other recipes in the firehouse's collection. He serves it for lunch—all by itself without any accompaniment. As you will find out for yourself once you've tried it, it doesn't need any.

SHRIMP AND SUN-DRIED TOMATOES

12 ounces angel hair pasta, linguine, or spaghetti

4 ounces oil-packed sun-dried tomatoes, drained and chopped

1¼ pounds large shrimp, peeled and deveined

2 cloves garlic

½ cup vegetable or chicken broth

½ cup dry white wine

1 teaspoon dried basil or to taste

½ pound imitation crabmeat, chopped

Grated Parmesan or Romano cheese (optional)

Prepare the pasta according to package directions.

Meanwhile, place the tomatoes in a deep skillet over medium-high heat. Add the shrimp and garlic and cook, stirring, for 5 minutes, or until the shrimp are opaque. Add the broth, wine, and basil and bring to a boil. Add the crabmeat and reduce the heat to low. Simmer for 5 minutes.

Place the pasta in a serving bowl and top with the shrimp mixture. Sprinkle with the cheese (if using).

Makes 6 servings
Per serving: 344 calories, 6 g fat

Guillermo Pernot

¡Pasión!, Philadelphia, Pennsylvania

A native of Buenos Aires, Argentina, Guillermo Pernot has taken nuevo Latino cooking to new heights in his adopted home of Philadelphia. As chef and owner of ¡Pasión!, he has garnered rave reviews including a James Beard award for Best Chef 2002 for his cuisine, a delicious blend of the foods of the Americas, incorporating such indigenous ingredients as boniato, yuca, plantain, and malanga.

BLACK BASS CEVICHE AND CHAYOTE MIRASOL SALAD

1   pound black sea bass fillet, with skin on and pinbones removed

½   cup fresh lime juice

2   tablespoons soy sauce

    Pinch salt

2   teaspoons Japanese toasted sesame oil

1   (2-inch) section fresh ginger, peeled and cut into julienne strips

1   whole fresh mirasol chile

¼   chayote squash, unpeeled, with large seed cut out, and cut into julienne strips

2   scallions, green part only, cut into julienne strips

Preheat the broiler (or use a small kitchen blowtorch). Place the sea bass fillet under the hot broiler for 1 to 2 minutes, only as long as it takes for the skin to get browned and bubbly. Remove the fillets from the broiler and wrap in plastic wrap. Freeze for about 30 minutes, or until firm. Using a sharp knife, cut on the bias into ½-inch slices. Arrange in a single layer in a shallow, nonreactive bowl or platter.

In a small bowl, whisk together the lime juice, soy sauce, salt, and sesame oil. Rub half of this marinade onto the fish, cover, and refrigerate for 30 minutes.

Bring a small saucepan of water to a boil. Add the ginger and cook 1 minute. Drain in a colander and rinse under cold water to stop the cooking.

Cut off the top of the chile. Scoop out the seeds and surrounding white membrane and discard. Open up the chile so that it lies flat and trim it into an even rectangle. Cut the chile into very thin julienne strips.

Combine the ginger, chile, chayote, and scallions with the remaining marinade. To serve, arrange sections of marinated sea bass in a circle in the center of 4 serving plates. Place a small mound of the salad on top. Drizzle the fish with any remaining dressing and serve immediately.

Makes 4 servings
Per serving: 164 calories, 4 g fat

SPICY GRILLED CHICKEN BREASTS

Prep time: 5 minutes ■ *Marinate time: 1 hour* ■ *Cook time: 10 minutes*

The tangy sauce is what makes this chicken special. You probably already have the ingredients in your pantry, so it's a snap to prepare.

⅓ cup ketchup

2 tablespoons lemon juice

1½ tablespoons reduced-sodium soy sauce

1½ teaspoons chili garlic sauce

¾ teaspoon toasted sesame oil

4 boneless, skinless chicken breast halves

4 cloves garlic, crushed

In a small bowl, combine the ketchup, lemon juice, soy sauce, chili garlic sauce, and oil.

Place the chicken in a large zip-top plastic bag. Add half of the ketchup mixture and the garlic. Turn the chicken to evenly coat with the sauce. Cover and marinate in the refrigerator for 1 hour.

Preheat the grill to medium-high or preheat the broiler. Coat the grill rack or broiler-pan rack with olive-oil cooking spray.

Remove the chicken from the marinade, discarding the marinade. Grill or broil the chicken, brushing frequently with the reserved sauce, for 10 minutes, turning once, or until a thermometer inserted in the thickest portion registers 160°F and the juices run clear.

Serve the chicken with the remaining sauce, if desired.

Makes 4 servings
Per serving: 164 calories, 2 g fat

Barbecued Dessert

Use the last of the warm coals from your barbecue to grill fruits for dessert. The grilling caramelizes the natural sugars in fruit, creating a particularly rich flavor. Try slices of pineapple, bananas in their skins, apple chunks skewered with pears, and whole peaches. Serve the grilled fruits with low-fat vanilla yogurt or soy alternative, and sprinkle with grated nutmeg or ground cinnamon.

PAN-GRILLED CHICKEN WITH GRAPES AND THYME

QUICK

Prep time: 10 minutes ■ Cook time: 20 minutes

4   boneless, skinless chicken breast halves

2   teaspoons chopped fresh thyme

½   teaspoon salt

¼   teaspoon freshly ground black pepper

1½ teaspoons extra-virgin olive oil

1½ cups halved seedless red and/or green grapes

½   cup vegetable broth

¼   cup dry white wine

½   teaspoon cornstarch

2   teaspoons cold water

Sprinkle the chicken with 1½ teaspoons of the thyme and the salt and pepper.

Coat a stove-top grill pan or skillet with olive-oil cooking spray and heat over medium heat for 2 minutes. Place the chicken in the pan. Grill for 4 minutes per side, turning once, or until a thermometer inserted in the thickest portion registers 160°F and the juices run clear. Place the chicken on a platter and cover loosely with foil to keep warm.

Heat the oil in the same pan or skillet over medium heat. Add the grapes and cook, shaking the pan often, for 3 minutes, or until the grapes are hot and begin to give up some juices. Place the grapes in a bowl.

Pour the broth and wine into the skillet and stir well. Increase the heat to medium-high and bring to a boil. Boil for 4 minutes, or until reduced to about ⅓ cup.

In a cup, combine the cornstarch and water and stir until dissolved. Add to the sauce in the skillet. Cook, stirring, until the sauce thickens and boils.

Stir in the grapes, any chicken juices from the platter, and the remaining ½ teaspoon thyme. Cook for 30 seconds; remove from the heat.

On a cutting board, cut the chicken diagonally into 1" pieces and arrange on the platter. Top with the sauce.

Makes 4 servings
Per serving: 195 calories, 4 g fat

A Game of Chicken

The single Buffalo wing, with its meager dollop of dressing, has more than three times the fat content of the Pan-Grilled Chicken with Grapes and Thyme. And it's much less food. If it's chicken you want, the wing gives you a taste; for the same number of calories, the grilled chicken with grapes gives you a meal.

1 Buffalo wing with 1 tablespoon blue cheese dressing
195 calories **14** grams fat

1 serving Pan-Grilled
Chicken with
Grapes and Thyme
195 calories 4 grams fat

Firefighter John Rohr

John Rohr started his firefighting career in 1993 at Ladder Company 10 in downtown Manhattan. He has been there ever since. His fellow firefighters, he says, are "harsh food critics," so Rohr has always been wary of cooking for them. Typically, when his turn to cook rolled around, he would more or less "adapt what others did," often experimenting with his adaptation at home. Rohr embarked on Picture-Perfect Weight Loss in December 2001 and lost 83 pounds by the summer. Credit the kind of "adaptation" he built into this lemon chicken recipe for the result. Where chicken served in the firehouse is almost invariably fried, Rohr "tried to put my own spin on it and just started fooling around here and there," adding vegetables and seasonings to enhance both the taste and the appearance of the dish. His wife and daughter liked the result, and his fellow firefighters asked for seconds and thirds. You will, too. Rohr recommends a balsamic vinegar salad as accompaniment.

LEMON CHICKEN WITH ASPARAGUS OVER RICE

½ cup rice

1 whole boneless, skinless chicken breast, cut into ½" slices

¾ teaspoon salt

¼ teaspoon freshly ground black pepper

4 cloves garlic, chopped

½ red bell pepper, chopped

8 ounces asparagus, cut into ½" pieces

1¼ teaspoons lemon peel

½ cup low-fat chicken broth or water

Prepare the rice according to package directions.

Meanwhile, season the chicken with ¼ teaspoon of the salt and the black pepper and place in a large nonstick skillet over medium heat. Cook, stirring occasionally, for 5 minutes, or until the chicken is no longer pink. Add the garlic, bell pepper, and asparagus and cook for 1 minute. Add the lemon peel, broth or water, and the remaining ½ teaspoon salt and bring to a simmer. Cover and cook for 4 minutes, or until the vegetables are tender. Serve over the rice.

Makes 2 servings
Per serving: 414 calories, 3 g fat

TURKEY SCALLOPS WITH TOMATO SAUCE AND SPINACH

QUICK

Prep time: 10 minutes ■ *Cook time: 15 minutes*

This is a great dish for a busy weeknight. The thin turkey cooks quickly, so you can have a healthy dinner on the table in less than a half hour.

2   bags (6 ounces each) baby spinach
    or flat-leaf spinach

⅓   cup chopped fresh basil

½   teaspoon salt

¼   teaspoon freshly ground black
    pepper

1   pound turkey breast cutlets,
    pounded to ⅛" thickness

1   tablespoon + 1 teaspoon olive oil

4   cloves garlic, crushed

1   pound tomatoes, peeled, seeded,
    and cut into rough ½" pieces

Heat a large nonstick skillet coated with olive-oil cooking spray over medium heat. Add the spinach, working in batches if necessary, and cook, stirring, for 2 minutes, or until the spinach is just wilted. Remove to a large platter. Wipe the skillet with a paper towel.

In a cup, combine 1 tablespoon of the basil, ¼ teaspoon of the salt, and the pepper. Rub over the turkey. In the same skillet, heat 1 tablespoon of the oil over high heat. Add half of the turkey and cook for 2 to 4 minutes, or until lightly browned on both sides and no longer pink. Place the turkey over the spinach on the platter. Repeat to cook the remaining turkey. Cover the platter loosely with foil.

Reduce the heat to low. Add the remaining 1 teaspoon oil and the garlic to the pan juices and cook, stirring occasionally and pressing down on the garlic, for 1½ to 2 minutes, or until golden.

Add the tomatoes and the remaining ¼ teaspoon salt and increase the heat to medium. Cook, stirring often, for 3 minutes, or until the tomatoes start to give off their juices.

Remove the pan from the heat and add the remaining basil. Spoon the sauce over the turkey and spinach.

Makes 4 servings
Per serving: 224 calories, 8 g fat

Tomato Tip

The red pigment of the tomato indicates the presence of lycopene, an antioxidant that helps neutralize cell-damaging free radicals before they can do any harm. While its well-studied cousin, beta-carotene, has gotten a lot of press over the past few years, studies indicate that red lycopene may pack twice the cancer-fighting wallop of orange beta-carotene. In addition, tomatoes are rich in vitamin C and contain appreciable amounts of vitamins A and B, potassium, iron, phosphorus, and beta-carotene. A medium tomato has about as much fiber as a slice of whole wheat bread and only about 30 calories. The moral? Eat your carrots, but be sure to eat plenty of tomatoes, too.

TURKEY CUTLETS MILANESE

Prep time: 10 minutes ■ *Cook time: 5 minutes*

Salad

2	teaspoons extra-virgin olive oil
2	teaspoons balsamic vinegar
½	teaspoon chopped fresh rosemary
⅛	teaspoon salt
⅛	teaspoon freshly ground black pepper
1½	cups halved yellow and/or red cherry tomatoes
½	red onion, chopped
4	cups Italian-style salad greens or baby greens with herbs

Turkey

2	teaspoons chopped fresh rosemary
1½	teaspoons grated lemon peel
½	teaspoon salt
¼	teaspoon freshly ground black pepper
1	pound turkey breast cutlets

To make the salad: In a large bowl, whisk together the oil, vinegar, rosemary, salt, and pepper. Add the tomatoes and onion and toss gently. Place the greens on top but do not toss. Set aside while preparing the turkey.

To make the turkey: Preheat the broiler. Coat the broiler-pan rack with olive-oil cooking spray.

In a cup, combine the rosemary, lemon peel, salt, and pepper. Rub over the turkey. Place the turkey on the prepared rack.

Broil the turkey 4" to 6" from the heat for 5 minutes, turning once, or until no longer pink.

Toss the salad and place on a platter. Top with the turkey.

Makes 4 servings
Per serving: 190 calories, 6 g fat

Concentrating on Cutlets

Dipped in batter and fried, this small morsel of wiener-schnitzel charges a high price in fat for a brief bit of cutlet. Concentrate instead on these Turkey Cutlets Milanese. For the same calories and less fat, you'll eat a meal unto itself.

2 ounces wienerschnitzel
190 calories **10** grams fat

**1 serving Turkey
Cutlets Milanese**
190 calories 6 grams fat

STEAK PIZZAIOLA

Prep time: 20 minutes ■ *Cook time: 25 minutes*

1 lean boneless sirloin beef steak (1 pound), well-trimmed

1 teaspoon dried Italian herb seasoning

½ teaspoon salt

½ teaspoon cracked black pepper

1 tablespoon olive oil

1 medium sweet onion, cut lengthwise into quarters and quarters thinly sliced

1 medium red bell pepper, cut into thin strips

1 medium yellow bell pepper, cut into thin strips

6 cloves garlic, thinly sliced

1 can (15 ounces) diced tomatoes, drained

1 teaspoon balsamic vinegar

Preheat the grill or broiler. Coat the grill rack or broiler-pan rack with cooking spray.

Place the steak on a plate. Rub ½ teaspoon of the Italian seasoning and ¼ teaspoon each of the salt and black pepper into both sides of the steak. Set aside.

Heat the oil in a large, nonstick skillet over medium heat. Add the onion, bell peppers, garlic, and the remaining ¼ teaspoon salt and cook, stirring often, for 12 minutes, or until the vegetables are tender and lightly browned.

Add the tomatoes, the remaining ½ teaspoon Italian seasoning, and the remaining ¼ teaspoon black pepper. Cook, stirring, for 1 minute. Reduce the heat to low, cover, and simmer for 5 minutes, or until the vegetables are tender. Remove from the heat and stir in the vinegar.

Meanwhile, grill or broil the steak 3" to 4" from the heat for 12 minutes, turning once, or until a thermometer inserted in the center registers 145°F for medium-rare. Remove the steak from the heat.

Place the steak on a cutting board and let stand for 5 minutes. Thinly slice the steak and arrange on a platter with the vegetables.

Makes 6 servings
Per serving: 175 calories, 7 g fat

Classic Contest

In one corner: a couple of mouthfuls of sausage that are high in fat, high in sodium, and high in heart-*un*healthy fat. In the other corner: an Italian classic offering not just steak grilled in oil but a plateful of fiber and nutrients—peppers, tomatoes, and onions—at half the fat content of the sausage. Bottom line? No contest.

1 piece (1¾ ounces) sausage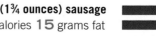
175 calories **15** grams fat

1 serving Steak Pizzaiola
175 calories **7** grams fat

Beef and Mushroom Stir-Fry with Tomatoes and Broccoli

Prep time: 5 minutes ■ Cook time: 40 minutes

1¼   cups brown rice

12   ounces lean, well-trimmed boneless beef top sirloin or London broil, cut into ¼"-thick slices

3   tablespoons reduced-sodium soy sauce

3   cloves garlic, minced

½   teaspoon toasted sesame oil

½   cup vegetable broth

1   tablespoon shao-hsing rice cooking wine or sherry (optional)

1   tablespoon cornstarch

1   tablespoon canola oil

2   teaspoons minced fresh ginger

12   ounces mixed mushrooms, such as white button, stemmed shiitake, cremino, and/or portobello, sliced

8   cups small broccoli florets

3   medium tomatoes, cut into thin wedges

¼   teaspoon salt

Prepare the rice according to package directions.

Meanwhile, in a small bowl, combine the beef, 1 tablespoon of the soy sauce, the garlic, and sesame oil. Toss well and marinate for 20 minutes. In a cup, combine the broth, wine (if using), cornstarch, and the remaining 2 tablespoons soy sauce until blended. Set aside.

Heat 1½ teaspoons of the canola oil in a large skillet over high heat. Add the ginger and cook, stirring, for 30 seconds. Carefully and quickly place the beef slices in the skillet. Cook, without stirring, for 1 minute (otherwise, the beef will steam instead of brown).

Begin stirring the beef, for 1 minute only, until it is browned but still pink in the center. Place in a clean bowl.

Add the remaining 1½ teaspoons oil to the skillet. Add the mushrooms and cook, stirring frequently, for 5 minutes, or until the mushrooms are browned and their juices have evaporated.

Add the broccoli and tomatoes. Sprinkle with the salt and cook, stirring occasionally, for 2 minutes, or until the vegetables begin to soften.

Stir the cornstarch mixture again and pour into the skillet. Cook, stirring, for 3 minutes, or until the mixture is thickened and bubbly and heated through. Stir in the beef and any juices in the bowl and heat briefly. Serve with the rice.

Makes 6 servings
Per serving: 350 calories, 8 g fat

Stirring It Up

This minute portion of rib steak—with its equally minute splash of high-calorie hollandaise—carries a heavy price in fat. For the same calories, eat a meal: beef and mushrooms with one-third the fat content *plus* all the nutrient goodness of the mushrooms.

1 piece (3 ounces) rib steak with
2 tablespoons bordelaise or hollandaise sauce
350 calories **26** grams fat

1 serving Beef and
Mushroom Stir-Fry with
Tomatoes and Broccoli
350 calories 8 grams fat

Herb Blends

The right combination of herbs and spices can magically transform the simplest foods into culinary treats to remember. Whether you're spicing a salad or seasoning meat, vegetables, or seafood, an herb blend adds exciting layers of flavor. And since you can prepare dried herb blends ahead of time, you don't have to fumble with half a dozen (or more) bottles at the last minute.

Whether you're mixing a small amount to use right away or an entire bottle for future meals, here are a few blends that you may want to try. Store leftovers in dark, airtight containers in a cool, dry, dark place. Heat, light, and exposure to air destroy the flavor of dried herbs and spices.

Poultry Seasoning

This savory herb blend brings out the best flavors of chicken and turkey without added salt. Use it to season soups, stews, casseroles, stuffings, and dumplings.

 2 teaspoons dried marjoram

 2 teaspoons onion powder

 1 teaspoon dried thyme

 ½ teaspoon dried sage

 ½ teaspoon dried savory

 ½ teaspoon freshly ground black pepper

Makes about 2 tablespoons

Lamb Seasoning

For great-tasting lamb, rub this herb blend into the meat before cooking.

 2 teaspoons dried parsley

 2 teaspoons dried rosemary

 2 teaspoons dried thyme

Makes about 2 tablespoons

Beef Seasoning

Beef has strong flavors of its own. So here's a simple blend to enhance those natural flavors without overpowering them. Add this seasoning to almost any beef dish during cooking.

 2 teaspoons dried parsley

 2 teaspoons garlic powder

 2 teaspoons onion powder

 2 teaspoons freshly ground black pepper

Makes about 2½ tablespoons

Italian Herb Seasoning

This all-purpose blend perks up the flavor of soups, stews, gravy, tomato sauce, meat, or vegetables. Or sprinkle it on baked potatoes and pizza.

 1 tablespoon dried oregano

 1 tablespoon dried basil

 1 teaspoon dried thyme

Makes about 2 tablespoons

Variation

For a more zesty blend, add ½ teaspoon onion powder, ¼ teaspoon garlic powder, and ¼ teaspoon crushed red-pepper flakes.

Vegetable Seasoning

A few shakes of this salt-free herb blend will keep your cooked vegetables from tasting bland and boring. You can use it in soups and casseroles, too.

 1 teaspoon dried basil

 1 teaspoon dried chervil

 1 teaspoon dried chives

 1 teaspoon dried marjoram

 1 teaspoon dried parsley

 ½ teaspoon dried savory

 ½ teaspoon dried thyme

Makes about 2½ tablespoons

CURRY POWDER

Similar to the curry powders sold in stores, this recipe lends a delicious, exotic flavor to vegetable, bean, and rice dishes. For the most flavor, sauté the curry powder in a little oil before adding the other ingredients. Because you're using whole seeds, you'll want to grind the mixture to a fine powder with a mortar and pestle or with a spice mill or a coffee mill reserved just for spices. Alternatively, use already ground forms of the same herbs and spices.

3½ teaspoons coriander seeds
2½ teaspoons turmeric
1 teaspoon cumin seeds
1 teaspoon fenugreek seeds
½ teaspoon black peppercorns
½ teaspoon dry mustard
½ teaspoon allspice berries
¼ teaspoon crushed red-pepper flakes
¼ teaspoon ground ginger

Makes about 3 tablespoons

CAJUN SPICE

Lend a bit of zip to any Creole or Cajun dish with this Louisiana seasoning. Or rub it into catfish or red snapper fillets as a "blackening" seasoning before cooking.

2 teaspoons paprika
2 teaspoons freshly ground black pepper
1½ teaspoons garlic powder
1 teaspoon crushed red-pepper flakes
1 teaspoon dried thyme
1 teaspoon dried oregano
1 teaspoon onion powder
¼ teaspoon dry mustard

Makes about 3 tablespoons

CHILI POWDER

Commercial chili powders often contain added salt. Here's a spicy salt-free recipe that's great in chili, sloppy joes, bean dishes, soups, stews, and savory sauces. For a milder mix, cut back on the ground red pepper.

1 tablespoon ground cumin
1 teaspoon dried oregano
1 teaspoon garlic powder
1 teaspoon onion powder
½ teaspoon ground red pepper
½ teaspoon paprika
¼ teaspoon ground allspice

Makes about 2½ tablespoons

PUMPKIN PIE SPICE

This delicious blend isn't just for pumpkin pie. Try it on sweet potatoes, acorn or butternut squash, carrots, or soups.

2 teaspoons ground cinnamon
2 teaspoons ground nutmeg
1 teaspoon ground ginger
½ teaspoon ground cloves
½ teaspoon ground mace

Makes about 2 tablespoons

BEEF STEW WITH WINTER VEGETABLES

Prep time: 15 minutes ■ *Marinate time: overnight* ■ *Cook time: 2 hours 40 minutes*

Beef fillet tips work well in this stew. They're often available at a discount, so check at your market or local butcher shop.

¾ pound well-trimmed beef tenderloin, cut into 1" cubes

½ cup dry red wine

4 cloves garlic, minced

½ teaspoon dried thyme, crushed

½ teaspoon ground cinnamon

¼ teaspoon freshly ground black pepper

3 cups fat-free beef or vegetable broth

3 medium onions, each cut into 6 wedges

1 can (28 ounces) diced tomatoes

1 medium butternut squash, peeled and cut into 1" pieces

1 bag (6 ounces) baby spinach

In a zip-top plastic bag, combine the beef, wine, garlic, thyme, cinnamon, and pepper. Seal and marinate in the refrigerator overnight.

The next day, preheat the oven to 325°F. Place the meat mixture, broth, onions, and tomatoes (with juice) in an ovenproof Dutch oven. Place over high heat and bring to a boil. Cover and place in the oven. Bake for 1 hour.

Stir in the squash. Cover and bake for 1½ hours. Remove from the oven and stir in the spinach until wilted.

Makes 6 servings
Per serving: 284 calories, 13 g fat

Love That Cinnamon

The ancient Romans used cinnamon in love potions and perfumes and regarded it as an exotic ingredient, highly prized. They were right: Cinnamon is the inner bark of a tropical evergreen tree harvested during the rainy season in jungle-like climates. When dried, the bark curls into long quills that are then sold as cinnamon sticks or ground into powder. While we tend to use cinnamon mostly in sweet dishes—and to top off cappuccino and hot chocolate—it makes an intriguing addition to such dishes as stews and curries.

Kevin Taylor

Restaurant Kevin Taylor, Denver, Colorado

Chef Taylor's career began in his home state of Colorado when he was just in his teens. Now the owner of four restaurants in Denver and one in the neighboring city of Boulder, he may be best known for the opulent Restaurant Kevin Taylor. He is nationally recognized for serving down-to-earth, unpretentious, and uniquely American food. "I am not interested in food that looks good and has no flavor," Chef Taylor says. "In my restaurants, flavor is paramount." His succulent Colorado Lamb with Serrano Blackberry Sauce is a superb example of his cooking style and panache.

COLORADO LAMB WITH SERRANO BLACKBERRY SAUCE

¼ onion, diced

¼ carrot, diced

1 serrano chile pepper, chopped

1½ teaspoons + ½ cup chopped mixed herbs (fresh sage, parsley, rosemary, thyme)

½ tablespoon olive oil

1½ teaspoons tomato paste

½ cup red wine

1½ cups lamb or veal stock or canned beef or chicken broth

½ pint blackberries, pureed, reserving 8 berries for garnish

 Salt and pepper

2 racks lamb, cleaned and defatted

1 teaspoon chopped fresh garlic

Procedure for sauce: Sauté the onion, carrot, chile pepper, and 1½ teaspoons of the herbs in the oil until dark brown in color. Add the tomato paste and continue cooking for 2 to 3 minutes. Deglaze the pan with red wine and reduce until thick. Add the stock or broth and reduce until approximately ¾ cup remains. Strain through a fine sieve along with the blackberry puree and season to taste with salt and pepper.

Procedure for lamb: Rub lamb with garlic and the remaining ½ cup of the chopped herbs.

Cut each rack in half. Cook the lamb in a hot sauté pan over medium-high heat for 6 minutes on each side. Transfer to a 350°F oven and cook until a thermometer inserted in the center registers 145°F for medium-rare.

Serve the lamb with the sauce. Garnish with the reserved blackberries.

Makes 4 servings
Per serving: 217 calories, 9 g fat

GRILLED PORK CHOPS WITH GEORGIA PEACH CHUTNEY

Prep time: 15 minutes ▪ *Cook time: 20 minutes*

Chutney

- ½ red bell pepper, chopped
- ½ small onion, chopped
- ¼ cup vegetable broth
- 2 large ripe peaches, peeled and cut into ½" pieces
- 1 teaspoon honey
- 1 teaspoon cider vinegar
-    Pinch of sage
-    Pinch of salt
-    Pinch of coarsely cracked black pepper

Pork Chops

- ½ teaspoon dried sage leaves, crushed
- ½ teaspoon coarsely cracked black pepper
- ¼ teaspoon salt
- 4 boneless center-cut pork loin chops (4 ounces each) or bone-in pork rib chops (6 ounces each), trimmed

To make the chutney: In a medium saucepan, combine the bell pepper, onion, and broth. Bring to a boil over high heat. Reduce the heat to low and simmer for 4 minutes, or until the vegetables are tender and the broth is reduced. Add the peaches, cover, and cook, stirring frequently, for 4 minutes, or until the peaches are tender and start to release their juices. Remove from the heat. Stir in the honey, vinegar, sage, salt, and pepper. Place in a serving bowl, cover loosely, and let cool to room temperature (or serve hot).

To make the pork chops: Preheat the grill or broiler. In a cup, combine the sage, pepper, and salt and rub over the chops.

Grill or broil for 4 minutes per side, or until a thermometer inserted in the center of a chop registers 160°F and the juices run clear. Serve the chops with the chutney.

Makes 4 servings
Per serving: 266 calories, 13 g fat

Choose Chutney

The grilled pork chop with chutney is an inventive, appetizing, absolutely delicious dish—the centerpiece of an elegant meal. The two ribs with just 3 ounces of meat cost the same in calories but much more in fat—and seem barely enough to constitute a side dish. The choice? Choose the pork chop with chutney.

2 medium ribs
266 calories **20** grams fat

1 serving Grilled Pork Chops
with Georgia Peach Chutney
266 calories 13 grams fat

ROASTED PORK LOIN AND VEGETABLES

Prep time: 20 minutes ■ *Cook time: 50 minutes*

3   cloves garlic, minced

1½ teaspoons dried rosemary, crushed

1   teaspoon salt

1   teaspoon coarsely ground black
    pepper

3   medium red onions, each cut into 6
    wedges

1   large sweet potato, peeled and cut
    into 1" chunks

1   medium yellow bell pepper, cut into
    1" chunks

¼   cup apple cider

1   well-trimmed boneless center pork
    loin (12 to 16 ounces)

Preheat the oven to 425°F. Coat a 13" × 9" roasting pan with olive-oil cooking spray.

In a small bowl, combine the garlic, rosemary, salt, and black pepper.

Place the onions, sweet potato, and bell pepper in the prepared pan. Sprinkle with 2 tablespoons of the garlic mixture and the cider and toss to coat.

Rub the remaining garlic mixture over the pork; set aside.

Roast the vegetables for 20 minutes. Place the pork in the pan with the vegetables and roast for 30 minutes, or until a thermometer inserted in the center of the pork registers 155°F and the juices run clear. Let stand for 10 minutes before slicing.

Remove the pork to a cutting board and slice thinly on an angle. Serve with the vegetables.

Makes 4 servings
Per serving: 266 calories, 9 g fat

Appetizer Alert!

Take a hard look at these appetizers. Each represents approximately one bite of food, yet together they cost more in calories and far more in fat than this scrumptious meal of Roasted Pork Loin and Vegetables. The photographs send a strong signal: Forgo the tidbits and feast on the meal—tasty, low calorie, and rich with the health benefits of vegetables.

1 ounce cheese
110 calories 9 grams fat

+

1 meatball (1 ounce)
80 calories 6 grams fat

+

1 ounce paté
130 calories 10 grams fat

320 calories 25 grams fat   **VS.**

**1 serving Roasted Pork
Loin and Vegetables**
266 calories **9** grams fat

PORK CUTLETS WITH MUSHROOMS, MARSALA, AND SAGE

Prep time: 15 minutes ■ *Marinate time: 1 hour* ■ *Cook time: 15 minutes*

The Marsala adds a rich, smoky flavor that brings out the earthiness of the mushrooms. Enhance the earthiness even more by serving with a nutty brown rice pilaf.

1¼ teaspoons dried sage, crumbled

½ teaspoon salt

¼ teaspoon freshly ground black pepper

1 pound thin-sliced well-trimmed boneless pork loin cutlets

2 medium lemons

2 cloves garlic, crushed

1 pound small cremino mushrooms, rinsed and sliced

1 tablespoon Marsala or dry sherry

¼ cup chopped flat-leaf parsley

In a cup, combine ¾ teaspoon of the sage, ¼ teaspoon of the salt, and the pepper. Rub over both sides of the cutlets. Place the cutlets in a glass dish large enough to hold them in a single layer. Slice 1 lemon and place the slices over the cutlets. Add the garlic to the dish. Cover and marinate in the refrigerator for 1 hour. Squeeze enough juice from the remaining lemon to measure 1 tablespoon and reserve.

Heat a large, deep, heavy skillet coated with olive-oil cooking spray over medium-high heat. Add the cutlets and cook for 6 minutes, turning once, or until lightly browned and no longer pink in the center. Transfer the pork to a platter and cover loosely with foil.

Recoat the skillet with cooking spray. Add the mushrooms, the remaining ½ teaspoon sage, and the remaining ¼ teaspoon salt. Cook, stirring often, for 7 minutes, or until the mushrooms are tender and their juices have evaporated.

Stir in the Marsala or sherry, the reserved lemon juice, and any pork juices from the platter. Let the mixture bubble for 1 minute. Remove from the heat and stir in the parsley. Spoon the mushrooms and any pan juices over the pork.

Makes 4 servings
Per serving: 217 calories, 6 g fat

Salt Saga

Salt has long been a highly prized commodity. At the lavish banquets of ancient Rome, only members of the highest nobility at the head of the table could season their food with salt. Lesser folk had to make do with herbs; they were "below the salt," an expression that to this day connotes someone or something common or "plebeian." Salt is an important part of many cuisines, and thus of many cultures. When the British rulers of India taxed salt, essential to Indian cooking, Gandhi led the salt march to the sea, where salt could be made from sea water evaporation, and won some important constitutional reforms.

Today, salt remains a staple of cuisines the world over. In the United States, it is readily available in numerous forms.

Table salt is most commonly used in cooking and as a condiment for the table. It consists of small, dense, granular cubes that adhere poorly to food, dissolve slowly in solution, and are difficult to blend.

Iodized salt is table salt to which iodine has been added as a preventive against goiter, the enlargement of the thyroid gland caused by iodine deficiency.

Kosher salt is granular salt that has been compressed to give each grain a greater surface area. It is flaky, and compared with table salt, it is lighter in weight, dissolves more readily, and adheres better to food, which is why it is a favorite of professional chefs. Diamond Crystal kosher salt is formed through an evaporation process similar to that used for sea salt; it's a lighter version of regular kosher salt.

Sea salt and bay salt are collected through the evaporation of natural salt water, which leaves thin, flaky layers of salt. Sea and bay salts adhere well to food and dissolve quickly. They also contain various other trace minerals that occur naturally in the waters from which they are collected. For this reason, sea and bay salts will taste different depending on where in the world they were collected. In general, however, all are more complex in flavor than table and kosher salts. You can find them in fine-grain and larger crystal forms.

Canning and pickling salts contain no additives and are very pure. They are processed specifically to prevent clouding of the brine and discoloration of food undergoing salt curing.

Popcorn salt is a superfine salt; its most prominent use is obvious from its name.

Rock salt is a very coarse salt. It's used in crank ice-cream makers and as a bed for shellfish. Rock salt has a gray tint from the usually harmless impurities it contains. Some rock salt may contain arsenic; if so, it will be labeled as inedible, while the rock salts that are safe to consume are labeled as edible.

Curing salt is a blend of 94 percent salt and 6 percent sodium nitrate. It is used in a variety of meat processing procedures, especially for cold smoking. Curing salt is usually dyed pink to differentiate it from other salts. Saltpeter, which is potassium nitrate, is occasionally used in place of curing salt.

Whatever salt you use, it should be stored in a dry place. In very humid weather, salt may cake together. Mixing a few grains of rice in with the salt will help prevent this.

Roasted Lamb with Mediterranean Vegetables

Prep time: 30 minutes ▩ Cook time: 1 hour 30 minutes

6 large cloves garlic, minced

1 teaspoon dried thyme, crushed

1 teaspoon dried rosemary, crushed

1 teaspoon salt

½ teaspoon freshly ground black pepper

1 pound ripe tomatoes, cut into ½" chunks

1 large sweet white onion, cut into ½" chunks

2 small zucchini, cut into ½" slices

2 small yellow summer squash, cut into ½" slices

4 medium thin-skinned potatoes, scrubbed and cut into thin slices

1 well-trimmed boneless lamb leg roast (1½ pounds), rolled and tied

Preheat the oven to 425°F. Coat a large roasting pan with olive-oil cooking spray.

In a small bowl, combine the garlic, thyme, rosemary, salt, and pepper.

Place the tomatoes, onion, zucchini, yellow squash, and potatoes in the prepared pan. Add 1½ tablespoons of the garlic mixture and toss to coat. (The pan will be very full.) Roast for 30 minutes.

Meanwhile, rub the lamb with the remaining garlic mixture. Let stand at room temperature while the vegetables cook.

Place the lamb on top of the vegetables. Roast for 15 minutes, or until lightly browned. Turn the vegetables and spoon some juices over the lamb. Reduce the heat to 350°F and roast for 45 minutes, or until a thermometer inserted in the center of the lamb registers 145°F for medium-rare.

Place the lamb on a cutting board. Let stand for 10 minutes before slicing. Slice the lamb and serve with the vegetables.

Makes 8 servings
Per serving: 190 calories, 5 g fat

More of the Mediterranean

Want a taste of the Mediterranean? You could down two bites of spanakopita. Or, for the same calorie count and half the fat content, you could eat a full meal rich with the taste and fragrance of the warm South. With the roasted lamb dish, you gain the health bonus of the fiber and phytochemical nutrients in such vegetables as zucchini, summer squash, potatoes, onions, and tomatoes.

2 pieces (1 ounce each) spanakopita
190 calories **10** grams fat

1 serving Roasted Lamb with Mediterranean Vegetables
190 calories 5 grams fat

Salads and Accompaniments

At the Heart of Culinary Creativity

*L*ong ago and far away, the word *salad* connoted a few leaves of green lettuce lightly dressed and served when it was time for a pause in the meal.

Today, the salad contains just about every kind of food in every combination. The most sophisticated chefs vie with one another to invent yet more stunning permutations of ingredients. And they'll serve the end result as an appetizer, a side dish, to provide a pause for the palate, or to constitute the entire meal.

The recipes in this chapter give you an idea of the possibilities inherent in the word *salad* today. You'll find salads with fruit, salads with vegetables, salads with fruit *and* vegetables. You'll use ingredients like nuts, cheese, and spices.

As if that weren't enough, we've added some vegetable dishes that can serve in place of a salad. We call them accompaniments, but they're not there simply to embellish another dish; rather, they complete it. Every one of these accompaniments can be used as a starter, a side dish, or a main course all on its own.

Best of all for Picture-Perfect Weight-Loss cooks, the recipes for both salads and accompaniments show that the possibilities for creating your own dish ideas are endless. Build your own salad—and name it after yourself. Mix and match the ingredients to stuff into an artichoke, or try the artichoke stuffing called for here in another vegetable. In short, make the recipes in this chapter your starting point—and take it from there.

MESCLUN WITH PEARS, PECANS, AND BLUE CHEESE

QUICK

Prep time: 5 minutes ■ Cook time: 1 minute

Blue cheese contributes a tartness that's just right for this salad of greens and sweet fruit. If you don't have blue cheese, you can use feta cheese instead.

Dressing

¼ cup apple juice

2 tablespoons balsamic vinegar

2 tablespoons extra-virgin olive oil

1 teaspoon Dijon mustard

½ teaspoon salt

¼ teaspoon freshly ground black pepper

Salad

⅓ cup pecans

¾ pound mesclun or salad mix

2 Bartlett or Bosc pears, cored and thinly sliced

1 small red onion, sliced

¼ cup (2 ounces) finely crumbled blue cheese

To make the dressing: In a small bowl, whisk together the apple juice, vinegar, oil, mustard, salt, and pepper.

To make the salad: Place the nuts in a small nonstick skillet over medium heat and toast, shaking the pan often, for 1 to 2 minutes, or until fragrant.

Place the mesclun and pears in a large serving bowl. Toss with the dressing. Sprinkle with the onion, cheese, and pecans.

Makes 6 servings
Per serving: 182 calories, 12 g fat

The Move to Mesclun

Mesclun, also known as spring mix, has become increasingly popular as it has become increasingly available. Low in calories and high in nutrition, these "designer greens" are a mix of tender baby lettuces and other ingredients. Originally from the south of France, where mesclun means chervil, arugula, lettuce, and endive, mescluns in the United States have extended the definition to include mustards, purslane, chicory, cresses, parsleys, escarole, and fennel. Exotic greens like mizuna and tatsoi also figure in some mescluns, along with the petals of edible flowers. The mix of ingredients makes for a mix of tastes—from bitter to sweet—and for a mix of colors that ranges from lime green to deep red.

GREEK CHOPPED SALAD

Prep time: 10 minutes

The cool lemon-mint dressing makes this salad especially refreshing. Try serving it with broiled salmon or scallops.

Dressing

½ cup low-fat plain yogurt or soy
     alternative

2 tablespoons chopped fresh mint

1 teaspoon grated lemon peel

1 teaspoon lemon juice

1 teaspoon honey

1 clove garlic, minced

½ teaspoon salt

¼ teaspoon freshly ground black
     pepper

Salad

1 large tomato, cut into ½"-thick
     wedges

1 medium cucumber, partially
     peeled, halved, seeded, and cut
     into ½"-thick slices

½ small head romaine lettuce,
     trimmed and cut into 1" pieces

2 cups packed fresh spinach, stems
     removed

½ small red onion, cut into thin
     wedges

¼ cup pitted kalamata olives,
     quartered

¼ cup (2 ounces) low-fat feta cheese,
     crumbled

To make the dressing: In a small bowl, combine the yogurt, mint, lemon peel, lemon juice, honey, garlic, salt, and pepper. Cover and refrigerate.

To make the salad: In a large bowl, combine the tomato, cucumber, romaine, spinach, onion, olives, and cheese. Add the dressing and toss to blend well.

Makes 4 servings
Per serving: 89 calories, 3 g fat

Dressings to Live By

Do you know the number-one source of fat in the average American woman's diet? Hang on to your hats: It's salad dressing. So how can you get your greens—with all their health essentials—and still hold down the calorie count? Here are some satisfying, but not sabotaging, salad dressings. Refrigerate them in a small jar with a tight-fitting lid for several days. Then just shake and pour over your salad as needed.

Each recipe makes enough to coat about 6 cups of greens, or 4 servings.

CREAMY RANCH DRESSING

   2 tablespoons 1% cottage cheese

   2 teaspoons grated Parmesan cheese or soy alternative

1½ teaspoons low-fat buttermilk

   1 teaspoon lemon juice

   1 teaspoon water

   1 shallot, finely chopped

   1 clove garlic, minced

   ½ teaspoon chopped fresh basil

   ½ teaspoon chopped fresh oregano

      Pinch of freshly ground black pepper

In a jar with a tight-fitting lid, combine the cottage cheese, Parmesan, buttermilk, lemon juice, water, shallot, garlic, basil, oregano, and pepper. Seal the jar and shake well.

TAHINI DRESSING

   2 tablespoons extra-virgin olive oil

   1 tablespoon tahini (sesame paste)

   2 tablespoons cider vinegar

   1 teaspoon Dijon mustard

   ¼ teaspoon salt

   ⅛ teaspoon freshly ground black pepper

In a jar with a tight-fitting lid, combine the oil, tahini, vinegar, mustard, salt, and pepper. Seal the jar and shake well.

BASIL-YOGURT DRESSING

   ¼ cup fat-free plain yogurt or soy alternative

   1 shallot, finely chopped

   1 scallion, chopped

   1 garlic clove, minced

   2 tablespoons red wine vinegar

   2 tablespoons balsamic vinegar

   2 tablespoons water

   1 tablespoon chopped fresh basil

   ½ teaspoon freshly ground black pepper

   ½ teaspoon chopped fresh thyme

   ¼ teaspoon chopped fresh cilantro

In a jar with a tight-fitting lid, combine the yogurt, shallot, scallion, garlic, red wine vinegar, balsamic vinegar, water, basil, pepper, thyme, and cilantro. Seal the jar and shake well.

ROASTED GARLIC LEMON DRESSING

1 whole head garlic

3 tablespoons lemon juice

1 tablespoon oil

1 tablespoon water

⅛ teaspoon salt

2 tablespoons chopped parsley

Preheat the oven to 400°F.

Wrap the garlic in foil and bake for 45 minutes, or until soft. Cool slightly. Squeeze the garlic from its skins into a blender or food processor. Add the lemon juice, oil, water, and salt. Blend or process until smooth. Stir in parsley.

FDNY SALAD DRESSING

¼ cup balsamic vinegar

1 teaspoon Gulden's spicy brown or Dijon mustard

1 tablespoon Sorrell Ridge or similar low-calorie raspberry jam

2 tablespoons water (if you want to dilute the mixture)

In a jar with a tight-fitting lid, combine the vinegar, mustard, jam, and water. Seal the jar and shake well. (This makes a great marinade, too!)

Randy Zweiban

Nacional 27, Chicago

Randy Zweiban did not begin his working life as a chef. By day, he was a diamond setter, by night he was a drummer. Between jobs, this Queens, New York, native spent his time sampling dishes in Manhattan eateries. Fine dining fueled a passion for cooking and led him to Miami, where he immersed himself in the culture and cooking of the Latino community. Chef Zweiban has taken his bold nuevo Latino cuisine to Chicago, where he is executive chef and partner at Nacional 27. His zesty mojo-marinated roasted vegetable salad shows off his talent—combining exciting flavors and different textures, while keeping the calories and fat to a minimum.

TOMATO AND ORANGE MOJO MARINATED VEGETABLE SALAD

Mojo

- 3 tablespoons canola or safflower oil
- 7 tablespoons chopped fresh garlic
- 3 tablespoons chopped jalapeño chile
- 2 teaspoons chopped Scotch bonnet chile
- 2 tablespoons toasted cumin seeds
- 1½ cups fresh orange juice
- 4 cups fresh tomato fillets or good quality canned tomato fillet (6 to 8 large tomatoes)
- 2 tablespoons red wine vinegar
- ½ cup chopped fresh cilantro
- 2 teaspoons freshly ground black pepper
- 1 teaspoon kosher or sea salt

In a large heavy skillet, heat the oil over medium-high heat until hot. Sauté the garlic, chiles, and cumin. Add the orange juice and reduce by half. Add the tomatoes and the vinegar and cook over medium heat for 4 to 5 minutes. Add the cilantro, black pepper, and salt. Remove from the heat and process in a blender until smooth.

Makes 1⅓ cup

Vegetables

- 2 cups calabaza, pumpkin, or acorn squash, cut into ¼" dice
- 2 cups chayote squash, peeled, seeded, and cut in ½" dice
- 2 cups white button mushrooms, sliced
- 2 cups slender French green beans, blanched and cut in half
- 2 red bell peppers, cut into ¼" squares
- 1 medium yellow summer squash, cut in half lengthwise and sliced in ¼" half-moon slices

Preheat the oven to 350°F. Put the calabaza on a jelly-roll pan and toss with 2 tablespoons of the mojo. Bake until the calabaza can be pierced easily with a knife, 10 to 12 minutes.

Mix each of the remaining vegetables with 2 tablespoons of the mojo and sauté each separately over medium-high heat until tender.

To serve, mix all the vegetables in a large bowl and toss with more of the mojo.

Makes 6 servings
Per serving: 144 calories, 4 g fat

OLD-FASHIONED POTATO SALAD

Prep time: 10 minutes ▪ Cook time: 15 minutes

This potato salad is based on the popular mayonnaise-laden version. Here, yogurt takes the place of the fat, resulting in a deliciously creamy dressing.

Dressing

¾ cup low-fat plain yogurt or soy alternative

¼ cup chopped fresh dill

1½ tablespoons apple cider vinegar

½ teaspoon salt

¼ teaspoon freshly ground black pepper

Salad

1½ pounds baby red-skinned potatoes, quartered

2 medium carrots, chopped

1 small onion, finely chopped

1 rib celery, chopped

To make the dressing: In a large bowl, combine the yogurt, dill, vinegar, salt, and pepper. Cover and refrigerate.

To make the salad: Place a steamer basket in a large saucepan with ½" of water. Place the potatoes in the steamer and bring to a boil over high heat. Reduce the heat to medium, cover, and cook for 15 minutes, or until tender. Drain the potatoes and set aside until cooled.

Add the potatoes, carrots, onion, and celery to the dressing and toss to coat well.

Makes 6 servings
Per serving: 116 calories, 1 g fat

Yacking about Yogurt

We all know that yogurt is good for us—not the sweetened or heat-treated version but plain, low-fat or fat-free yogurt with live cultures—especially as a source of calcium and protein. It's often prescribed for people taking antibiotics, may help prevent osteoporosis, can counter gastrointestinal ailments, and may even protect against colon cancer. But the really exciting news is yogurt's potential benefit to the immune system. A growing body of evidence suggests that yogurt has "immunostimulatory effects" that may prove especially helpful to the elderly or to those whose immune systems have been weakened by illness or even by medical treatment.

WINTER GREENS, PEAR, AND GOAT CHEESE SALAD

Prep time: 20 minutes ■ Cook time: 25 minutes

The intense flavor of winter greens is nicely complemented by an onion-and-shallot vinaigrette—delightful topped off with creamy goat cheese.

Dressing

1	tablespoon olive oil
2	shallots, minced
1	medium onion, chopped
¼	cup vegetable broth
2	tablespoons chopped parsley
1½	tablespoons sherry wine vinegar
¼	teaspoon salt
⅛	teaspoon freshly ground black pepper

Salad

1	head Belgian endive, cut into 1" pieces
½	small head frisée, cut into 1" pieces
½	small head escarole, cut into 1" pieces
1	red-skinned pear, cored and thinly sliced
¼	cup (2 ounces) low-fat goat cheese, crumbled

To make the dressing: Heat the oil in a small nonstick skillet over medium heat. Add the shallots and onion and cook, stirring occasionally, for 10 minutes. Reduce the heat to low, cover, and cook, stirring occasionally, for 10 minutes. Uncover and continue cooking, stirring occasionally, for 5 minutes, or until tender and browned.

Remove ½ cup of the cooked onion to a small bowl and set aside. Place the remaining cooked onion, the broth, parsley, vinegar, salt, and pepper in a food processor or blender and process until almost smooth.

To make the salad: In a large bowl, combine the endive, frisée, escarole, and pear. Top with the cheese and reserved onion and drizzle with the dressing.

Makes 4 servings
Per serving: 141 calories, 6 g fat

TOMATO SALSA SALAD

Prep time: 10 minutes

This flavorful summer salad can also make a delicious showing served as a topping for bruschetta.

1 tablespoon canola oil

2 teaspoons apple cider vinegar

2 teaspoons lime juice

1 teaspoon grated lime peel

⅛ teaspoon sugar

3 cups cherry or pear tomatoes, quartered

3 scallions, chopped

2 tablespoons packed fresh cilantro leaves

1 tablespoon minced jalapeño chile pepper (wear plastic gloves when handling)

In a large bowl, whisk together the oil, vinegar, lime juice, lime peel, and sugar. Add the tomatoes, scallions, cilantro, and chile pepper. Toss to combine.

Makes 4 servings
Per serving: 65 calories, 3 g fat

JICAMA AND ORANGE SALAD

QUICK

Prep time: 10 minutes

Jicama is a large root vegetable grown in South America and Mexico. You can find it year-round in Latin American markets and in large supermarkets.

¼ cup orange juice

2 tablespoons canola oil

2 teaspoons grated orange peel

½ teaspoon salt

¾ teaspoon ground cumin

4 oranges

2 medium jicama, peeled and cut into ¼" matchsticks

2 small red onions, cut into thin wedges

In a large bowl, whisk together the orange juice, oil, orange peel, salt, and cumin.

Cut off the peel and pith from the oranges and discard. Working over the bowl with the dressing, cut out the segments of fruit from the membranes, letting the segments fall into the bowl. Squeeze any remaining juice from the membranes over the orange segments; discard the membranes.

Add the jicama and onions and toss to combine.

Makes 8 servings
Per serving: 130 calories, 4 g fat

PARSNIP AND PEAR PUREE

Prep time: 15 minutes ■ *Cook time: 40 minutes*

If you're looking for a new accompaniment for meat or fish, look no further than this naturally sweet puree. Your family will love it!

1 tablespoon canola oil

1 medium onion, chopped

1 pound parsnips, peeled and sliced

2 medium pears, peeled, cored, and chopped

½ cup vegetable broth

1 tablespoon finely chopped fresh ginger

Heat the oil in a large saucepan over medium heat. Add the onion and cook, stirring occasionally, for 5 minutes. Add the parsnips. Reduce the heat to low, cover, and cook, stirring occasionally, for 20 minutes, or until tender. Add the pears, broth, and ginger. Cover and cook for 15 minutes longer, or until very tender.

In a food processor or with an electric mixer, blend the parsnip mixture until smooth.

Makes 4 servings
Per serving: 184 calories, 4 g fat

Leafy Greens

Rich in beta-carotene, folic acid, iron, calcium, and other phytonutrients, leafy greens can help protect against cancer, circulatory diseases, macular degeneration, and many problems linked to aging. When it comes to health-giving foods, these go to the head of the class. Fortunately, there are lots of leafy greens, offering a range of tastes and textures and providing a range of cooking options.

Green	Appearance	Taste
Arugula (roquette)	Long, medium-green, sometimes scalloped leaves	Aggressive peppery taste
Beet	Reddish stems with tender leaves	Mild cabbage flavor
Belgian endive	Tight, elongated head with blanched white to pale yellow-green leaves	Slightly bitter flavor
Chard	Narrow, fan-shaped loose green leaf, with white or red veins and stems	Tastes slightly of mustard
Chicory	Bushy, frizzy head made of thick, crisp, narrow leaves with curly, frilly edges	Ranges from slightly bitter when young to extremely bitter when old
Collard greens	Large, smooth, silvery green leaves	Tastes like a cross between spinach and watercress
Dandelion	Jagged, medium-green leaves	Ranges from slightly bitter when young to more pungent when old
Escarole	Broad, curly-edged, dark green leaves with pale, yellowish heart	Bitter flavor
Kale	Very curly, dark green, coarse leaves with frilly edges	Fresh, grassy flavor
Lettuce, butterhead	Small, round, loosely formed head of soft leaves	Buttery, slightly sweet flavor
Lettuce, red leaf	Red-tinged, large, loose leaves	Delicate flavor
Lettuce, romaine	Elongated head with large, medium to dark green leaves that branch out from a white base	Mild, sweet, nutty flavor
Mizuma (mizuna)	Light green, lacy leaves	Mildly bitter, with a slight mustard taste
Radicchio	Red, cabbagelike leaves	Sweetly bitter flavor
Sorrel	Bright green, tongue-shaped leaves	Sour flavor
Spinach	Dark green, tender leaves	Mild but musky flavor
Watercress	Dark green, dime-size glossy leaves	Spicy, peppery flavor

Edamame Salad

Prep time: 5 minutes ■ Cook time: 5 minutes

1   pound edamame (frozen blanched shelled soybeans)

3   tablespoons seasoned rice wine vinegar

2   tablespoons lite soy sauce

1   teaspoon canola oil

1   teaspoon sesame oil

¼   teaspoon red-pepper flakes

4   scallions, sliced diagonally

1   medium cucumber, peeled, halved, seeded, and chopped

1   medium red bell pepper, chopped

    Lettuce leaves (optional)

In a large pot over high heat, bring 6 cups salted water to a boil. Add the edamame and cook for 5 minutes, or until tender. Drain well.

Meanwhile, in a large bowl, whisk together the vinegar, soy sauce, canola oil, sesame oil, and red-pepper flakes. Add the drained soybeans, scallions, cucumber, and bell pepper. Toss to coat. Serve on a bed of lettuce (if using).

Makes 6 servings
Per serving: 160 calories, 7 g fat

Beating Caesar

Edamame, the fresh green soybean, is among the hottest of the trendy new "designer foods," yet it has been cultivated across Asia as both food and medicine for some 5,000 years. The current vogue for edamame seems to have been launched in Japan, where it gained popularity as a bar snack, typically served boiled and salted. Today, it's available in American supermarkets and gourmet shops in both fresh and frozen versions, and its pungent taste and crisp texture have made edamame a welcome ingredient in a range of dishes. This colorful recipe features edamame but blends a variety of tastes and textures, and it's a nutritionist's dream as well. The soy is an excellent source of protein, fiber, and disease-fighting phytochemicals; the other vegetables—bell pepper, cucumber, scallion—add more nutrients; and the dressing, featuring both canola and sesame oil, offers just 7 grams of the best kind of fat. Caesar salad made with 3 ounces of chicken seems old hat by comparison, while its calorie count and fat content show it is not as benign as it looks.

1 serving chicken Caesar salad
450 calories **24** grams fat

1 serving Edamame Salad
160 calories **7** grams fat

Louise Bourgeois

*L*ouise Bourgeois was born in Paris in 1911 and moved to New York City in 1938. In 1982, she became the first woman to have a large-scale retrospective at the Museum of Modern Art in New York. Bourgeois has had solo exhibitions in the art world's major venues and was awarded the National Medal of Arts by President Clinton in 1997. A distinctive and influential figure in the art world for decades, Bourgeois continues to make art every day. An exhibition of her sculpture at the Hermitage Museum in St. Petersburg, Russia, in 2001, was the first there for a living American artist; the exhibition later moved to Scandinavia.

What is the worst experience you've ever had as a cook?

LB: There is an anecdote about a *gigot*—a beautiful leg of lamb. I had been toiling all day in the kitchen, preparing it for my husband and my three children. You know, preparing a gigot is a lot of work, and it's a wonderful dish, one of my favorites. When it was finally ready, I called everybody to dinner and brought it to the table. We sat down, and for some reason they were all silent; there was no response. I had been working so hard to please them and then nothing, no exclamation of admiration. I became enraged, so angry at their lack of reaction that I opened the window and threw out the gigot. We lived on the fifth floor above the parking lot, so of course it landed on a car, bounced off a couple of times, and then rolled around on the gravel of the parking lot.

So what happened?

LB: Well, my son Jean-Louis went downstairs to retrieve it, and he brought it back to me. It was filthy, so I cleaned it up thoroughly, put it back on the serving dish, and brought it to the table again. Then we had dinner.

Did it happen more than once?

LB: Well, there was the day I pulled a dish from the oven and put it on the fire escape to cool it down. Then I went about my business, and when I went to get it, it was gone, stolen. Someone just took it. I never knew who it was, but it doesn't matter. I just hope they ate it and liked it.

Is there any food you cannot resist?

LB: I can resist anything but temptation . . . caviar.

Is there any relation between food and your childhood?

LB: We were a family of gourmets. My mother ate very little, but my father gobbled up everything in sight.

What is your favorite smell in the kitchen?

LB: I like the smell of frying garlic.

What is your favorite seasoning?

LB: A pinch of salt.

As a child, what was your least favorite food?

LB: Pigeon. We used to feed them and I could not bear the idea of eating pets.

What is your least favorite food now?

LB: All alcohols—wine and beer included.

What is your favorite food?

LB: Raw salmon and *marrons glacés*.

If you were on a desert island, which five food items would you have?

LB: Sardines, spaghetti, coffee ice cream, orange marmalade, and chocolate.

Which food items do you keep in your refrigerator on a regular basis?

LB: Coke, cheese, fish, and milk.

Whom would you most like to have dinner with?

LB: My son Jean-Louis.

BEET AND APPLE SALAD

Prep time: 10 minutes ■ *Cook time: 1 hour*

Beets will keep in the refrigerator for up to 3 weeks. As soon as you get them home, trim the greens, leaving about an inch of stem, then place the beets in a zip-top plastic bag, and save the greens in a separate bag. The greens can sap moisture and nutrients from the bulb, so trimming keeps the vegetable fresher longer.

1 pound medium beets with tops

1 teaspoon mustard seeds

1 tablespoon olive oil

2 shallots, cut into thin wedges

1 tablespoon white balsamic vinegar

1 teaspoon Dijon mustard

¼ teaspoon salt

1 Granny Smith apple, cored and cut into ¼" matchsticks

1 head Boston lettuce, separated into leaves

Preheat the oven to 400°F.

Trim the tops from the beets, leaving ½" of the stems and the roots intact. Place the beets on a piece of foil. Fold the foil up and over the beets and fold the edges to seal. Place the foil packet on a baking sheet and roast for 50 minutes, or until tender. Remove the beets and set aside until cool enough to handle. Peel the beets and cut into thin wedges. Place in a large bowl.

Meanwhile, toast the mustard seeds in a small skillet over medium heat for 2 minutes, or until fragrant. Remove to a small bowl.

Heat the oil in the same skillet over medium heat. Add the shallots and cook, stirring occasionally, for 6 minutes, or until tender. Remove the skillet from the heat. Whisk in the vinegar, Dijon mustard, salt, and the reserved mustard seeds. Add to the beets along with the apple. Toss to combine.

Place a few lettuce leaves on 4 salad plates. Evenly divide the salad among the plates.

Makes 4 servings
Per serving: 114 calories, 4 g fat

Don't Throw Out the Beet Greens!

When you save the beet greens, you're saving what is actually the most nutritious part of the plant. Unlike other cooking greens, there's nothing pungent about beet greens, especially if you have bought baby beets or tender young specimens. And along with the good taste, you'll be taking in a healthy supply of folate, calcium, iron, and antioxidant phytochemicals. You can find beet greens in markets from June through October; look for crisp, unwilted, unblemished leaves. Stored in plastic in the refrigerator, they will last for as many as 5 days. They're delicious sautéed, then eaten hot or cold, and they're a wonderful ingredient in sauces.

Bean Salad

Prep time: 10 minutes

A colorful bean salad is always popular at buffets and picnics. And this one couldn't be any easier! A few cans of beans and a little chopping are all it takes.

3   tablespoons spicy vegetable juice

2   teaspoons lime juice

1   tablespoon extra-virgin olive oil

½   teaspoon salt

½   teaspoon grated lime peel

½   teaspoon Dijon mustard

¼   teaspoon ground cumin

1   can (15½ ounces) black beans, rinsed and drained

1   can (15½ ounces) red kidney beans, rinsed and drained

1   can (15 ounces) soybeans, rinsed and drained

1   medium green bell pepper, chopped

1   small tomato, chopped

½   small red onion, chopped

¼   cup packed fresh cilantro leaves

In a large bowl, whisk together the vegetable juice, lime juice, oil, salt, lime peel, mustard, and cumin. Add the black beans, kidney beans, soybeans, pepper, tomato, onion, and cilantro and toss to coat.

Makes 8 servings

Per serving: 174 calories, 7 g fat

The Scent of Cilantro

Cilantro—also known as Chinese parsley or coriander—has a lively, pungent fragrance. Particularly apt for spicy foods, it is a common ingredient in Asian, Latin American, and Caribbean cuisines. Choose bright, evenly col-ored leaves and store cilantro for up to a week in a plastic bag in the refrigerator. Or place the bunch, stems down, in a glass of water, cover with a plastic bag, and refrigerate, changing the water every 2 days or so.

Color Me Healthy

Pigment in food indicates the presence of a phytonutrient. In fact, pigment works as a thermometer that measures the nutrients: The deeper the color, the more nutrients there are—and the deeper the flavor. Take winter squash, for example. The yellow-orange color of its flesh shows you that it's high in beta-carotene; the deeper that yellowish-orangish tint, the more beta-carotene it has. But even "pale" colors announce the presence of nutrients, so don't neglect them. Here's an index of phytonutrients and their health benefits.

Apricots. Vitamin A, potassium

Artichokes. Iron, magnesium, potassium

Asparagus. Riboflavin, folate

Avocado. Vitamin B_6, vitamin E, potassium

Bananas. Potassium, vitamin B_6

Beans. Folate, pantothenic acid, thiamin, calcium, iron, magnesium, potassium, zinc

Beet greens. Potassium, vitamin A, vitamin C, riboflavin

Bok choy. Vitamin A, vitamin C, calcium, potassium

Broccoli. Folate, vitamin A, vitamin C, calcium, riboflavin, vitamin B_6

Brussels sprouts. Vitamin A, vitamin C, vitamin K, folate, potassium

Cantaloupe. Vitamin A, potassium

Cauliflower. Vitamin C, folate

Curly endive. Vitamin A, folate, vitamin K

Kale. Vitamin A, vitamin C, calcium

Lentils. Folate, iron, magnesium, zinc

Mango. Vitamin A, vitamin C

Mustard greens. Vitamin A, vitamin C, folate, calcium

Oranges. Vitamin C, folate, potassium

Peaches. Vitamin A

Peanut butter. Vitamin E, magnesium

Peanuts. Vitamin B_6, folate, niacin, vitamin E, magnesium

Peas. Folate, riboflavin, thiamin, calcium, iron, magnesium

Peppers. Vitamin C

Potatoes. Vitamin B_6, niacin, riboflavin, thiamin, vitamin C, iron, magnesium, potassium

Pumpkin seeds. Iron, magnesium, potassium, zinc

Rice. Vitamin B_6, riboflavin, thiamin, iron

Romaine lettuce. Vitamin A, vitamin C

Soybeans. Vitamin B_6, folate, riboflavin, iron, magnesium, potassium, zinc

Spinach. Vitamin A, vitamin C, vitamin B_6, vitamin B_{12}, folate, riboflavin, magnesium, potassium

Strawberries. Vitamin C

Sunflower seeds. Vitamin E, folate, thiamin, iron, magnesium, zinc

Sweet potatoes. Vitamin A, vitamin B_6, vitamin C, vitamin E, potassium

Tofu. Calcium, iron, magnesium

Tomatoes. Vitamin C, potassium

Watermelon. Vitamin B_6, thiamin, vitamin C, magnesium, potassium

Nutrient	What It Does
Vitamin A	Essential for vision; enhances immunity; builds and maintains bone
Thiamin (B$_1$)	Helps turn food into energy; essential for nerve impulses
Riboflavin (B$_2$)	Helps turn food into energy; regulates hormones and red blood cells
Niacin (B$_3$)	Helps turn food into energy
Pantothenic acid (B$_5$)	Helps metabolize foods; helps produce red blood cells and neurotransmitters
Vitamin B$_6$	Helps metabolize proteins and fats; helps make red blood cells
Vitamin B$_{12}$	Helps make new cells; protects and maintains sheath around nerve fibers
Biotin	Necessary for energy metabolism; makes fatty acids; breaks down amino acids
Folic acid	Helps form DNA in new cells
Vitamin C	An antioxidant; strengthens resistance to infections; helps in absorption of iron
Vitamin D	Promotes bone mineralization by raising calcium and phosphorus levels in blood
Vitamin E	An antioxidant; helps protect cells from damage
Calcium	Essential in bone formation and maintenance
Iron	Helps carry oxygen in the bloodstream
Magnesium	Helps metabolize food and transmit messages between cells
Potassium	Helps transmit nerve impulses, contract muscles, and maintain normal blood pressure
Zinc	Necessary for growth, immune function, wound healing, and sperm production

STUFFED ARTICHOKES

Stuffed artichokes are usually drizzled with butter for a fat-laden dish. Not so here where flavorful vegetables—onion, garlic, carrots, tomatoes, and fennel—are tossed in this cheesy bread-crumb mixture and stuffed between healthful artichoke leaves.

Artichokes

4   medium artichokes

1   lemon, halved

Filling

½   ounce dry-packed sun-dried tomatoes

1   tablespoon olive oil

3   medium carrots, chopped

2   large cloves garlic, minced

1   medium bulb fennel, cored and chopped

1   medium onion, chopped

¾   teaspoon salt

⅛   teaspoon freshly ground black pepper

1   slice light whole grain bread, toasted and cut into ¼" pieces

¼   cup (1 ounce) grated Asiago cheese

To make the artichokes: Trim the stems and 1" from the top of each artichoke. Rub all the cut edges of the artichokes with the lemon halves. Using kitchen shears, trim the thorny tips of the leaves.

Place the artichokes in a saucepot with 1" of water and bring to a boil over high heat. Reduce the heat to medium-low, cover, and cook for 20 minutes, or until tender. Drain well. Spread open the center of each artichoke and remove the inner, prickly leaves. Using a spoon, scrape out the fuzzy chokes.

To make the filling: Meanwhile, place the sun-dried tomatoes in a small bowl and cover with hot water. Soak for 10 minutes, or until soft. Remove the tomatoes from the liquid, reserving the liquid. Mince the tomatoes and set aside.

Heat the oil in a large nonstick skillet over medium heat. Add the carrots, garlic, fennel, onion, salt, and pepper and cook, stirring frequently, for 12 minutes, or until tender. Place in a bowl. Stir in the bread, the reserved tomatoes and liquid, and 2 tablespoons of the cheese.

Preheat the oven to 350°F. Pour ¾ cup water into a 13" × 9" baking pan.

Spoon some of the filling into the center of each artichoke and spoon the remaining filling between the leaves. Place the artichokes in the prepared pan. Sprinkle the tops of the artichokes with the remaining 2 tablespoons cheese. Cover with foil and bake for 25 minutes, or until the artichokes and the filling are heated through.

Makes 4 servings
Per serving: 221 calories, 6 g fat

CAPONATA

Prep time: 5 minutes ■ *Cook time: 30 minutes*

This combination of fresh vegetables can be served hot or at room temperature. For special occasions, sprinkle with just a hint of freshly grated Parmesan cheese.

1½ tablespoons olive oil

1 small onion, chopped

2 large cloves garlic, sliced

1 baby eggplant, cut into ¾" pieces

1 medium yellow bell pepper, chopped

3 cups cherry tomatoes, halved

¼ cup kalamata olives

1 teaspoon capers

½ teaspoon salt

⅛ teaspoon freshly ground black pepper

¼ cup water

¼ cup packed fresh basil leaves, sliced

1 tablespoon balsamic vinegar

Heat the oil in a large nonstick skillet over medium heat. Add the onion, garlic, and eggplant and cook, stirring frequently, for 8 minutes. Add the bell pepper and cook, stirring frequently, for 8 minutes longer. Add the tomatoes, olives, capers, salt, black pepper, and water and cook, stirring occasionally, for 10 to 15 minutes, or until the vegetables are tender. Stir in the basil and vinegar.

Makes 8 servings
Per serving: 65 calories, 4 g fat

The Story of Balsamic Vinegar

Balsamic vinegar seems to have burst on the scene in the past few years, but did you know that it has a history dating back several centuries? The first written reference to this condiment—called balsamic for its supposedly calming medicinal properties—was in 1046, and by the year 1700, it was known throughout Europe. The Emilia-Romagna region of Italy, stretching from the Adriatic Sea to the Gulf of Genoa, remains the center of production of the real balsamic, which is made with Spanish Trebbiano grape must (unfermented juice), concentrated in open vats over slow fires and aged in wooden casks. The aging is important. In fact, balsamic keeps on aging. When it is over 50 years old, it thickens and can be imbibed for an after-dinner liqueur! The quick-process industrialized balsamic vinegar available even in supermarkets does not qualify as true balsamic—and doesn't cost as much, either—but it, too, is supposed to be aged at least 3 years before being sold.

Oven Potato Medley

Prep time: 5 minutes　■　Cook time: 1 hour

Photo on page 151

1　pound baking potatoes, cut into ¾" chunks

1　pound sweet potatoes, cut into ¾" chunks

4　large shallots, sliced

1　teaspoon salt

¼　teaspoon ground nutmeg

¼　cup apple juice

¼　cup raspberry wine vinegar

Preheat the oven to 400°F. Coat a 13" × 9" baking pan with cooking spray.

Place the baking potatoes, sweet potatoes, shallots, salt, and nutmeg in the prepared pan and generously coat with cooking spray. Roast the potatoes, stirring occasionally, for 1 hour, or until tender. Remove to a serving bowl.

Stir the apple juice and vinegar into the pan, scraping any browned bits from the bottom of the pan. Pour over the potatoes, tossing to coat.

Makes 6 servings
Per serving: 155 calories, 0 g fat

Italian Potatoes and Fennel

Prep time: 10 minutes　■　Cook time: 25 minutes

This is a wonderfully warm-flavored dish, perfect for dinner on a chilly autumn evening. It goes nicely with beef or pork.

1　tablespoon olive oil

1　pound red potatoes, cut into thin wedges

2　bulbs fennel, cut lengthwise into thin strips

1　medium onion, cut into wedges

2　tablespoons dry-packed sun-dried tomatoes, finely chopped

2　large cloves garlic, crushed

1　teaspoon dried Italian seasoning

½　teaspoon salt

Heat the oil in a large nonstick skillet over medium heat. Add the potatoes, fennel, onion, tomatoes, garlic, Italian seasoning, and salt. Cook, stirring occasionally, for 25 minutes, or until the vegetables are tender.

Makes 6 servings
Per serving: 114 calories, 2 g fat

GARLIC AND CHIVE MASHED POTATOES

Prep time: 5 minutes ■ Cook time: 25 minutes

There's just enough spinach in these comfy mashed potatoes to provide a pretty speckling of green. Add an extra cup of spinach if you want to up the nutrition even more.

2 pounds Yukon gold potatoes, cut into 1" chunks

6 large cloves garlic

3 cups packed torn baby spinach leaves

½ cup reduced-fat sour cream

¼ cup chopped fresh chives

1 teaspoon salt

¼ teaspoon ground white pepper

Place the potatoes and garlic in a medium saucepan with enough water to cover. Bring to a boil over high heat. Reduce the heat to medium and cook for 20 minutes, or until the potatoes are very tender. Add the spinach to the pan and cook for 1 minute. Drain the potato mixture, reserving the cooking water. Return the potato mixture to the same pan. Add ½ cup of the cooking water, the sour cream, chives, salt, and pepper. Mash until smooth.

Makes 6 servings
Per serving: 138 calories, 2 g fat

MASHED SWEET POTATOES AND APPLES

Prep time: 10 minutes ■ Cook time: 30 minutes

Photo on page 169

1½ pounds sweet potatoes, peeled and cut into ¾" chunks

2 medium apples, peeled, cored, and sliced

¾ cup apple cider

1 teaspoon grated lemon peel

½ teaspoon salt

¼ teaspoon ground cinnamon

Place the potatoes in a large saucepan with enough water to cover. Bring to a boil over high heat. Boil for 15 minutes, or until fork-tender. Drain and place in a large bowl.

Meanwhile, heat a medium nonstick skillet coated with cooking spray over medium-high heat. Add the apples and coat with cooking spray. Cook, stirring occasionally, for 4 minutes, or until lightly browned. Reduce the heat to low, cover, and cook, stirring occasionally, for 10 minutes, or until very tender. Stir in the cider, lemon peel, salt, and cinnamon. Add to the bowl with the potatoes and beat with an electric mixer on medium speed until smooth.

Makes 6 servings
Per serving: 160 calories, 1 g fat

STUFFED TOMATOES

Prep time: 5 minutes ■ *Cook time: 55 minutes*

1½ cups vegetable broth

½ cup millet

6 medium tomatoes

2 teaspoons olive oil

1 large clove garlic, minced

½ small onion, finely chopped

1¼ cups packed baby spinach leaves

2 tablespoons pitted kalamata olives, chopped

¼ cup (1 ounce) grated Romano cheese

In a small saucepan over high heat, bring the broth to a boil. Add the millet. Reduce the heat to low, cover, and simmer for 40 minutes, or until the broth is absorbed and the millet is tender. Remove the pan from the heat.

Meanwhile, preheat the oven to 375°F. Slice the top quarter from each tomato and reserve. Remove the seeds from each tomato. Scoop out the pulp from each tomato and chop. Set the pulp aside.

Heat the oil in a medium skillet over medium heat. Add the garlic and onion and cook, stirring occasionally, for 5 minutes. Add the reserved tomato pulp, the spinach, and the olives and cook, stirring occasionally, for 5 minutes, or until tender. Add the millet and cheese.

Evenly divide the millet mixture among the tomatoes and replace the tops on each tomato. Place the tomatoes in an 11" × 8" baking pan. Bake for 15 minutes, or until heated through.

Makes 6 servings
Per serving: 225 calories, 6 g fat

Making a Meal of It

As thick and rich as quiche Lorraine is, this serving of Curried Yellow Split Pea Soup along with a delicious Stuffed Tomato offers a far greater quantity of food for the same calorie count, with a dramatic fat savings. A slice of quiche seems just a taste by comparison.

1 slice (7 ounces) quiche Lorraine
460 calories **32** grams fat

1 serving Stuffed Tomatoes
225 calories **6** grams fat

+

1 serving Curried Yellow Split Pea Soup (see page 90)
235 calories **3** grams fat

460 calories **9** grams fat

SUMMER SKILLET VEGETABLES

Prep time: 10 minutes ■ Cook time: 15 minutes

1½   teaspoons olive oil

½   small red onion, chopped

½   cup fresh or frozen corn

½   small yellow bell pepper, chopped

½   cup fresh or frozen and thawed
      sugar snap peas

1   teaspoon finely chopped fresh
      thyme

½   teaspoon salt

¼   teaspoon cracked black pepper

½   pint cherry or pear tomatoes,
      halved

½   medium cucumber, peeled,
      seeded, and cut into ¾" pieces

½   teaspoon grated lemon peel

Heat the oil in a large nonstick skillet over medium heat. Add the onion and cook, stirring occasionally, for 3 minutes. Add the corn, bell pepper, snap peas, thyme, salt, and black pepper and cook, stirring occasionally, for 5 minutes. Add the tomatoes, cucumber, and lemon peel and cook, stirring occasionally, for 5 minutes, or until the vegetables are tender.

Makes 4 servings
Per serving: 65 calories, 2 g fat

Monument of Taste

Vegetables are a mainstay of Picture-Perfect Weight Loss, the basis of the Picture-Perfect Weight-Loss Food Pyramid, and the healthiest path to achieving and maintaining weight loss. This huge, colorful vegetable platter—including onion, corn, yellow bell pepper, snap peas, cherry tomatoes, and cucumber and seasoned with a touch of lemon peel—is a monument to the low-calorie, low-fat deliciousness of grilled summer vegetables. It's a better, bigger way to take in vegetables than this meager portion of fried zucchini.

Fried zucchini sticks (3 ounces)
260 calories **11** grams fat

4 servings Summer Skillet Vegetables
260 calories **8** grams fat

Jerry Traunfeld

The Herbfarm, Seattle, Washington

Jerry Traunfeld is certain he has the best job in the world. As executive chef of The Herbfarm, in Woodinville, Washington, he is able to combine his two passions: gardening and cooking. Chef Traunfeld's cuisine employs the herbs grown at the restaurant's extensive kitchen gardens in inventive and surprising ways—always with the most delicious results. He is the recipient of the 2000 James Beard Foundation's Best Chef in the Northwest/Hawaii award. His light yet boldly flavored braised red cabbage comes from his award-winning cookbook, *The Herbfarm Cookbook*, which uses fresh herbs in every dish.

SPICY RED CABBAGE WITH APPLE AND CILANTRO

½ medium head red cabbage (about 1 pound)

2 tablespoons vegetable oil

½ teaspoon dried red pepper flakes

1 large or 2 small apples, peeled, cored, and cut into ¼-inch dice

¼ cup freshly squeezed lime juice

1½ tablespoons sugar

¾ teaspoon salt

3 green onions, thinly sliced

1 cup coarsely chopped fresh cilantro

1. Cabbage. Cut the ½ head of cabbage in half again and cut out the cores. Slice the cabbage very thin, less than ⅛ inch thick, preferably using a mandoline, cabbage shredder, or the shredding disk of a food processor.

2. Cooking. Heat the oil with the red pepper flakes in a large skillet or wide saucepan over medium heat. Add the apple and cook, stirring, for about 1 minute. Add the red cabbage and toss it with tongs to coat it with the hot oil. Add the lime juice, sugar, and salt, cover the pan, and reduce the heat to low. Cook until the cabbage is tender, 5 to 10 minutes. Add the green onions and cilantro and toss together with the tongs. Taste and season with additional salt or sugar if needed.

6 servings
Per serving: 104 calories, 5 g fat

Cauliflower with Chickpeas and Tomatoes

Prep time: 5 minutes ■ Cook time: 25 minutes

Fennel seeds, tomato, and chickpeas add intrigue and excitement to otherwise mild-flavored cauliflower. A wonderful new twist to an old standby.

1 teaspoon fennel seeds

1 medium onion, chopped

1 clove garlic, minced

1 head cauliflower, cut into florets

1 can (14½ ounces) diced tomatoes

1 can (15½ ounces) chickpeas, rinsed and drained

¼ cup chopped fresh basil leaves

Place the fennel seeds in a large nonstick skillet over medium-low heat and toast, shaking the pan often, for 1 to 1½ minutes, or until fragrant. Remove the seeds from the skillet and crush.

Coat the same skillet with olive-oil cooking spray and heat over medium heat. Add the onion and cook, stirring occasionally, for 5 minutes. Add the garlic and fennel seeds and cook for 1 minute. Add the cauliflower and tomatoes (with juice) and heat to boiling. Reduce the heat to low, cover, and simmer, stirring occasionally, for 15 minutes, or until tender. Stir in the chickpeas and basil and heat through.

Makes 8 servings
Per serving: 85 calories, 1 g fat

Sautéed Escarole with White Beans

Prep time: 5 minutes ■ Cook time: 10 minutes

You'll enjoy this dish hot, but it's equally delicious served at room temperature, or even cold. Try it all three ways to see which you like best.

2 large shallots, thinly sliced

1 clove garlic, minced

½ teaspoon red-pepper flakes

4 cups packed torn escarole

¼ teaspoon salt

1 can (15 ounces) cannellini beans, rinsed and drained

¾ cup vegetable broth

Heat a large nonstick skillet coated with cooking spray over medium-high heat. Add the shallots and cook, stirring occasionally, for 2 minutes. Add the garlic and red-pepper flakes and cook, stirring constantly, for 1 minute. Add the escarole and salt and cook, stirring constantly, for 2 minutes, or until the escarole is wilted. Stir in the beans and broth and cook, stirring occasionally, for 3 minutes, or until heated through.

Makes 6 servings
Per serving: 51 calories, 0.5 g fat

BRAISED BROCCOLI RABE

Prep time: 5 minutes ■ *Cook time: 15 minutes*

6 medium cloves garlic, sliced

⅛–¼ teaspoon crushed red-pepper flakes

1 large bunch broccoli rabe, 1½" from stem ends removed

½ cup vegetable broth

¼ cup (1 ounce) shredded Parmesan cheese or soy alternative

Coat a large saucepan with olive-oil cooking spray and place over medium heat. Add the garlic and pepper and cook, stirring occasionally, for 2 minutes, or until the garlic is lightly browned. Add the broccoli rabe and cook, stirring occasionally, for 2 minutes. Add the broth. Reduce the heat to low, cover, and simmer, stirring occasionally, for 10 minutes, or until tender. Top with the cheese.

Makes 4 servings
Per serving: 70 calories, 2 g fat

Green Virtue

White rice may look virtuous, but it's basically a low-nutrient, empty-calorie food. Compare this anemic-looking portion of it to one of these two hearty servings of green vegetables in tasty recipes.

⅓ cup plain boiled white rice
70 calories **0** grams fat

1 serving Braised
Broccoli Rabe
70 calories **2** grams fat

OR

1 serving Brussels Sprouts
with Hazelnuts
and Orange (see page 222)
70 calories **3** grams fat

BRUSSELS SPROUTS WITH HAZELNUTS AND ORANGE

QUICK

Prep time: 10 minutes ■ Cook time: 15 minutes

Photo on page 221

3 tablespoons hazelnuts

1 orange

1 pound Brussels sprouts, halved

½ teaspoon salt

Preheat the oven to 350°F.

Place the hazelnuts on a baking pan. Bake for 8 minutes, or until the skins loosen. Place the hazelnuts in a clean tea towel and rub together to remove the skins. Discard the skins and chop the nuts.

Meanwhile, grate ½ teaspoon peel from the orange and place in a small bowl. Cut off the remaining peel and pith from the orange and discard. Working over the bowl with the peel, cut out the segments of fruit from the membranes, letting the segments fall into the bowl. Squeeze any remaining juice from the membranes over the orange segments; discard the membranes.

Bring a saucepan of salted water to a boil over high heat. Add the Brussels sprouts and cook for 5 minutes, or until tender. Drain. Wipe the pan clean and return the Brussels sprouts to the pan.

Add the orange segments, salt, and hazelnuts to the pan with the Brussels sprouts and cook, stirring frequently, for 2 minutes, or until heated through.

Makes 6 servings
Per serving: 70 calories, 3 g fat

Winter Wonder

Benjamin Franklin introduced kale seeds into the United States. He brought them from Scotland, where this dark-green leafy vegetable flourishes in the cold, dark, long Scottish winters. In fact, kale is such a winter vegetable that frost actually enhances its strong flavor—a taste that works well as an accompaniment or in salads. A healthful green, kale is one of the best natural sources of calcium, iron, folate, beta-carotene, and a host of disease-preventing phytochemicals. When shopping for kale, look for unwilted leaves that are a dark bluish green in color.

KALE WITH BACON CRISPS

Prep time: 5 minutes ■ *Cook time: 20 minutes*

Kale, with its mild cabbagelike flavor, is available in supermarkets year-round, but it's best in the winter months. Keep it in the refrigerator for no longer than 2 to 3 days.

3 slices turkey bacon, cut crosswise into ½" pieces

2 shallots, sliced

2 large cloves garlic, sliced

1 cup fat-free vegetable broth

1 pound kale, tough stems removed and cut crosswise into 1" pieces

⅛ teaspoon salt

⅛ teaspoon freshly ground black pepper

Heat a large saucepan coated with olive-oil cooking spray over medium heat. Add the bacon and cook, stirring occasionally, for 3 minutes, or until browned. With a slotted spoon, remove the bacon to a plate.

Recoat the pan with cooking spray. Add the shallots and garlic and cook, stirring occasionally, for 5 minutes. Add the broth, kale, salt, and pepper and cook, stirring frequently, for 12 minutes, or until the kale is tender. Stir in the reserved bacon.

Makes 4 servings
Per serving: 73 calories, 3 g fat

The Facts about Folate

Folate—also known as folic acid or folacin—is a B vitamin that's essential for manufacturing new cells and regulating cell metabolism. You've heard about it as an essential vitamin for pregnant women and nursing mothers. The extra folate helps prevent neural tube defects—most notably, spina bifida.

But folate is also highly recommended for adults, particularly for its ability to help regulate homocysteine levels in the blood. Why is that important? Because high homocysteine levels can increase the risk of heart attacks. In fact, the recommendation for adults is 400 micrograms of folate per day. How can you boost your folate level? Try these suggestions.

Food	Folate (mcg)
½ cup cooked spinach	130
½ cup cooked navy beans	125
¼ cup wheat germ	80
½ medium avocado	55
1 medium orange	45
1 slice whole grain bread	15

GRAINS AND PASTA

Treating Yourself to the
Nutrients You Deserve

O f course, grains are good for you. There's a reason why bread is called the staff of life, a reason why rice is the basic food of more than half the people on the planet, a reason why "amber waves of grain" are celebrated as a national treasure. In fact, grain foods are standard fare not only for humans but for animals as well.

Grains have historically been a primary source of complex carbohydrates. Grain foods in many forms are also excellent sources of fiber, iron, plant protein, phytochemicals, vitamins—especially the B-complex vitamins—and minerals. Indeed, studies suggest that grain foods can help protect against chronic disease and cardiovascular ailments, and that they may reduce the risk of cancer.

But there's also a reason why grains—including pasta made from wheat flours—are some way up the Picture-Perfect Weight-Loss Food Pyramid. In fact, they're pretty much smack-dab in the middle. The reason is simple: Grains and pastas tend to be high in calories.

In the hierarchy of choices, make grains and pastas a lower-priority food. They should come third, after first-place fruits and vegetables and second-place protein foods like fish and legumes. The recipes that follow will give you plenty of delicious choices for the way you take in grains and pasta, but I want to add one important recommendation. Choose whole grain products whenever possible. That's where the nutrition is; the refined grain products have pretty much refined away the rich nutrients. And to be sure whole grain is what you're getting, check the package label. You'll know you're getting the real thing if whole grain flour is the first and only grain product listed, or if the words "100 percent whole" describe the particular grain you're buying. Marketing claims like "natural" or "seven grain" or "unbleached" don't cut it, unless the nutrition label carries the whole grain classification.

CREOLE-STYLE BROWN RICE

Prep time: 5 minutes ■ *Cook time: 1 hour*

Any variety of seasoned diced tomatoes will work well in this dish. Tomatoes with mild green chile peppers are an especially good choice.

2 large onions, chopped

1 medium green bell pepper, chopped

1 medium yellow bell pepper, chopped

2 ribs celery, sliced

2 cloves garlic, minced

1 cup brown rice

2 cups vegetable broth

½ teaspoon salt

1 can (14½ ounces) seasoned diced tomatoes, drained

2 tablespoons chopped parsley

Heat a medium saucepan coated with cooking spray over medium-high heat. Add the onions, peppers, and celery and coat with cooking spray. Cook, stirring occasionally, for 8 minutes, or until tender-crisp. Add the garlic and cook, stirring constantly, for 1 minute. Add the rice, broth, and salt and bring to a boil. Reduce the heat to low, cover, and simmer for 45 minutes, or until all of the liquid is absorbed and the rice is tender.

Stir in the tomatoes. Cover and cook for 5 minutes longer. Stir in the parsley.

Makes 8 servings
Per serving: 133 calories, 1 g fat

COUSCOUS TIMBALES

QUICK

Prep time: 20 minutes ■ *Cook time: 5 minutes*

Enjoy these timbales as an accompaniment to chicken or fish. For an extra kick, try topping the timbales with a spoonful of chunky salsa.

2 cups vegetable broth

1 cup rinsed and drained canned black beans

1 medium tomato, seeded and chopped

1 tablespoon Santa Fe-style spice blend

1 package (5.7 ounces) tomato lentil-flavored couscous

In a medium saucepan, combine the broth, beans, tomato, and spice blend. Bring to a boil over high heat. Stir in the couscous. Cover and remove from the heat. Let stand for 5 minutes.

Coat a ½-cup custard cup or measuring cup with cooking spray. Stir the couscous mixture and spoon into the cup, pressing to pack. Turn the cup over onto a serving plate and carefully remove the cup. Repeat with the remaining couscous to make 12 timbales.

Makes 12 servings
Per serving: 66 calories, 0 g fat

MILLET AND VEGETABLE STIR-FRY

Prep time: 5 minutes ■ Cook time: 20 minutes

Photo on page 229

⅓ cup millet

12 ounces shiitake mushrooms, thickly
   sliced

2 medium carrots, cut into
   matchsticks

1 large red onion, cut into thin
   wedges

2 cloves garlic, minced

½ cup vegetable broth

¼ cup stir-fry sauce

Cook the millet according to package directions.

Meanwhile, heat a large nonstick skillet coated with cooking spray over medium-high heat. Add the mushrooms, carrots, and onion and coat with cooking spray. Cook, stirring occasionally, for 8 minutes, or until tender-crisp. Add the garlic and cook, stirring, for 1 minute. Add the broth and bring to a boil. Reduce the heat to low, cover, and simmer for 10 minutes. Stir in the millet and stir-fry sauce and heat through.

Makes 4 servings
Per serving: 160 calories, 3 g fat

A Millet Minute

Millet is a tiny, fast-growing survivor, a grain that does well in numerous climates and can withstand both drought and flood. Its main use in the United States has been for cattle feed and birdseed, but it has long been the chief cereal in parts of northern Africa and Asia. In fact, history records millet as a holy plant in the China of 2800 B.C., and even today, it is the basis of Indian *roti* and Ethiopian *injera*, two classic flatbreads. Many cooks also use the tiny yellow millet grains, often toasted, in purees and soups.

WILD MUSHROOMS AND BARLEY

Prep time: 5 minutes ■ *Cook time: 55 minutes*

1   tablespoon olive oil

12   ounces assorted sliced wild
     mushrooms, such as shiitake,
     porcini, portobello, and/or
     cremino

1   red bell pepper, thinly sliced

½   teaspoon salt

½   cup pearl barley

1   tablespoon chopped fresh thyme or
     1 teaspoon dried

2   cups vegetable broth

Heat the oil in a medium saucepan over medium-high heat. Add the mushrooms, bell pepper, and salt and cook, stirring occasionally, for 8 minutes, or until tender and the liquid has evaporated. Add the barley and thyme and cook, stirring frequently, for 2 minutes. Stir in the broth and bring to a boil. Reduce the heat to low, cover, and simmer for 45 minutes, or until the barley is just tender.

Makes 4 servings
Per serving: 160 calories, 4 g fat

Much Nicer Than Rice

Rice seems like a healthy dish, but look again. As commonly prepared in a risotto like this one, it's very high in fat—the "bad" saturated kind. What's more, white rice is refined, which too often means that the nutrients have been lost. For more nutrition with less fat, far fewer calories, and some delicious variations in taste and texture, these barley and millet dishes are better ways to get your grain. In addition, of course, you're getting vegetables that supply fiber and even more nutrients.

1 serving (1¼ cup) risotto
420 calories **18** grams fat **VS.**

1 serving **Wild Mushrooms
and Barley**
160 calories **4** grams fat

OR

1 serving **Millet and
Vegetable Stir-Fry**
(see page 227)
160 calories **3** grams fat

Great Grains

Satisfying and nutritious—especially when the choice is whole grain—grains are also very versatile and relatively easy to prepare. Here are cooking instructions for some of the most common grains, and a few that aren't so common.

Grain	Cooking Tips	Uses
Amaranth	Simmer 1 part amaranth in 3 parts water for 20 to 25 minutes	Cereal
Barley, pearl	Simmer 1 part barley in 4 parts water for 30 to 40 minutes	Side dishes, pilafs
Buckwheat groats (kasha)	Simmer 1 part groats in 2 parts water for 15 minutes	Pilafs
Bulgur	Pour 1½ cups boiling water over 1 cup bulgur and let stand for 30 minutes	Side dishes, cold salads
Cornmeal (preferably whole grain)	Simmer 1 part cornmeal in 4 parts water for 30 minutes	Cereal, polenta
Couscous (preferably whole grain)	Pour 1½ cups boiling water over 1⅓ cups couscous and let stand for 5 minutes	Side dishes
Hominy	Soak overnight, then simmer 1 part hominy in 3 parts water for 2½ to 3 hours	Cereal, side dishes
Millet	Simmer 1 part millet in 2 parts water for 25 to 30 minutes	Soups, stews, side dishes
Oats, old-fashioned rolled	Simmer 1 part oats in 2 parts water for 10 minutes and let stand for 2 minutes	Cereal, baking
Oats, steel cut	Simmer 1 part oats in 4 parts water for 30 to 40 minutes	Cereal
Quinoa	Rinse before using. Simmer 1 part quinoa in 2 parts water for 15 to 20 minutes	Side dishes
Rice, brown	Simmer 1 part rice in 2 parts water for 30 to 40 minutes	Side dishes, casseroles, pilafs, soups
Rice, white, basmati	Simmer 1 part rice in 2 parts water for 15 to 20 minutes	Side dishes, casseroles, pilafs, soups
Rye berries	Soak overnight, then simmer 1 part rye berries in 4 parts water for 1 hour	Side dishes, casseroles, stews
Triticale	Simmer 1 part triticale in 4 parts water for 1 hour	Cereal, casseroles, pilafs
Wheat berries	Soak overnight, then simmer 1 part wheat berries in 3 parts water for 2 hours	Stuffings, casseroles, side dishes, cereal
Wheat, cracked	Simmer 1 part cracked wheat in 2 parts water for 25 minutes	Cereal, side dishes, salads, casseroles
Wild rice	Simmer 1 part rice in 3 parts water for 45 to 60 minutes	Stuffings, casseroles, side dishes

Michael Romano

Union Square Café, New York City

Michael Romano is executive chef and co-owner of Union Square Café in New York City, which has been hailed many times over as the most popular restaurant in the Big Apple. Winner of the James Beard Foundation's Best Chef in New York award, Chef Romano has made an art of creating unique, delicious dishes that keep customers coming back again and again. This warmly spiced pilaf showcases the nutty flavors of basmati rice, a grain popular in Indian cuisine.

BASMATI RICE PILAF

1½	cups basmati rice
3	tablespoons butter
1	cinnamon stick
4	cardamom pods
2	cloves
5	peppercorns
1	bay leaf
¾	teaspoon black cumin or cumin
1½	cups chopped onion
4	cups thinly sliced cremini mushrooms
2	teaspoons kosher salt
⅛	teaspoon freshly ground black pepper

1. Preheat the oven to 400 degrees F.

2. In a large bowl, cover the rice with cold water and stir with your fingers until the water becomes cloudy. Carefully pour off the water, reserving the rice. Repeat 2 or 3 times, until the water is almost clear. Cover with fresh, cold water and soak for 10 minutes.

3. Bring 2 cups of water to a boil and set aside.

4. Heat the butter over medium-high heat in a 3-quart straight-sided saucepan until it begins to turn nut-brown. Add the spices and cook until fragrant, 30 to 60 seconds. Add the onion and cook until it begins to brown, 4 to 5 minutes. Add the mushrooms and cook until softened, 2 to 3 minutes.

5. Drain the rice, add it to the pan, and cook, stirring, for 1 minute to coat the rice with the butter. Season with the salt and pepper, and pour in the reserved hot water. Bring to a boil and cook for 1 minute. Cover with a tight-fitting lid or aluminum foil, place in the oven, and bake for 10 minutes. Remove from the oven and let stand, still covered, for 5 minutes. Uncover the rice, fluff with a fork, and serve hot.

Serves 4
Per serving: 386 calories, 9 g fat

GRILLED GAZPACHO WITH POLENTA

QUICK

Prep time: 10 minutes ■ *Cook time: 10 minutes*

1   medium orange or red bell pepper, chopped

1   medium onion, chopped

2   cloves garlic, minced

1   tablespoon olive oil

1   package (24 ounces) prepared polenta, cut into ½"-thick slices

2   medium tomatoes, seeded and chopped

1   small cucumber, peeled, if desired, halved, seeded, and chopped

3   tablespoons red wine vinegar

1   tablespoon chopped fresh thyme

½   teaspoon salt

¼   teaspoon freshly ground black pepper

Preheat the grill.

In a large bowl, combine the bell pepper, onion, garlic, and oil and toss to coat. Grill the vegetable mixture in a grill wok or on a grill screen, stirring occasionally, for 10 minutes, or until tender.

Meanwhile, coat one side of the sliced polenta with cooking spray and grill, coated side down, for 5 minutes. Coat the second side with cooking spray, turn the slices over, and grill for 5 minutes longer, or until heated through.

In the bowl, combine the grilled vegetables, tomatoes, cucumber, vinegar, thyme, salt, and black pepper until evenly coated. Serve over the polenta.

Makes 8 servings
Per serving: 95 calories, 2 g fat

Italian Exchange

While gnocchi and polenta are nutritionally similar, this dish of gnocchi in traditional butter sauce loads you with tons of saturated fat. When you want an Italian taste, try this vegetable-based Grilled Gazpacho with Polenta for lots of food, lots of taste, and very few calories.

**1 cup gnocchi
in 1 tablespoon butter sauce**
485 calories **24** grams fat

VS.

1 serving Grilled
Gazpacho with Polenta
95 calories **2** grams fat

Quinoa Salad

Prep time: 35 minutes ◾ *Cook time: 20 minutes*

Dressing

- 2 tablespoons mustard
- 2 tablespoons white balsamic vinegar
- 1 tablespoon extra-virgin olive oil
- 1 tablespoon honey

Quinoa

- 1¾ cups vegetable broth
- 1 cup quinoa, well-rinsed and drained
- ½ pound broccoli, cut into small florets, stems peeled and chopped
- 2 scallions, sliced
- 1 red-skinned apple, cored and chopped
- 1 rib celery, chopped
- 2 tablespoons flaxseeds

To make the dressing: In a small bowl, whisk together the mustard, vinegar, oil, and honey. Cover and set aside.

To make the quinoa: Pour the broth into a large measuring cup and add enough water to measure 2 cups. Pour into a large saucepan and bring to a boil over high heat. Add the quinoa. Reduce the heat to low, cover, and simmer for 10 minutes. Add the broccoli florets and stems. Cover and cook for 10 minutes, or until all the liquid is absorbed and the broccoli and quinoa are tender. Spoon the quinoa mixture into a large bowl. Cover and refrigerate until cool.

Add the scallions, apple, celery, flaxseeds, and the reserved dressing and toss to coat.

Makes 6 servings
Per serving: 195 calories, 6 g fat

From the Andes to You

Ready to try something new? Quinoa may be new to you, but it was a favorite of the ancient Aztecs and other Andean peoples. And its whole grain, nutty flavor is quickly finding favor among 21st-century North Americans as well. Nutritionally, it towers over a traditional macaroni salad, which gives you lots of calories empty of nutrients but filled with refined carbohydrates and saturated fat.

1 cup macaroni salad
360 calories **21** grams fat

1 serving Quinoa Salad
195 calories **6** grams fat

ROASTED RATATOUILLE WITH QUINOA

Prep time: 10 minutes ■ Cook time: 1 hour 20 minutes

Serving this traditional French dish over quinoa allows you to soak up every savory drop of the vegetable juices.

1   eggplant, peeled, halved
      lengthwise, and cut into ½"
      pieces

1   medium zucchini, cut into ½"
      rounds

2   cups frozen small white onions,
      thawed

2   tomatoes, seeded and coarsely
      chopped

4   cloves garlic, crushed

1   teaspoon dried oregano

1   teaspoon salt

½   cup quinoa, well-rinsed
      and drained

¼   cup balsamic vinegar

Preheat the oven to 375°F. Coat a 13" × 9" baking pan with cooking spray.

Place the eggplant, zucchini, onions, tomatoes, garlic, oregano, and ½ teaspoon of the salt in the prepared pan and generously coat with cooking spray. Toss to coat. Roast the vegetables, stirring occasionally, for 1 hour 15 minutes, or until tender.

Meanwhile, bring 1 cup water to a boil in a small saucepan. Stir in the quinoa and the remaining ½ teaspoon salt. Cover and simmer for 20 minutes, or until tender. Keep warm.

When the vegetables are done, remove to a serving bowl and place the pan over medium heat. Stir the vinegar into the pan, scraping any browned bits from the bottom. Pour over the vegetables.

Serve the vegetables with the quinoa.

Makes 6 servings
Per serving: 137 calories, 1 g fat

BAKED VEGETABLE NOODLE KUGEL

Prep time: 15 minutes ■ *Cook time: 1 hour 15 minutes*

This baked pudding is a traditional favorite among Jews of eastern European origin. Experiment by trying different frozen vegetables, such as peas and carrots or broccoli, corn, and red bell peppers.

1   bag (12 ounces) yolk-free egg
      noodles

1   bag (16 ounces) frozen assorted
      vegetables such as broccoli,
      cauliflower, and/or carrots,
      thawed

1   jar (7 ounces) roasted red peppers,
      drained and chopped

1¾ cups vegetable broth

1   cup liquid egg substitute

1   can (12 ounces) low-fat evaporated
      milk

1½ teaspoons dried thyme or basil
      leaves

½   teaspoon salt

¼   teaspoon ground black pepper

Preheat the oven to 350°F. Coat a 13" × 9" baking dish with cooking spray.

Prepare the noodles according to package directions. Drain and cool.

In a large bowl, combine the noodles, assorted vegetables, roasted peppers, broth, egg substitute, evaporated milk, thyme or basil, salt, and black pepper. Pour into the prepared baking dish.

Bake for 55 minutes, or until a knife inserted in the center comes out clean. Let stand for 10 minutes before cutting.

Makes 12 servings
Per serving: 145 calories, 2 g fat

How to Roast Peppers

If you prefer roasting your own peppers rather than using the jarred variety, here's how. Cook them directly over a flame till they become thoroughly black and bubbly, turning them occasionally with tongs to make sure they cook evenly. Or, spread them on a baking sheet covered with foil and roast under a broiler—about 3 inches below the heat source—turning them often with tongs. When the peppers are charred and slightly cooled, pull out the stem and seed core, then peel off the blackened skin with your fingers or the edge of a knife or a sheet of paper towel.

The World's Easiest Sauces

Pesto originated in Genoa, Italy, as an easy, no-cook fresh basil and olive oil sauce for pasta. But the basic method lends itself to many variations that are lower in calories and fat. Use them not just on hot pasta but on raw or cooked vegetables or other foods as well.

Asian pesto. In a blender or food processor, combine 1 can (16 ounces) rinsed and drained water chestnuts, 1 tablespoon peanut butter, ½ cup soy sauce, 1 or 2 packs low-calorie sweetener, ⅓ cup rice wine vinegar or white wine vinegar, 3 large cloves garlic, and 1 tablespoon toasted sesame oil. Process until pureed. Makes 1½ cups.

Olive pesto. In a blender or food processor, combine 1 tablespoon olive oil, ¼ cup vegetable broth, 2 large cloves garlic, ½ cup chopped fresh or drained canned tomatoes, 3 tablespoons pitted olives, 1½ cups loosely packed fresh basil leaves, 1 tablespoon balsamic vinegar, and a pinch each of salt and freshly ground black pepper. Process until pureed. Makes 1 cup.

Roasted red pepper pesto. In a blender or food processor, combine 1⅓ cups diced roasted red peppers (patted dry), ¾ cup fresh parsley, ⅓ cup toasted pine nuts, 2 large cloves garlic, 1 tablespoon wine vinegar, 1 tablespoon grated Parmesan cheese, and a pinch each of salt and freshly ground black pepper. Process until pureed. Makes 1 cup.

South-of-the-border pesto. In a blender or food processor, combine 1 can (19 ounces) rinsed and drained black beans, 1 seeded jalapeño chile pepper (wear plastic gloves when handling), 2 cloves garlic, ½ cup loosely packed fresh cilantro leaves, 1 teaspoon chili powder, and 2 tablespoons fat-free sour cream. Process until coarsely pureed. Makes 1½ cups.

Sun-dried tomato pesto. In a blender or food processor, combine ⅔ cup reconstituted dry-pack sun-dried tomatoes, 1 cup fresh oregano leaves, 1 tablespoon olive oil, 1 tablespoon reduced-sodium vegetable broth, 1 small onion, 2 large cloves garlic, 1 tablespoon wine vinegar, and a pinch each of salt and freshly ground black pepper. Process until pureed. Makes 1 cup.

LINGUINE WITH ROASTED RED PEPPER SAUCE

Prep time: 10 minutes ■ *Cook time: 15 minutes*

The yogurt and flour help make this sauce thick and rich, so it really coats the pasta well. If you prefer a thinner sauce, reserve about ½ cup of the pasta cooking water and add a little of it to the sauce as it finishes cooking.

8	ounces whole wheat linguine
2	jars (7½ ounces each) roasted red peppers
1	medium onion, chopped
2	cloves garlic, minced
3	tablespoons balsamic vinegar
¾	cup low-fat plain yogurt or soy alternative
1½	teaspoons flour
3	tablespoons grated Parmesan cheese (optional)

Prepare the linguine according to package directions.

Meanwhile, drain the roasted peppers and place in a blender. Puree until smooth.

Heat a large nonstick skillet coated with cooking spray over medium-high heat. Add the onion and cook, stirring occasionally, for 5 minutes, or until tender. Add the garlic and cook, stirring constantly, for 1 minute. Stir in the roasted pepper puree and vinegar. Bring to a boil, reduce the heat to low, and simmer for 4 minutes, or until heated through.

In a cup, combine the yogurt and flour. Add to the skillet with the onion mixture and heat through.

Toss the linguine with the red-pepper sauce. Sprinkle with the cheese (if using).

Makes 4 servings
Per serving: 289 calories, 3 g fat

Romesco Sauce

Want to try something absolutely sensational on fish, poultry, or grilled vegetables? Romesco sauce is a classic from Catalonia, Spain. You'll need tomatoes, red peppers, onion, garlic, almonds, and olive oil. Roast the peppers and skin the tomatoes, brown the almonds in olive oil or on a baking sheet, then puree everything in a food processor, adding olive oil as you do so.

Beverly Sills

*B*everly Sills is widely recognized as one of the 20th century's great opera divas. Born in Brooklyn in 1929, she was a childhood radio performer, appearing on *Major Bowes' Amateur Hour* and in bit parts in soap operas. She went on to become a reigning interpreter of an extraordinary diversity of operatic roles. She retired from the stage at the age of 51 and went on to lead the New York City Opera as its director and, in 1994, to assume the post of chairwoman of Lincoln Center, New York's premier arts complex, until her retirement in 2002. Beverly Sills has received numerous awards and honors, including the Heinz Award in the Arts and Humanities, the French Order of Arts and Letters, the Presidential Medal of Freedom, and the Kennedy Center Honor for lifelong accomplishment.

Is there one food that you cannot resist under any circumstances?

BS: Ice cream, definitely. Preferably with nuts.

What is the comfort food you turn to in times of stress?

BS: Bread.

What's the most unusual combination of food you eat?

BS: My husband invented a sandwich of peanut butter, onions, mayonnaise, and bacon, and people look horrified, but it's very good.

What is your favorite ethnic food?

BS: Chinese food, but very good Chinese food. I'm very fussy about Chinese food, even though on a cold, snowy night, I will order from the local takeout.

Do you find supermarket shopping a pleasant experience—and do you check the food labels when you shop?

BS: I love shopping, and I love going to supermarkets, but unfortunately I hate checking out. I always wish someone else would get on the line and do that for me. And no, I don't check labels. But I get very inspired when I see an ingredient such as morel mushrooms, as I can create a whole meal around that.

How does food relate to you and your career?

BS: When I perform, I usually have a steak around 3 P.M. and that's it. It's kind of like an athlete; I don't think they can perform on a full stomach, either. The leaner the better.

Do you like to cook? What do you like about it?

BS: I love to cook, and I have a wonderful time when I'm left to my own.

Do you like to entertain?

BS: Well, again because of my work, my entertaining is done in restaurants, so I have not entertained at home in 40 years.

How does food relate to your childhood?

BS: I come from a Russian-Rumanian background. We ate a lot of Russian cooking, a lot of blini, rice prepared in a special way. My maternal grandmother cooked a great many dishes with eggplant and oil and spices. My mother made the best borscht imaginable and all sorts of exotic pasta pastries.

Did you ever watch your mother cook?

BS: She ruled the kitchen. She used to brag that my father didn't even know what color the kitchen was painted. And since in her mind I was always going to be an opera star, she did not want me to cook. In fact, my husband graduated from Le Cordon Bleu in Paris. When we were married, my mother came for her first dinner to Ohio where we lived, and he made oysters Rockefeller for her and a wonderful stuffed turkey, and she said to me, "See, I always knew you could cook. All you have to do is set your mind to it." I said, "I didn't cook anything; he made the whole dinner." And she put the fork down and said, "I'm not going to eat anything in this house unless you cook it." I said, "How can you say that? You never taught me." But my husband taught me. And that was when I began to enjoy it a lot.

How were family gatherings?

BS: We gathered almost every Sunday when we were children. My father had 15 brothers and sisters, and my mother had six brothers and sisters, so it was a very large gathering, and the two families were very close. We never stopped talking. The decibel level was very high. We were very noisy people.

What's your favorite smell in the kitchen?

BS: Bread baking.

What is your favorite seasoning?

BS: Coriander. I'd probably put it on ice cream if I could. I just love it; I use it an awful lot.

As a child, what was your least favorite food?

BS: Eggs. I didn't mind them so much when they were involved in a dish. But I hated the idea of eggs for breakfast.

What is your least favorite food now?

BS: I don't like bonefish, because as an opera singer, I have a fear of bones. I still have that fear left over from my singing.

What's your favorite food?

BS: I love escargots. I can make a whole meal out of that and butter. I'm also crazy about soft-shelled crabs.

If you were on a desert island, which five food items would you have?

BS: Ice cream of course, bread and butter, a good Châteaubriand, pommes soufflées.

As a child, before you were a great star, if you could have dinner with anyone, who would have been your choice?

BS: Lily Pons. She was my idol.

FUSILLI WITH GREEN SAUCE

QUICK

Prep time: 10 minutes ■ Cook time: 15 minutes

8 ounces whole wheat fusilli

1 tablespoon olive oil

2 medium zucchini, thinly sliced

½ teaspoon salt

¼ teaspoon freshly ground black pepper

2 cloves garlic, thinly sliced

¼ cup packed fresh basil leaves

½ cup vegetable broth

Prepare the pasta according to package directions.

Meanwhile, heat the oil in a large nonstick skillet over medium-high heat. Add the zucchini, salt, and pepper and cook, stirring occasionally, for 10 minutes, or until very tender. Add the garlic and cook, stirring frequently, for 2 minutes. Remove from the heat and let cool for 5 minutes.

In a blender, process the zucchini mixture, basil, and ¼ cup of the broth, scraping the sides occasionally, until smooth. Add more broth if the mixture is dry. Toss the pasta with the sauce.

Makes 8 servings
Per serving: 240 calories, 5 g fat

Pasta Preference

Pasta provokes culinary creativity. Traditional Bologna-style means meat and butter—here adorning refined grain pasta to create a high-calorie dish that is high in saturated fat. Try instead this very tasty recipe using whole wheat fusilli, zucchini, basil, and olive oil.

1 serving (2 ounces) pasta
Bolognese (½ cup sauce)
380 calories **10** grams fat

VS.

**1 serving Fusilli
with Green Sauce**
240 calories **5** grams fat

FIESTA PASTA

Prep time: 5 minutes ■ Cook time: 15 minutes

8   ounces whole wheat pasta

1   medium onion, chopped

1   can (15 ounces) black beans, rinsed and drained

1   can (14½ ounces) Mexican-seasoned diced tomatoes

1   can (8 ounces) tomato sauce

1   can (4½ ounces) chopped green chile peppers

1   cup (4 ounces) shredded reduced-fat Monterey Jack or Cheddar cheese or soy alternative

Prepare the pasta according to package directions.

Meanwhile, coat a large nonstick skillet with cooking spray and heat over medium-high heat. Add the onion and cook, stirring occasionally, for 5 minutes, or until tender. Stir in the beans, tomatoes (with juice), tomato sauce, and chile peppers (with juice) and bring to a boil. Reduce the heat to low, cover, and simmer for 3 minutes, or until heated through.

Toss the pasta with the sauce. Sprinkle with the cheese.

Makes 4 servings
Per serving: 395 calories, 4 g fat

Leaving a Legend Behind

The legendary fettuccine Alfredo is a minefield of carbohydrates and saturated fat. When you yearn for a rich pasta taste, try this recipe for Fiesta Pasta. With black beans, onion, diced tomatoes, green chile peppers, and reduced-fat cheese, this whole wheat dish is a luxurious treat for far fewer calories and far less fat.

1 serving fettuccine Alfredo
520 calories **28** grams fat

1 serving Fiesta Pasta
395 calories **4** grams fat

DESSERTS

Sweets without Fear

recipes

*I*f you were on a diet, your automatic reaction would probably be to skip this chapter altogether. After all, any dieter knows that desserts are a no-no—something to be avoided until the diet is over and you can get back to real life.

Picture-Perfect Weight Loss, however, is not a diet. It's a way of eating and of cooking that insists that no food is off-limits, and that every category of food contains lower-calorie choices that are perfectly delicious, completely filling, and utterly satisfying.

The recipes in this chapter are a case in point.

Here are recipes for chocolate mousse, cheesecake, even a soufflé—hardly the items that leap to mind when your intent is to lose weight or maintain weight loss. Yet in all three cases—indeed, in all the recipes that follow—lower-calorie choices are made at every step along the way: in the ingredients list, the preparation, the cooking methods. The result is a collection of desserts as scrumptious as their names would lead you to believe—bread pudding, chocolate fondue, pizzelle—but with the calorie count ratcheted way down.

Desserts are an integral part of our eating habits, and trying to kill a craving for sweets is an exercise in futility. Instead of fighting or fearing dessert, take your cue from this chapter of the book and make dessert the Picture-Perfect Weight-Loss way.

All the recipes in this book that call for artificial sweeteners were tested with Splenda, but other artificial sweeteners are available. See page 250 for information on each of them.

CHOCOLATE MOUSSE

Prep time: 5 minutes ■ Cook time: 2 minutes ■ Chill time: 3 hours

6 ounces semisweet chocolate

1 package (12.3 ounces) reduced-fat silken tofu, firm or extra-firm

1½ teaspoons vanilla extract

⅓ cup pasteurized egg whites

Shaved chocolate for garnish (optional)

Place the semisweet chocolate in a small microwaveable bowl. Microwave on high power for 2 minutes. Stir until smooth.

In a food processor, pulse the tofu until very small pieces form. Add the semisweet chocolate and vanilla extract and process until smooth.

Place the egg whites in a large bowl. With an electric mixer on medium speed, whip until foamy. Increase the speed to high and whip until stiff peaks form. Gradually fold the chocolate mixture into the egg-white mixture.

Spoon the mousse into dessert bowls. Cover and chill for at least 3 hours. Garnish with the shaved chocolate (if using).

Makes 6 servings
Per serving: 190 calories, 8 g fat

Nutritionally Correct Chocolate

Chocolate Mousse and Espresso-Chocolate Fondue are the quintessential luxury desserts, so how is it possible for them to be "nutritionally correct"? Well, studies have shown that while the fat in chocolate is certainly of the saturated variety, it does not seem to raise cholesterol levels. That means all you have to do is find a way around the other ingredients in these sumptuous items, and you've got a nutritionally correct dessert. We've done it for you, in recipes based on egg whites, tofu, and soy or fat-free milk, but with real chocolate. A delight for the senses and as nutritionally correct as chocolate desserts can get.

1 serving (¾ cup) traditional chocolate mousse
450 calories **33** grams fat

**1 serving
nutritionally correct
Espresso-Chocolate Fondue
(see page 250)**
120 calories 0 grams fat

OR

**1 serving nutritionally
correct Chocolate Mousse**
190 calories 8 grams fat

ESPRESSO-CHOCOLATE FONDUE

QUICK

Prep time: 5 minutes ■ *Cook time: 5 minutes*

Photo on page 249

1   package (3.4 ounces) regular
    chocolate pudding mix (not
    instant)

1   cup espresso

1   cup fat-free milk or soy milk

1   tablespoon rum or 1 teaspoon rum
    extract

In a medium saucepan, cook the pudding mix, espresso, and milk according to package directions. Remove from the heat and stir in the rum or rum extract. Serve warm.

Makes 4 servings

Per tablespoon: 120 calories, 0 g fat

Sweet Talk

The story of artificial sweeteners has long been one of conflicting studies with no small amount of controversy. Finally, the Food and Drug Administration (FDA) stepped in with a rigorous and exhaustive study on the safety of these nonnutritives. The result? The FDA approved four for use in the United States, certifying them as safe even for pregnant women and people with diabetes.

The four are saccharin, aspartame, acesulfame potassium, and sucralose. Here's the skinny on these artificial sweeteners.

Saccharin, sold as Sweet'n Low, has zero calories and, along with sucralose, tends to offer the sweetest taste. Even heating does not lessen saccharin's sweetness.

Aspartame—NutraSweet or Equal on supermarket shelves—is the one sweetener that may produce a nominal rise in blood sugar levels. Aspartame products, which contain 4 calories per gram but in so concentrated a form as to be insignif-

icant, can lose their sweetness through cooking or baking; add the sweetener after the cooking.

Acesulfame potassium, known as acesulfame K and sold as Sunette, gets even sweeter when there are other sweet ingredients present; it parlays their sweetening power to create a very honeyed taste—something to be aware of when you cook with it.

Sucralose, sold as Splenda, has zero calories, is very sweet, and stays sweet with heating.

None of these four, by the way, causes tooth decay.

All the recipes in this book that call for artificial sweeteners were tested with Splenda, the sucralose product, but any of the other sweeteners will do just as well. Whichever sweetener you use, read the package to see how much of the sweetener equals the sweetening power of sugar. Concentrations differ, and so will your measurements for different recipes.

WARM APPLE COMPOTE WITH FROZEN YOGURT

QUICK

Prep time: 5 minutes ■ *Cook time: 10 minutes*

1 tablespoon butter

2 tablespoons packed brown sugar

⅛ teaspoon ground nutmeg

4 crisp apples such as Fuji, Braeburn, or Gala, peeled, cored, and cut into ⅜"-thick slices

1 cup low-fat vanilla frozen yogurt or soy alternative

¼ cup chopped toasted pecans

Melt the butter in a large skillet over medium heat. Add the brown sugar and nutmeg and stir until smooth. Add the apples, cover, and cook, stirring occasionally, for 8 minutes, or until the apples are tender.

Spoon the apples into dessert bowls. Top with the frozen yogurt and pecans.

Makes 4 servings
Per serving: 230 calories, 9 g fat

Comfort Food

Nothing is as warm and homey as an apple concoction. This traditional tarte Tatin, however, starts with apples cooked in butter, so it's sky-high in fat. The Warm Apple Compote captures the same comforting apple flavor, accompanied by brown sugar and nutmeg, capped by the cool sweetness of frozen yogurt, and at half the calories and fat.

1 serving (3 ounces) tarte Tatin
450 calories **19** grams fat

VS.

1 serving Warm Apple Compote with Frozen Yogurt
230 calories **9** grams fat

CITRUSY PUMPKIN PUDDING

Prep time: 5 minutes ■ *Chill time: 3 hours*

1 can (15 ounces) pumpkin

1 package (1 ounce) instant sugar-free vanilla pudding

½ cup + 2 tablespoons water

¼ cup orange juice

½ teaspoon grated orange peel

½ teaspoon ground cinnamon

½ teaspoon pumpkin pie spice, or a mixture of cloves, allspice, ginger, and nutmeg

Whipped topping and cinnamon sticks for garnish (optional)

In a blender or food processor, combine the pumpkin, pudding, water, orange juice, orange peel, cinnamon, and pumpkin pie spice or spice mixture. Process on low speed until smooth. Spoon into dessert dishes and refrigerate for several hours before serving. Garnish with the whipped topping and cinnamon sticks (if using).

Makes 4 servings
Per serving: 70 calories, 1 g fat

Native Virtues

The pumpkin is a nutritional powerhouse, and this Citrusy Pumpkin Pudding just happens to be one of the healthiest low-calorie dessert recipes in the book. It gives you all the virtues of the pumpkin—lots of beta-carotene and high fiber—without the high calorie count of pumpkin pie. And it tastes fabulous. Indulge yourself. This one has everything that's good and nothing that's bad. By the way, you can substitute pureed winter squash for the canned pumpkin.

1 slice (4 ounces) pumpkin pie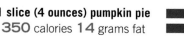
350 calories **14** grams fat

5 servings Citrusy Pumpkin Pudding
350 calories **5** grams fat

MANGO-COCONUT BREAD PUDDING

Prep time: 50 minutes ■ Cook time: 1 hour

If you like extra-fruity bread pudding, stir a cup of fresh or thawed frozen blueberries into the pudding along with the bread. The sauce will keep in the refrigerator, covered, for up to 2 days.

Bread Pudding

  3 cups 1% milk or soy milk

  ¾ cup liquid egg substitute

  3 tablespoons light margarine, melted

  2 tablespoons sugar

  1 loaf (about 14 ounces) day-old light Italian or French bread, cut into ½" cubes

  ⅓ cup flaked coconut, toasted

Sauce

  2 large ripe mangoes, peeled

  2 tablespoons sugar

To make the bread pudding: Preheat the oven to 350°F. Lightly coat a 2-quart baking dish with cooking spray.

In a large bowl, whisk together the milk, egg substitute, margarine, and sugar. Add the bread and toss to coat. Let stand for 30 minutes.

Place the bread mixture in the prepared baking dish and bake for 45 minutes. Sprinkle the top with the coconut and bake for 15 minutes longer, or until a knife inserted in the center comes out clean. Let stand for 20 minutes before serving.

To make the sauce: Meanwhile, cut the flesh of the mangoes away from the pits and cut the mangoes into chunks. Place in a blender with the sugar. Puree until smooth. Serve the sauce at room temperature over the bread pudding.

Makes 8 servings
Per serving: 290 calories, 8 g fat

The Coconut

The fabulous coconut—a hard, fibrous outer shell filled with meat and liquid—is actually the fruit of the palm tree. Coconuts were known to Marco Polo, who came upon them during his travels in India, but it was Portuguese explorers who gave them the name we know them by—all because the three holes at the base of the nut made it look like a grinning face, or "coco" in Portuguese. In the islands of the Pacific, the region perhaps most closely associated with the coconut, it is a multiple-use item. It provides a nutritious food, satisfies thirst, and yields oil that islanders drink, massage into their skin, turn into soaps and other products, and process for export. The outer husk can serve as a dish or cup, or it can be burned for fuel. One typical recipe is to marinate raw fish in cut-up coconut meat with the coconut liquid right in the coconut shell. The result is a kind of Polynesian sushi.

Lidia Matticchio Bastianich

Felidia, Becco, and Esca in New York City; Lidia's Kansas City, in Missouri; and Lidia's Pittsburgh, in Pennsylvania

For Lidia Matticchio Bastianich, cooking is an art borne out of love. As a young girl growing up in Italy, she learned from her grandmother all about traditional Italian cooking and about using only the freshest ingredients. Now, in her top-rated New York City restaurants, she happily continues those traditions, staying true to her native Italian heritage. Her sincere and heartfelt love of cooking has made her a dedicated student of culinary history. She has taught numerous courses on the anthropology of food and has frequently lectured on the history of Italian food. Cooking is true contentment for Chef Bastianich, inspired by a deep love of family.

"UGLY BUT GOOD" NUT COOKIES

Butter, softened, for the pans
(if using)

8 large egg whites

Pinch salt

2 cups confectioners' sugar, sifted

2 cups shelled hazelnuts, toasted,
skins removed, and chopped fine

Preheat the oven to 275°F. Lightly grease two baking sheets, or line them with parchment paper.

Beat the egg whites and salt in a bowl with a handheld electric mixer until foamy. As you continue beating, add the sugar gradually, until it is all incorporated and the egg whites hold soft and shiny peaks. Scrape the beaten whites into a wide, heavy saucepan and set over medium-low heat. Stir in the hazelnuts and cook, stirring, until the batter is light golden brown, about 20 minutes. (The batter will deflate quite a bit as it cooks.)

Remove the pan from the heat. Drop the batter by rounded teaspoonfuls onto the prepared baking sheets, leaving about 1 inch between them. Bake until golden brown and firm to the touch, about 30 minutes. Remove, and cool completely before serving. Store at room temperature in an airtight container for up to 1 week.

Makes about 48 cookies
Per serving: 35 calories, 2 g fat

TRIO OF MELON ICES

Prep time: 20 minutes ■ *Chill time: 3 hours*

Cantaloupe Ice

3 cups cubed cantaloupe

⅓ cup sugar

¼ cup water

1 tablespoon lemon juice

⅛ teaspoon grated lemon peel

Honeydew Ice

3 cups cubed honeydew melon

⅓ cup sugar

¼ cup water

1 tablespoon lime juice

⅛ teaspoon grated lime peel

Watermelon Ice

3 cups cubed watermelon, seeded

⅓ cup sugar

¼ cup water

1 tablespoon Campari

To make the cantaloupe ice: Place the cantaloupe in a plastic container, cover, and place in the freezer for 3 to 4 hours.

In a small saucepan, combine the sugar and the water. Cover and bring to a boil. Boil for 1 minute, or until the sugar is completely dissolved. Transfer the sugar syrup to a small glass bowl. Stir in the lemon juice and lemon peel. Cover and refrigerate for 45 minutes.

Place the frozen cantaloupe in a food processor and pulse just until pureed. With the machine running, gradually add the syrup. Process the cantaloupe mixture just until smooth. Serve immediately. (Can be frozen, covered, for up to 1 week. Allow to soften slightly before serving.)

To make the honeydew ice: Prepare as directed above.

To make the watermelon ice: Prepare as directed above.

Makes 10 servings
Per serving: 132 calories, 0 g fat

Scoop It Up

When you crave a frozen dessert, think beyond the customary banana split. Yes, it offers a potpourri of flavor, but at a high price in calories and in saturated fat—the "bad" kind of fat. Here's an alternative that offers just as much flavor at about a quarter of the calories. What's more, you could get six scoops of the melon ices—as if anyone could down that much—versus just three scoops of split. And it's worth keeping in mind that the sorbet in the melon ice dessert is a food you find on the Anytime List, so you can reach for this dessert any time.

1 banana split (3 scoops ice cream)
1,340 calories **78** grams fat

3 servings melon ices
396 calories 0 grams fat

PHYLLO CUPS WITH RICOTTA CREAM AND BERRIES

Prep time: 20 minutes ■ *Cook time: 5 minutes*

You can find phyllo dough in the freezer section of the supermarket. It will keep in your freezer for up to a year. Once it's thawed, however, don't refreeze it, or it will become brittle.

Ricotta Cream

- 1 cup lite ricotta cheese
- ⅓ cup Neufchâtel cheese, softened
- 2 tablespoons sugar
- 1 tablespoon orange juice
- 1 tablespoon Grand Marnier or orange liqueur
- 1 teaspoon grated orange peel

Phyllo Cups

- 1 tablespoon sliced almonds, toasted
- 3 sheets whole wheat phyllo dough
- ½ teaspoon sugar
- 1 cup assorted fresh berries

To make the ricotta cream: In a blender or food processor, combine the ricotta, Neufchâtel, sugar, orange juice, Grand Marnier or liqueur, and orange peel. Blend, scraping down the sides, until smooth. Place in a bowl, cover, and refrigerate.

To make the phyllo cups: Preheat the oven to 350°F. Lightly coat 4 muffin cups with butter-flavored cooking spray.

Finely chop 2 teaspoons of the almonds. Reserve the remaining almonds for garnish.

Place 2 phyllo sheets on a work surface and cut each into six 5" squares. Coat with butter-flavored cooking spray. Sprinkle the squares with sugar and chopped almonds. Place one square over another, turning so that the corners are not aligned. Add a third layer, turning so that the corners are not aligned. Set aside. Repeat layering the remaining squares, three layers each, to make 4 stacks.

Place the remaining sheet of phyllo on the work surface and cut four 5" squares. Place one square over each stack, alternating corners. Lightly coat with cooking spray. Place the squares in the prepared muffin cups, lightly pressing the center of the squares to take the shape of the muffin cups. Bake for 5 minutes, or until golden brown. Allow the phyllo cups to cool in the pan.

Place 1 phyllo cup on each of 4 dessert plates. Divide the ricotta cream evenly among the cups. Top with the berries and the remaining almonds.

Makes 4 servings
Per serving: 248 calories, 11 g fat

RASPBERRY SOUFFLÉ

If fresh raspberries aren't available, you can substitute 1½ cups frozen raspberries or frozen mixed berries.

Raspberry Puree

- 1 pint fresh raspberries
- 3 tablespoons sugar

Soufflé

- 1 teaspoon + 3 tablespoons sugar
- 4 large egg whites, at room temperature

To make the raspberry puree: Combine the raspberries and sugar in a blender and blend until smooth. Strain the puree through a fine mesh strainer, discarding the seeds (there should be at least ½ cup puree).

To make the soufflé: Preheat the oven to 350°F. Lightly coat the inside of 4 individual soufflé dishes with butter-flavored cooking spray. Sprinkle the bottom and sides of each dish with ¼ teaspoon of the sugar.

Place the egg whites in the large bowl of an electric mixer. Beat the whites on medium speed until foamy. Add the remaining 3 tablespoons sugar, increase the speed to high, and beat the whites just until stiff peaks form. With a rubber spatula, gently fold ⅓ cup of the raspberry puree into the egg white mixture; reserve the remaining puree.

Evenly divide the raspberry–egg white mixture among the prepared dishes. With a small spatula, level the tops and angle the sides in from the edge of the dishes.

Bake for 12 minutes, or until the soufflés rise and the tops are brown.

To serve, place the soufflés on individual dessert plates. Cut an X in the center of each soufflé and spoon 1 tablespoon of the remaining raspberry puree into each.

Makes 4 servings
Per serving: 118 calories, 0 g fat

STRAWBERRIES MARINATED IN BALSAMIC VINEGAR

Prep time: 10 minutes ■ *Marinate time: 1 hour*

2 tablespoons balsamic vinegar

1 tablespoon Splenda

¼ teaspoon freshly ground black
   pepper

2 teaspoons orange peel

1 pound strawberries, hulled, halved
   or quartered if large

1 cup fat-free vanilla frozen yogurt or
   soy alternative

In a medium bowl, combine the vinegar, Splenda, pepper, and orange peel. Add the strawberries and toss to coat. Cover and marinate for 1 to 2 hours.

Spoon the strawberries into dessert bowls and top each with the frozen yogurt.

Makes 4 servings
Per serving: 95 calories, 1 g fat

Tart Fruit, Fruit Tart

It's the hottest new trend in desserts: Add a pungent touch to what's naturally candy-sweet. Today's inventive chefs are sprinkling balsamic vinegar, pepper, cardamom, even chiles onto extravagantly sweet concoctions. These strawberries are marinated in balsamic vinegar for pungency, then mellowed by cool frozen yogurt. They're delicious, and compared with the rather pathetic-looking strawberry tart, they give you a lot of strawberry taste at a much lower calorie cost.

**1 strawberry tart (4 ounces)
with cream filling**
380 calories **14** grams fat

**4 servings Strawberries
Marinated in
Balsamic Vinegar**
380 calories **4** grams fat

PIZZELLE WITH FRUIT AND SORBET

Prep time: 10 minutes + stand time ■ *Cook time: 7 minutes*

It's easy to vary this recipe to suit your family's tastes—just substitute different kinds of pizzelles, fruit, or sorbet. Try plain pizzelles with orange sorbet and segments of mandarin oranges, or lime sorbet topped with sliced fresh kiwifruit.

4	chocolate pizzelles (4" diameter)
½	cup fat-free milk or soy milk
1	cup vanilla and/or chocolate sorbet
4–5	strawberries, sliced (about ½ cup)

Preheat the oven to 300°F. Place four 6" ramekins, right side up, on a baking pan.

Place one pizzelle on each ramekin and brush with milk. Place in the oven and bake for 3 minutes, or until the pizzelles soften. Remove from the oven and gently press the pizzelles into the ramekins to form cups. Return to the oven and bake for an additional 4 minutes.

Cool the ramekins on a rack. Remove the pizzelles from the ramekins and let stand overnight, or until crisp.

Scoop ¼ cup sorbet into each pizzelle cup and top with the strawberries.

Makes 4 servings
Per serving: 109 calories, 2 g fat

Carnie Wilson

The multitalented Carnie Wilson, daughter of legendary Beach Boy Brian Wilson, is a member of the musical pop trio Wilson Phillips, a talk show host, an actress, a voice-over artist, and the author of *Gut Feelings*. She is also a veteran of gastric bypass surgery, a radical weight-loss procedure that enabled her to lose more than 150 pounds. Eager to raise awareness of morbid obesity, Carnie chose to have her surgery performed live over the Internet. Today, she runs an obesity support group, does monthly chats at spotlighthealth.com, and travels around the country telling the story of her journey with weight and food issues and discussing the options available to help control obesity and the co-morbidities associated with this disease.

What is the one food you cannot resist under any circumstances?

CW: Chocolate or macaroni and cheese.

What is the comfort food that you turn to in times of distress—and why that food?

CW: I find all food comfort food. I guess just the act of eating is itself comforting.

What is the most unusual combination of food that you eat?

CW: Hands down: pickles and peanut butter. Everyone thinks I am out of my mind, but don't knock it till you try it.

What is your favorite ethnic food and why?

CW: Sushi. I think it's the purest, healthiest, most mouthwatering food there is, and I love the combination of ginger with the fish. I also adore Indian food. I think that the flavors and spices are out of this world. Yum.

How does food relate to you and your career?

CW: My eating, dieting, and weight-loss surgery have been very public, and I am open to sharing what I have eaten in the past and what I eat now. It's actually a huge part of my career. It's a great feeling to not be neurotic about food and overeating anymore, but I still share with the world my love for food and passion for cooking. I hope to write a cookbook one day.

Do you like to cook? Why?

CW: Cooking is one of my favorite things. It calms me down. It centers me and makes me feel productive. I like to put on some great music—maybe old standards—and sing away in the kitchen. I love to make a great meal for my family and friends and watch them eat it. Seeing their faces and listening to them say "Mmm" is the best—especially my sweet husband, Rob.

What's the worst experience you've ever had as a cook?

CW: It was around Thanksgiving time, and I was supposed to cook Thanksgiving dinner that year. Now this was a time when I was approaching 300 pounds and was eating everything in sight, including snacking in the middle of the night. That year, I was so anxious to start cooking that 2 days before Thanksgiving at like 3 in the morning I started making the stuffing. I was half asleep and hovering over the stove, and I was so hungry and so obsessed with the ideas of cooking and eating that my shirt sleeve caught fire on one of the stove burners. I managed to smother the fire, but it was terrifying.

What does food mean to you, and does it make you feel good?

CW: Food has always been an important part of my life, but from a young age, I have always overeaten. I always felt like I couldn't get enough. I had many reasons for overeating, but now I can separate those feelings from food and not abuse my body anymore by stuffing my face. I don't eat to numb out or shove feelings down anymore. I don't overeat. I now appreciate food. I still love food, and whatever I eat, I savor every bite. In fact, since my surgery, eating is a better experience for me because I eat less and feel better about it. It's the most liberating feeling I've ever had.

Is there any relation between food and your childhood?

CW: Please—where do I begin? Most of my issues are from childhood and food. For my entire life, food has been the reason I feel good or bad. And it's also true that eating certain foods brings me back to childhood. Green beans, ice cream, peanut butter, pie: They all trigger a feeling inside of being young again and experiencing taste sensations of different foods. It's powerful.

What's your favorite food?

CW: Cheese. All varieties. I like cheese in and on so many things: pasta, tortillas, eggs, pizza. It's creamy and delicious.

If you were on a desert island, which five food items would you have?

CW: My nightmare: having to choose. That's a hard one, but I would say French bread, cheese, filet mignon, peanut butter, and bananas. Maybe we'd find some coconuts on the island.

Which food items do you keep in your refrigerator on a regular basis?

CW: Cottage cheese, fresh fruit, cheese, tortillas, eggs, salsa, veggies, vanilla nut creamer for the coffee, and leftovers.

Whom would you most like to have dinner with?

CW: Jim Carrey. I want to get inside that mind. I find him funny, smart, and attractive. I wouldn't mind feeding him some chocolate-covered strawberries.

PAN-GRILLED PINEAPPLE WITH MANGO SORBET

Prep time: 10 minutes ▪ *Cook time: 10 minutes* ▪ *Chill time: 1 hour*

2 tablespoons seasoned rice wine vinegar

2 tablespoons chopped fresh mint

1 tablespoon lime juice

1 tablespoon brown sugar

1 teaspoon grated lime peel

1 teaspoon grated fresh ginger

1 small ripe pineapple, peeled, cored, and cut into ½"-thick semicircles

1½ cups mango sorbet

In a medium bowl, combine the vinegar, chopped mint, lime juice, brown sugar, lime peel, and ginger. Set aside.

Heat a heavy griddle lightly coated with cooking spray over medium-high heat. Add the pineapple and cook for 5 minutes per side, or until lightly browned. Place the pineapple in a dish and top with the reserved sauce. Cover and refrigerate for 1 hour.

Evenly divide the pineapple among 4 dessert plates and top with the sorbet.

Makes 6 servings
Per serving: 125 calories, 1 g fat

Something to Chew On

Why waste all those calories on a teeny serving of something that just slides down your gullet in an instant? Give yourself some taste to chew on, lingeringly, while gaining the health benefits of sweet, nutritious fruit.

**1 serving (½ cup)
super-premium ice cream**
280 calories **19** grams fat

1 serving Pan-Grilled
Pineapple with
Mango Sorbet
125 calories 1 gram fat

OR

1 serving Roasted Pears
with Chocolate Sauce
(see page 266)
150 calories 3 grams fat

Photo on page 265

ROASTED PEARS WITH CHOCOLATE SAUCE

Prep time: 10 minutes ■ *Cook time: 35 minutes*

Pears

4 ripe Bartlett pears, peeled, cored, and halved lengthwise

2 teaspoons lemon juice

1 tablespoon sugar

Chocolate Sauce

¼ cup 1% soy milk

1 square (1 ounce) semisweet chocolate, finely chopped

Mint sprigs for garnish (optional)

To make the pears: Preheat the oven to 425°F. Lightly coat a 13" × 9" baking pan with cooking spray.

In a large bowl, toss the pears with the lemon juice and sugar. Arrange the pears in a single layer in the prepared baking pan. Roast for 35 minutes, or until the pears are tender and light brown.

To make the chocolate sauce: Meanwhile, heat the milk in a small saucepan over medium heat just until it begins to bubble. Remove from the heat and stir in the chocolate. Whisk until smooth.

Spoon the chocolate sauce onto 4 dessert plates and top each with 2 pear halves. Garnish with the mint (if using).

Makes 4 servings
Per serving: 150 calories, 3 g fat

The Pear Package

Pears are packed with vitamin C, but most of it is in the skin, so at least when you're snacking on a pear, keep it unpeeled. This fruit is also a powerhouse of folate, potassium, and iron, and it's an excellent source of fiber. As a bonus, pears are a versatile fruit: Bake them, poach them, sauté them, or, as in this recipe, roast them. Adding to this versatility is the great variety of pears available—including Bosc, Comice, Anjou, and the Bartletts called for here.

ORANGE-ALMOND BISCOTTI

Prep time: 20 minutes ■ *Cook time: 40 minutes* ■ *Cool time: 10 minutes*

For a change of taste, substitute hazelnuts for some or all of the almonds. You can keep biscotti in an airtight container in the refrigerator for 2 weeks.

1 cup unbleached all-purpose flour

½ cup whole grain pastry flour

1 teaspoon baking powder

¼ teaspoon salt

2 eggs

2 tablespoons canola oil

¼ cup sugar

¼ cup Splenda

2 tablespoons orange juice

2 teaspoons grated orange peel

½ teaspoon vanilla extract

½ teaspoon almond extract

¾ cup whole natural almonds, toasted

Preheat the oven to 350°F. Lightly coat a large baking sheet with cooking spray.

In a medium bowl, combine the all-purpose flour, pastry flour, baking powder, and salt.

In a large bowl, with an electric mixer on medium speed, beat the eggs, oil, sugar, and Splenda for 2 minutes, or until pale yellow and thickened. Beat in the orange juice, orange peel, vanilla extract, and almond extract. With the mixer on low speed, gradually add the flour mixture. Stir in the almonds.

Divide the dough in half. With floured hands, form the dough into two 1½" × 14" logs on the prepared baking sheet. Lightly pat the logs to smooth the tops. Bake for 20 minutes, or until firm. Cool the pan on a rack for 10 minutes.

Reduce the oven temperature to 325°F. Transfer the logs to a cutting board and with a serrated knife, slice diagonally into ½"-thick slices. Place the slices, cut side down, on the baking sheet. Bake for 10 minutes. Turn each slice and bake for 10 minutes longer. Remove to a rack to cool.

Makes 48 cookies
Per cookie: 38 calories, 2 g fat

FRUITCAKE

Prep time: 15 minutes ■ *Cook time: 1 hour*

- 1 cup unbleached all-purpose flour
- 1 cup whole grain pastry flour
- 1½ teaspoons pumpkin pie spice
- ½ teaspoon baking soda
- ½ teaspoon cardamom
- ½ teaspoon salt
- ½ cup packed brown sugar
- ½ cup vegetable oil
- ½ cup liquid egg substitute
- 1 teaspoon vanilla extract
- ½ cup fat-free milk or soy milk
- 2 cups small pieces mixed candied fruit
- 1 cup raisins
- 1 cup chopped pecans

Preheat the oven to 325°F. Coat a 9" × 5" loaf pan with cooking spray.

In a medium bowl, combine the all-purpose flour, pastry flour, pumpkin pie spice, baking soda, cardamom, and salt.

In a large bowl, beat together the brown sugar, oil, egg substitute, and vanilla extract. Add the flour mixture and beat well. Add the milk and beat until smooth. Stir in the candied fruit, raisins, and pecans.

Pour the batter into the prepared pan and bake for 1 to 1¼ hours, or until a wooden pick inserted in the center comes out clean. Invert the cake onto a rack and cool completely.

Makes 16 servings
Per serving: 270 calories, 11 g fat

A Slice of Deception

This pound cake looks bland, virtuous—just the sort of "dessert" you would force yourself to have when what you really wanted was something rich and delicious. It's proof that looks can be deceptive. Go for the rich and delicious Fruitcake. For all its appealing substance, it comes in at far fewer calories and less than half the fat of the pound cake.

1 slice (3 ounces) pound cake
420 calories **27** grams fat

1 slice Fruitcake
270 calories **11** grams fat

CREAMY LEMON-LIME CHEESECAKE

Prep time: 30 minutes ▪ Cook time: 55 minutes ▪ Cool/chill time: 4 hours

Crust

1	cup low-fat graham cracker crumbs (about 8 crackers)
2	teaspoons grated lemon peel

Filling

16	ounces ⅓-less-fat cream cheese
8	ounces fat-free cream cheese
2	packages (12.3 ounces) firm silken tofu
¾	cup sugar
½	cup reduced-fat sour cream
½	cup liquid egg substitute
¼	cup lemon juice
¼	cup lime juice
1	tablespoon grated lemon peel
2	teaspoons grated lime peel

To make the crust: Preheat the oven to 325°F. Lightly coat a 10" springform pan with cooking spray.

In a medium bowl, combine the graham cracker crumbs and lemon peel. Press the crust evenly into the bottom of the prepared pan.

To make the filling: In a food processor, combine the cream cheeses, tofu, sugar, and sour cream. Pulse for 1 to 2 minutes, or until smooth. Add the egg substitute, lemon juice, lime juice, lemon peel, and lime peel. Pulse until smooth. Pour the cheese mixture over the crust and smooth the top. Bake for 55 minutes. Turn off the oven and leave the cheesecake in the oven for 20 minutes, or until the center seems firm to the touch. Cool on a rack for 1 hour.

Remove the sides of the pan, cover the cheesecake, and refrigerate for at least 3 hours before serving.

Makes 16 servings
Per serving: 225 calories, 9 g fat

Sour Note

That small, flat wedge of lemon tart looks like the virtuous choice; after all, it eschews the lavish creaminess of the cheesecake. But while it looks bland and innocent enough, it actually contains more than twice the calories and almost twice as much fat as this lush, very tasty cheesecake.

1 wedge (3½ ounces) lemon tart
480 calories **16** grams fat

**1 serving Creamy
Lemon-Lime Cheesecake**
225 calories **9** grams fat

FUN FOOD FOR FAMILIES

Nutritious, Low-Calorie Eating Is Fun!

recipes

The U.S. food industry is the nation's second-largest advertiser. What do they mostly sell? Soft drinks. Candy. Snacks. Fast food.

And just who is it the food industry really wants to capture and hold with this advertising blitz? You guessed it: children. *Your* children. "Get 'em early and you've got 'em for life" is the clear philosophy here. It may be part of the reason why childhood obesity is an epidemic in the United States, an epidemic that will only lead to health problems and serious unhappiness in adolescence and later in life.

There's probably little you can do about the onslaught of advertising. But there's plenty you can do about what your family eats, especially if you're the one in the kitchen who's preparing the meals.

Start here, with a slew of recipes for dishes that are more fun, more appetizing, more all-around alluring than anything the glossiest magazine or most Technicolor TV ad could ever produce. Recipes that are also more healthful and far lower in calories.

Here are breakfasts for a bright start to the day, conversation-starting lunchbox ideas, special-treat after-school snacks, full dinners, desserts, even party platters. We've made them to look as good as they taste.

Of course, these dishes are not just for kids. But the emphasis is on fun, and much of the fun for you can come from teaching your children early that the world is filled with wonderful things to eat—and that the tastiest among them are packed with nutrients and low in calories.

FRUIT PIZZA

Prep time: 10 minutes ■ Chill time: overnight ■ Cook time: 1 minute

1 cup lite vanilla yogurt or soy alternative

1 orange

1 cup raspberries

1 cup blueberries

¼ teaspoon cardamom

4 honey-wheat English muffins, split

1 teaspoon cinnamon sugar

Line a sieve with 2 pieces of paper towel. Place the sieve over a bowl. Spoon the yogurt into the sieve. Cover with plastic wrap and place in the refrigerator overnight.

Preheat the broiler. Cut the peel and pith from the orange and discard. Working over a small bowl, cut out the segments of fruit from the membranes, letting the segments fall into the bowl. Squeeze any remaining juice from the membranes over the orange segments; discard the membranes. Add the raspberries, blueberries, and cardamom.

Place the English muffin halves on a broiler-pan rack. Coat lightly with cooking spray. Sprinkle each muffin half with some of the cinnamon sugar. Broil for 1 to 2 minutes, or until golden brown. Remove the muffin halves to a plate.

Evenly divide the yogurt cheese among the muffin halves. Top with the fruit.

Makes 4 servings (1 whole muffin per serving)
Per serving: 200 calories, 1 g fat

Pizza for Breakfast

Is there a kid who doesn't love pizza? Give yours a change-of-pace treat and concoct this high-nutrition Fruit Pizza for breakfast. It starts with a honey-wheat English muffin, adds fresh fruit and berries, yogurt as the pizza "cheese," even some cinnamon flavor. A great way to incorporate fruit into your child's diet, a delicious start to the day, and a healthful and satisfying alternative to the nutrition-free calories of this bagel half.

½ 5-ounce bagel
200 calories **1** gram fat

1 serving Fruit Pizza
200 calories **1** gram fat

Stuffed French Toast

Prep time: 15 minutes ■ Cook time: 15 minutes

1 cup liquid egg substitute

½ teaspoon grated orange peel

8 slices light whole wheat or white bread

½ cup light cream cheese spread

9 large strawberries, hulled and sliced

⅓ cup lite pancake syrup

1 cup raspberries or blueberries

Preheat the oven to 450°F. Coat a baking sheet with cooking spray.

In a pie plate, combine the egg substitute and orange peel. Dip each slice of bread into the egg mixture, turning to coat, until each slice has soaked up some batter. Place on the prepared baking sheet.

Bake for 12 minutes, turning once, or until golden brown.

Spread 2 tablespoons cream cheese on each of 4 slices of the bread. Arrange the strawberries on top. Cover each with 1 of the remaining bread slices to make 4 sandwiches.

To serve, cut each sandwich diagonally in half. Evenly divide the syrup over each sandwich and sprinkle with berries.

Makes 4 servings
Per serving: 240 calories, 9 g fat

Certainly Sweet

Sometimes, only something very sweet and very rich will do. At such times, it's all too easy to pick up a Cinnabon and start munching. But just consider what that momentary pleasure costs in calories, fat, and nutrition-free eating. Even when sweet, rich pleasure is the aim, there are alternatives. Here's one you can rustle together easily. It's a lavish treat of fruit sweetness that is also a calorie bargain! Just as satisfying as the Cinnabon and just as filling, it adds the bonus of whole grain goodness, fiber, and healthful fruit.

1 Cinnabon cinnamon roll
670 calories **34** grams fat

**1 serving Stuffed
French Toast**
240 calories **9** grams fat

BREAKFAST BURRITOS

Prep time: 10 minutes ■ Cook time: 25 minutes

¼ pound fully cooked chicken sausages or 1 frozen meatless soy smoked sausage

4 whole wheat flour tortillas (10" diameter)

1½ teaspoons canola oil

1 medium red-skinned potato, chopped

¾ cup liquid egg substitute

¼ cup (1 ounce) shredded light extra-sharp Cheddar cheese or soy alternative

3 tablespoons chopped fresh cilantro

⅛ teaspoon salt

½ cup thick and chunky salsa

Preheat the oven to 350°F.

If using the meatless sausage, prepare according to package directions. Cool slightly, then coarsely chop.

Stack the tortillas on a piece of foil. Fold the edges to seal. Place the foil packet in the oven and bake for 8 minutes, or until warm and pliable. Turn off the oven, leaving the tortillas in the oven to keep warm.

Meanwhile, heat the oil in a medium nonstick skillet over medium heat. Add the potato and cook, stirring occasionally, for 15 minutes, or until tender and browned. Add the cooked sausage and cook, stirring occasionally, for 1 minute, or until heated through. Add the egg substitute, cheese, cilantro, and salt and cook, stirring, for 1 to 2 minutes, or until scrambled.

Place 1 tortilla on a plate. Spoon about ½ cup of the egg mixture down the center. Top with 2 tablespoons of the salsa. Fold up the bottom of the tortilla and fold the sides over to cover the filling. Repeat with the remaining tortillas, egg mixture, and salsa to make 4 burritos.

Makes 4 burritos
Per burrito: 360 calories, 16 g fat

Bet on the Burrito

One diminutive sausage-and-egg biscuit, sky-high in both calories and saturated fat, or this burly burrito, stuffed with yummy taste? The burrito offers the same kind of food and more of it, but at a big savings in calories and fat.

1 sausage-and-egg biscuit (6 ounces)
510 calories **35** grams fat

1 Breakfast Burrito
360 calories **16** grams fat

FRUIT KEBABS WITH STRAWBERRY-GINGER DIP

Prep time: 10 minutes ■ Chill time: 30 minutes

2 cups low-fat strawberry yogurt or
    soy alternative

2 tablespoons finely chopped
    crystallized ginger

1 tablespoon finely chopped fresh
    mint

1 cantaloupe, flesh scooped out with
    a melon baller

6 ounces red and/or green seedless
    grapes

24 dried apricot halves

In a medium bowl, combine the yogurt, ginger, and mint until well-blended. Refrigerate for at least 30 minutes.

Meanwhile, thread the melon balls, grapes, and apricots onto 12 small skewers. Serve the kebabs with the dip.

Makes 12 kebabs
Per kebab: 65 calories, 0 g fat

No Chips for a Change

It's time for hors d'oeuvres, and chances are you're tired of the usual potato chips. Not only have they become boring but they're also high in calories and fat, especially because we tend to just keep eating them. The minuscule amount shown here, for example, looks like just the first handful of many. For a change of pace, try these high-nutrition, low-calorie, zero-fat fruit kebabs or even the spinach-packed mini calzones, and whet your appetite with something both tasty and completely different.

2⅔ ounces potato chips
390 calories **29** grams fat

6 Mini Spinach Calzones
(see page 282)
390 calories **12** grams fat

OR

6 servings Fruit Kebabs
with Strawberry-Ginger Dip
390 calories **0** grams fat

MINI SPINACH CALZONES

Prep time: 25 minutes ■ *Cook time: 15 minutes*

Photo on page 281

1 package (10 ounces) frozen chopped spinach, thawed and squeezed dry

¾ cup lite ricotta cheese

½ cup (2 ounces) shredded reduced-fat mozzarella cheese or soy alternative

¼ teaspoon salt

⅛ teaspoon freshly ground black pepper

⅛ teaspoon ground nutmeg

1 loaf (1 pound) frozen honey-wheat or white bread dough, thawed

⅔ cup marinara sauce + additional, if desired, for dipping

Preheat the oven to 400°F. Coat a baking sheet with cooking spray.

In a medium bowl, combine the spinach, ricotta, mozzarella, salt, pepper, and nutmeg.

On a lightly floured surface, roll the dough to ⅛" thickness. Using a 3" round cookie cutter or glass, cut out dough rounds. Gather the scraps together, reroll, and cut out rounds again until all of the dough has been used.

Evenly divide the sauce among the rounds, spooning it in the center of each. Top with the spinach mixture. Dip your finger in water and rub around the edges of the dough to moisten. Fold the rounds in half, pressing the edges together. Using a fork, firmly press the seams to seal the edges. Place on the prepared baking sheet and coat with cooking spray.

Bake for 15 minutes, or until the crust is golden brown. Let cool for 5 minutes, then remove from the baking sheet. Serve with additional marinara sauce (if using).

Makes 28 calzones
Per calzone: 65 calories, 2 g fat

SMOKED TURKEY QUESADILLAS

Prep time: 10 minutes ■ Cook time: 15 minutes

Mexican-style dinners are always fun for the whole family. You can personalize these quesadillas by adding some of your favorite vegetables, perhaps sliced red and green bell peppers. Serve with individual cups of chunky salsa for dipping.

1 teaspoon canola oil

1 clove garlic, minced

2 teaspoons ground cumin

¾ teaspoon ground coriander

1 can (14–19 ounces) black beans, rinsed and drained

3 tablespoons water

⅛ teaspoon salt

8 whole wheat flour tortillas (6" diameter)

1 large tomato, thinly sliced

¼ pound deli-sliced smoked turkey or meatless soy alternative

1 cup (4 ounces) shredded reduced-fat Monterey Jack cheese or soy alternative

Preheat the oven to 400°F. Coat a baking sheet with olive-oil cooking spray.

Heat the oil in a medium saucepan over low heat. Add the garlic, cumin, and coriander and cook for 1 minute, or until the garlic is lightly browned. Add the beans, water, and salt. Using a potato masher or fork, mash the beans and heat through.

Place a tortilla on the work surface. Spread about ¼ cup of the bean mixture on the tortilla. Place some of the tomato, turkey, and cheese on top. Place another tortilla on top of the cheese and lightly press to seal. Repeat with the remaining tortillas, beans, tomatoes, turkey, and cheese to make 4 quesadillas.

Place the quesadillas on the prepared baking sheet and coat with cooking spray. Bake for 5 minutes. Carefully turn the quesadillas and bake for 5 minutes longer, or until lightly browned. Cut each quesadilla into wedges.

Makes 4 quesadillas
Per quesadilla: 363 calories, 8 g fat

Photo on page 69

CUBAN BLACK BEAN SOUP

Prep time: 10 minutes ■ *Cook time: 30 minutes*

1   tablespoon olive oil

2   medium ribs celery with some
    leaves, chopped

1   large onion, chopped

1   large green bell pepper, chopped

2   cloves garlic, minced

1   teaspoon Spanish paprika

½   teaspoon salt

½   teaspoon freshly ground black
    pepper

2   cans (14–19 ounces each) black
    beans, rinsed and drained

2   cups water

1   cup vegetable broth

2   tablespoons dry sherry

2   tablespoons lime juice

Heat the oil in a Dutch oven over medium heat. Add the celery, onion, bell pepper, and garlic and cook, stirring frequently, for 8 minutes, or until tender. Stir in the paprika, salt, and black pepper.

Add the beans, water, and broth and bring to a boil over high heat. Reduce the heat to low, cover, and simmer for 20 minutes to blend the flavors.

Working in batches, puree the soup in a food processor or blender until smooth. Return the soup to the pot and reheat if necessary.

Remove the soup from the heat and stir in the sherry and lime juice.

Makes 9 servings
Per serving: 100 calories, 3 g fat

CHICKEN SOUP WITH GREENS

Prep time: 20 minutes ■ *Cook time: 30 minutes*

Boneless, skinless chicken breast makes this soup easy to prepare—it's on the table in less than an hour. You'll enjoy the hearty addition of kidney beans and couscous.

12 ounces boneless skinless chicken breast

½ teaspoon dried oregano, crumbled

½ teaspoon salt

¼ teaspoon crushed red-pepper flakes

1 tablespoon olive oil

1 medium bunch escarole, torn, rinsed, and dried

4 large cloves garlic, minced

2½ cups fat-free chicken broth

2½ cups water

1 can (14–19 ounces) chickpeas or kidney beans, rinsed and drained

¼ cup whole wheat couscous

Cut the chicken into ½" cubes. Place in a bowl.

In a cup, combine the oregano, salt, and red-pepper flakes. Sprinkle ½ teaspoon of the herb mixture over the chicken and toss to coat.

Heat 1½ teaspoons of the oil in a Dutch oven over high heat. Add the chicken and cook, stirring often, for 3 to 4 minutes, or until lightly browned and no longer pink in the center. Remove the chicken to a clean bowl and cover to keep warm.

Add the remaining 1½ teaspoons oil to the pot. Add the escarole, garlic, and the remaining herb mixture and toss to mix. Reduce the heat to medium-high and cook, stirring, for 4 minutes, or until the escarole has wilted and the garlic is fragrant.

Add the broth, water, and beans and bring to a boil. Reduce the heat to low, cover, and simmer for 10 minutes, or until the flavors have blended.

Stir in the couscous, chicken, and any juices from the bowl. Cover and let stand for 10 minutes, or until the couscous has softened.

Makes 4 servings
Per serving: 294 calories, 5 g fat

Taking the Pulse of Chickpeas

Chickpeas, also known as garbanzos, are what is called a pulse crop. It means that their seeds are produced in pods, and that in turn means that they contain a particularly high percentage of protein. Chickpeas originated in the Middle East nearly 8,000 years ago and are a mainstay not only of the cooking in that region but also of the cuisines of India, Italy, Spain, and Latin America.

In addition to their high protein content, chickpeas are rich in fiber and filled with phytochemicals. But if chickpeas are almost a perfect food nutritionally speaking, they also rate pretty high in terms of flavor and usefulness. Buy them dried, cooked, or in a can, and let them add flavor and texture to salads, soups, dips, and grain dishes.

Bean Burgers with Lime-Scallion Yogurt Sauce

Prep time: 15 minutes ▪ *Cook time: 10 minutes*

½ cup low-fat plain yogurt or soy alternative

1 scallion, white and green parts, finely chopped

1 teaspoon lime juice

1 can (15½ ounces) black beans, rinsed and drained

1 large egg white or ¼ cup liquid egg substitute

¼ cup chopped fresh cilantro

½ red onion, coarsely grated

1 jalapeño chile pepper, seeded and finely chopped (wear plastic gloves when handling)

1 tablespoon unseasoned whole wheat bread crumbs

½ teaspoon ground cumin

¼ teaspoon garlic salt

4 whole wheat pitas or lavashes, warmed

4 large leaves Romaine lettuce, shredded

4 thick slices tomato

In a small bowl, combine the yogurt, scallion, and lime juice. Chill the sauce until ready to serve.

In a large bowl, mash the beans with the egg white or egg substitute until only slightly lumpy. Stir in the cilantro, onion, chile pepper, bread crumbs, cumin, and garlic salt until well-combined. With floured hands, shape the bean mixture into 4 burgers.

Heat a large nonstick skillet coated with cooking spray over medium heat. Add the burgers and cook for 4 minutes per side, or until lightly browned and firm.

Place the burgers in the pitas or lavashes. Top each with the sauce, lettuce, and tomato.

Makes 4 burgers
Per burger: 305 calories, 3 g fat

Fast-Food Object Lesson

Here's proof, if more were needed, that mass-producing food for speedy delivery and low cost carries a high price tag in calories and saturated fat. And while some fast-food places are now opting for low-calorie options, chicken does not necessarily qualify. Instead, go for this quick-to-make bean burger. Flavored with a zesty salsa and wrapped in pita or lavash bread, it's a quick and healthy treat.

1 Burger King chicken sandwich
660 calories **39** grams fat

**1 Bean Burger with
Lime-Scallion Yogurt Sauce**
305 calories 3 grams fat

Firefighter Sal D'Angelo

In his 24 years as a firefighter, mostly with Engine 204 in Brooklyn but also on Staten Island, Sal D'Angelo did "a lot of cooking in the firehouse." In fact, D'Angelo loves to cook anywhere. He has a feel for it, too—and a sense of adventure about putting foods together. That's how he devised his Sautéed Shrimp with Broccoli and Peppers recipe. "I just tried shrimp instead of chicken with broccoli one day," D'Angelo says, then "fooled around with the other ingredients." The resulting dish was a hit with his fellow firefighters, and it was a mainstay of D'Angelo's own Picture-Perfect Weight-Loss program, on which he lost 47 pounds in 10 months. The recipe can be even more Picture Perfect if you substitute cooking spray for olive oil, D'Angelo says. And although the dish is a meal unto itself, he likes to accompany it with his favorite salad: beets, chickpeas, red onions, and cucumbers in a lite balsamic dressing.

SAUTÉED SHRIMP WITH BROCCOLI AND PEPPERS

1   pound whole wheat pasta or spaghetti

2   tablespoons olive oil

4–6 cloves garlic, minced

1   head broccoli, cut into florets

1   large red bell pepper, chopped

1   large yellow bell pepper, chopped

1   cup white wine

2   pounds medium shrimp, peeled and deveined

Prepare the pasta according to package directions.

Meanwhile, heat the oil in a large skillet over medium-high heat. Add the garlic and cook, stirring, for 1 minute. Add the broccoli and bell peppers and cook, stirring frequently, for 8 minutes, or until the vegetables are tender-crisp. Add the wine and bring to a boil. Add the shrimp and cook for 5 minutes, or until the shrimp are opaque.

Makes 8 servings
Per serving: 372 calories, 6 g fat

TURKEY BURGERS WITH SECRET SAUCE

Prep time: 10 minutes ■ *Cook time: 10 minutes*

The tangy sauce gives these burgers a sweet smack of flavor that kids will love.

Burgers

1   pound lean ground turkey

¼   cup seasoned dried bread crumbs

¼   cup chopped fresh parsley

1   tablespoon grainy Dijon mustard

¼   teaspoon salt

¼   teaspoon freshly ground black pepper

Sauce

¼   cup fat-free mayonnaise

2   tablespoons chopped red onion

1   tablespoon dill pickle relish

1   teaspoon grainy Dijon mustard

1   teaspoon mild hot-pepper sauce

8   slices lite whole wheat bread, toasted
     Green leaf lettuce

1   tomato, sliced

To make the burgers: Preheat the broiler. Coat a broiler-pan rack with cooking spray.

In a large bowl, combine the turkey, bread crumbs, parsley, mustard, salt, and pepper. Shape the mixture into 4 burgers.

Place the burgers on the prepared rack. Broil 4" to 6" from the heat for 10 minutes, turning once, or until a thermometer inserted in the thickest portion registers 165°F and the juices run clear.

To make the sauce: Meanwhile, in a small bowl, combine the mayonnaise, onion, relish, mustard, and hot-pepper sauce.

To serve, place 1 slice of toast on each of 4 plates. Top each with a burger, lettuce, and tomato and spoon some sauce over each. Top with the remaining toast slices.

Makes 4 burgers
Per burger: 343 calories, 12 g fat

Spreads Sheet

Try any of these delightful spreads on a sandwich or as a topping or dip for vegetables.

Asian spread. Combine equal parts ketchup and hoisin sauce with hot-pepper sauce to taste.

Creamy herb spread. For every ½ cup reduced-fat cream cheese or homemade yogurt cheese, mix in 3 tablespoons chopped fresh herbs.

Horseradish spread. Combine 2 tablespoons low-fat mayonnaise, 1 teaspoon drained prepared horseradish, and 1 teaspoon Dijon mustard. For added interest, use beet horseradish.

Roasted garlic spread. Combine 1 tablespoon fat-free sour cream, 1 tablespoon chopped sun-dried tomatoes, and 1 tablespoon roasted garlic until smooth.

Sweet-and-spicy spread. Combine equal parts bottled spicy chutney, Dijon mustard, and reduced-fat cream cheese or homemade yogurt cheese.

Tex-mex mayonnaise. Mix ¼ cup low-fat mayonnaise, 1 tablespoon chopped scallions, 1 tablespoon chopped cilantro, ½ teaspoon ground cumin, and hot-pepper sauce to taste.

Chicken and Vegetable Stir-Fry

Prep time: 15 minutes ■ *Marinate time: 20 minutes* ■ *Cook time: 10 minutes*

Zesty orange juice replaces heavy oil in this tasty dish. For a change of pace, substitute pineapple juice.

½ teaspoon grated orange peel

⅓ cup orange juice

2 tablespoons reduced-sodium soy sauce

2 tablespoons dry sherry

2 cloves garlic, minced

¼ teaspoon crushed red-pepper flakes

12 ounces boneless skinless chicken breast, cut into ¼"-thick strips

1 tablespoon cornstarch

2½ teaspoons vegetable oil

5 packed cups cut bok choy (½" pieces)

1 large red bell pepper, cut into thin strips

1 medium onion, thinly sliced

¼ teaspoon salt

¼ cup shredded fresh basil leaves

In a medium bowl, combine the orange peel, 2 tablespoons of the orange juice, 1 tablespoon of the soy sauce, 1 tablespoon of the sherry, the garlic, and red-pepper flakes until blended. Add the chicken and toss to coat. Cover and let stand for 20 minutes.

Meanwhile, to the remaining orange juice, add the cornstarch, the remaining 1 tablespoon soy sauce, and the remaining 1 tablespoon sherry. Mix well and set aside.

Heat 1½ teaspoons of the oil in a large, deep nonstick skillet or wok over medium-high heat. Using a slotted spoon, remove the chicken from the bowl and add to the skillet; reserve the marinade. Cook, stirring often, for 2 to 3 minutes, or until no longer pink in the center. Transfer to a clean bowl.

Heat the remaining 1 teaspoon oil in the skillet. Add the bok choy, bell pepper, onion, and salt. Cook, stirring constantly, for 3 minutes, or until the greens of the bok choy start to wilt.

Return the chicken and its juices and the reserved marinade to the skillet. Cook for 3 minutes. Stir the cornstarch mixture again and pour into the skillet. Cook, stirring constantly, for 2 minutes, or until the juices are thickened and bubbly.

Remove from the heat and sprinkle with the basil.

Makes 4 servings
Per serving: 187 calories, 4 g fat

Lime and Spice Chicken Drumsticks

Prep time: 10 minutes ■ *Marinate time: 1 hour* ■ *Cook time: 15 minutes*

For a spicier dish, substitute a chopped serrano or jalapeño chile pepper for the canned green chiles.

8 skinless chicken drumsticks (about 2 pounds)

1 teaspoon grated lime peel

¼ cup lime juice

½ can chopped green chile peppers, undrained (2 ounces)

1 tablespoon honey

2 cloves garlic, minced

1½ teaspoons ground cumin

1 teaspoon toasted sesame oil

½ teaspoon salt

½ cup chopped fresh cilantro

Lime wedges

Cut 2 or 3 diagonal slashes in the fleshy part of each drumstick. Place the drumsticks in a large bowl or glass baking dish.

In a measuring cup, combine the lime peel, lime juice, chile peppers, honey, garlic, cumin, oil, and salt until well-blended. Pour over the drumsticks, rubbing the mixture into the meat and the slashes. Cover and marinate in the refrigerator for 1 hour.

Coat a grill rack with cooking spray. Preheat the grill to medium.

Remove the drumsticks from the marinade. Bring the remaining marinade to a boil in a small saucepan over medium-high heat. Place the drumsticks on the grill and brush with the marinade. Cover and grill, turning the drumsticks often, for 15 to 20 minutes, or until a thermometer inserted in the thickest portion registers 170°F and the juices run clear. Place on a clean platter.

Sprinkle the drumsticks with the cilantro and drizzle with the juice from 2 or 3 lime wedges. Serve with additional lime wedges.

Makes 4 servings
Per serving: 189 calories, 6 g fat

Getting Your Garlic

Garlic comes in three major versions: white-skinned, strongly flavored American garlic; Mexican and Italian, with mauve skins and a milder flavor; and the white-skinned elephant garlic, not a true garlic but a relative of the leek, which is the mildest in flavor. As befits its name, elephant garlic is gigantic, with bulbs the size of a small grapefruit and cloves weighing in at 1 ounce each.

When buying garlic, look for firm, plump bulbs with dry skins. (Unless you're shopping for green garlic—this is young garlic before it has begun to form cloves, and it's usually sold as a specialty item.) Avoid garlic with soft or shriveled cloves, and don't buy garlic that is stored in the refrigerated section. Store your fresh garlic in an open container away from other foods in a cool, dark place—it'll last up to 8 weeks.

Peter Beard

*P*eter Beard is a man who manages to accommodate varied personalities and opposing ideas, all of which live within him. Inspired by the writings of Isak Dinesen, he traveled to Africa and became a wildlife supporter and surveyor. His photography offers an intimate vision of elephants and other endangered wildlife. Beard is also a hoarder of beauty—and a man with a fatalistic approach to life. He is famous for discovering some of the world's most beautiful supermodels, for partying across New York and haunting Studio 54, for his friends and admirers—among them such literary and artistic luminaries as Truman Capote, Andy Warhol, and the great British painter Francis Bacon. Beard has documented life, beauty, and decline in diaries filled with collages that are themselves works of art.

Tell me about a meal in the wild.

PB: The best meals depend on how hungry you are and where you are. Usually, out of doors is the best place to eat them. One of my favorite places to be is Lake Rudolph, between Kenya and Ethiopia. I went there when I was 30 years old to do a survey of crocodiles with my friend Alistair Graham, a scientist. We were there for 6 years, give or take. I had a lot of good fireside meals with lions roaring in the distance, crocodiles popping their heads out of the water, big winds, and big problems. We would eat catfish, tilapia, Ritz crackers—with Hellmann's mayonnaise and bread-and-butter pickles.

Do you still eat all of those things?

PB: Yes, I still do.

What are some of your favorite foods?

PB: Boar's Head cheese, clamato juice, pâté, vichyssoise, barbecued chips, Tora Bora cheese, crème fraîche and Danish, tube caviar, clam salsa, wild duck, red currant jelly, stuffed squash, cashew nuts, hot dogs off the street or in Madison Square Garden with a beer or with French fries and pepper sauce, maple sugar, Smith & Wollensky crab claws with the most amazing mustard sauce in the world.

Which five ingredients do you keep in your refrigerator on a regular basis?

PB: Hellmann's mayonnaise, Worcestershire sauce, honey mustard, Colman's hot English mustard, clamato juice.

Is there any combination of foods that you consider unusual?

PB: Artichokes and milk.

Desert island question: Which five foods would you want with you if you were marooned on a desert island?

PB: Hellmann's, bread-and-butter pickles, Ritz crackers, vodka, and tomatoes.

Is there any food that you cannot resist under any circumstances?

PB: Crème fraîche, Ritz crackers.

What's your favorite smell in the kitchen?

PB: Bacon.

What's your favorite seasoning?

PB: Worcestershire sauce.

What was your least favorite food as a child?

PB: Applesauce and rhubarb.

And now?

PB: Applesauce and rhubarb. Also anything raw—like pigs' feet.

If you could have dinner with anybody, alive or dead, who would that be?

PB: Ava Gardner.

VEGGIE-TOFU TACOS

Prep time: 15 minutes ■ *Cook time: 10 minutes*

¼ cup (2 ounces) crumbled feta
    cheese

1 cup crumbled firm tofu, excess
    water squeezed out

1 teaspoon extra-virgin olive oil

2 medium zucchini, finely chopped

1 large red onion, diced

1 clove garlic, minced

1 jalapeño chile pepper, seeded and
    finely chopped (wear plastic
    gloves when handling)

4 scallions, white and green parts,
    minced

2 medium tomatoes, chopped

1 can (15 ounces) sweet corn
    kernels, drained

½ cup chopped fresh cilantro

¼ teaspoon freshly ground black
    pepper

12 taco shells

3 cups shredded lettuce

¾ cup salsa

In a small bowl, combine the cheese and tofu. Set aside.

Heat the oil in a large nonstick skillet over medium-high heat. Add the zucchini, onion, garlic, and chile pepper and cook, stirring occasionally, for 5 minutes. Add the scallions, tomatoes, and corn. Cook, stirring occasionally, for 3 minutes, or until the vegetables are cooked through. Remove from the heat. Stir in the cilantro and black pepper. Drain the mixture in a sieve. Stir in the lettuce and salsa.

Evenly divide the vegetable mixture and cheese mixture among the taco shells.

Makes 12 tacos
Per taco: 160 calories, 7 g fat

Twice the Taco

Get twice the amount of Tex-Mex flavor for fewer calories when you make your own taco and fill it with vegetables. Even the fat in this Veggie-Tofu Taco comes mostly from the tofu and olive oil, which are both sources of "good" fat.

1 Taco Bell Beef Burrito
Supreme
430 calories **18** grams fat

1 Veggie-Tofu Taco
160 calories 7 grams fat

GRILLED VEGGIE PIZZA

Prep time: 15 minutes ■ Cook time: 45 minutes

Veggies

2   red bell peppers, cut into thin strips

1   small red onion, cut into wedges

1   medium zucchini, halved
    lengthwise and sliced

1   medium yellow squash, halved
    lengthwise and sliced

16   asparagus spears, cut into 1" pieces

1   tablespoon extra-virgin olive oil

Pizza

¾   pound frozen whole wheat bread or
    pizza dough, thawed

½   teaspoon garlic salt

16   pieces vegetarian pepperoni

¼   cup (2 ounces) grated Parmesan
    cheese or soy alternative

¼   cup chopped fresh basil and/or
    oregano

¼   teaspoon freshly ground black
    pepper

To make the veggies: Preheat the oven to 425°F.

Place the peppers, onion, zucchini, yellow squash, and asparagus in a 13" × 9" baking dish. Drizzle with the oil and toss to coat. Roast the vegetables, stirring occasionally, for 30 minutes, or until tender-crisp. Do not turn off the oven.

To make the pizza: Coat a pizza pan or 15" × 10" baking pan with cooking spray. Spread the dough evenly on the prepared pan into a flat crust and coat with cooking spray.

Sprinkle the dough with ¼ teaspoon of the garlic salt. Top with the vegetables and pepperoni. Sprinkle with the remaining ¼ teaspoon garlic salt and the cheese.

Bake for 15 minutes, or until cooked through and the crust is golden brown. Remove the pizza from the pan and place on a cutting board. Top with the basil and/or oregano and pepper. Slice into 10 squares.

Makes 10 servings
Per serving: 174 calories, 4 g fat

Homemade Pizza

Pizza started as a dish made from leftover bread at home in southern Italy, and maybe it's time to bring it home to your house. This recipe is fun to make—a good activity in which to involve the kids—and it's healthful. You'll give your children a good lesson in cooking, lots of vegetables, and a helping of soy in the veggie pepperoni.

**1 Pizza Hut Ultimate
Veggie Lover's Personal Pan Pizza
610 calories 24 grams fat**

**3½ slices Grilled
Veggie Pizza**
610 calories **14** grams fat

Cucumber-Hummus Tortilla Pizza

Prep time: 15 minutes ■ Cook time: 10 minutes

Flour tortillas baked in the oven make wonderful pizza shells. Topped with a tangy hummus, these little pizzas will disappear quickly. The baked tortillas can be stored in an airtight container for up to 1 week, and the hummus can be made up to 2 days in advance and refrigerated.

Hummus

1　small yellow onion, sliced

½　English cucumber, peeled, halved, seeded, and sliced

1　can (15½ ounces) chickpeas, rinsed and drained

1　large clove garlic

1　tablespoon tahini

　　Juice of 1 lemon (about 3 tablespoons)

¼　teaspoon salt

Pizza

4　whole wheat flour tortillas (8" diameter)

½　English cucumber, thinly sliced into rounds

4　plum tomatoes, seeded and diced

To make the hummus: In a blender or food processor, combine the onion, cucumber, chickpeas, garlic, tahini, lemon juice, and salt. Process for 3 minutes, or until smooth.

To make the pizza: Preheat the oven to 400°F. Coat both sides of the tortillas with olive-oil cooking spray. Place the tortillas on baking sheets, working in batches if necessary, and bake for 8 minutes, or until the tortillas are lightly browned and crisped on each side.

Evenly divide the hummus among the tortillas. Top with the cucumber and tomatoes.

Makes 4 pizzas
Per pizza: 246 calories, 5 g fat

Hummus: A Staple of the Middle East

Hummus is a virtually obligatory ingredient of Middle Eastern cuisine, yet about the only absolute in its preparation is that it is made from chickpeas. Differences in the ingredients and manner of preparing hummus differ from region to region, even from family to family. Some Syrian families, for example, use olive oil, cumin, and allspice, while the typical Palestinian and Israeli way of making it includes tahini (sesame seed paste) and lemon juice. Some chefs prefer sesame oil to olive oil; some add garlic; some turn to food processors to make the hummus silky smooth. Experiment; just make sure you peel and discard the thin white skins of the chickpeas. On the other hand, canned chickpeas work just fine. As for tahini, you can find jars of it in just about any supermarket.

CARAMEL POPCORN

Prep time: 5 minutes ■ Cook time: 5 minutes

Here's a healthier version of caramel popcorn, which is often surprisingly high in the bad kind of fat. Be sure to remove any unpopped kernels from the popcorn before serving, because those little nuggets are really hard on your teeth if you bite into them. For variety, you could form the caramel popcorn into balls.

10 cups air-popped popcorn

3 tablespoons reduced-calorie butter or margarine

½ cup light corn syrup

½ cup packed brown sugar

Place the popcorn in a very large glass or metal bowl. Set aside.

In a large heavy saucepan, melt the butter or margarine, corn syrup, and brown sugar. Cook over medium heat, stirring occasionally, until the mixture comes to a boil and thickens. Continue cooking, stirring occasionally, for 1 minute.

Remove the pan from the heat. (The syrup will be very hot; be careful not to get any on your hands.)

Carefully pour some of the syrup over the popcorn. Stir to coat using 2 large wooden spoons. Repeat several more times until all the syrup has been used and the popcorn is well-coated. Cool completely before serving.

Makes 15 servings
Per serving: 86 calories, 1 g fat

Pumped-Up Popcorn

Some brands of microwave popcorn contain as much fat as potato chips. By tossing your own plain popped corn with seasoning combinations, such as Chinese five-spice powder or Cajun seasoning, you can enjoy this great snack without excess fat. Or, make your own seasoning mixes from this selection.

To make a batch of flavored popcorn, place 6 cups of plain popped popcorn (popped in an air popper or microwave oven) in a large bowl. Toss while coating with cooking spray. Sprinkle with the selected seasoning and toss to mix. Spread onto 2 foil-lined baking sheets coated with cooking spray. Lightly coat the popcorn with cooking spray. Bake at 300°F for 3 to 5 minutes, or until it looks dry.

Harvest. ½ teaspoon each ground cinnamon and ground ginger with ¼ cup each dried apples and raisins

Indian. ½ teaspoon each curry powder, dry mustard, turmeric, ground coriander, and ground cumin

Italian. ½ teaspoon each dried basil and oregano, ⅛ teaspoon dried red-pepper flakes, and ¼ cup (1 ounce) grated Parmesan cheese

Jamaican. ½ teaspoon each onion powder, allspice, jerk seasoning, and ground cinnamon

Mediterranean. ½ teaspoon each thyme, sage, marjoram, and grated lemon peel

Mexican. ½ teaspoon each ground cumin and ground coriander, with ¼ teaspoon each chili powder and ground red pepper

SUMMER FRUIT POPS

Prep time: 15 minutes ■ *Chill time: 2 hours*

1 cup frozen unsweetened
   strawberries

2 tablespoons sugar-free orange
   syrup

2¾ cups + 1¼ cups lite vanilla yogurt
   or soy substitute

1 cup frozen unsweetened
   blueberries

Place the strawberries and 1 tablespoon of the orange syrup in a blender and process until smooth. Evenly divide among 8 paper cups. Evenly divide the 2¾ cups yogurt among the cups, spooning it over the strawberries.

Place the blueberries, the remaining 1 tablespoon orange syrup, and the remaining 1¼ cups yogurt in the blender. Process until smooth. Evenly divide among the cups, spooning it over the yogurt.

Insert a pop stick in the center of each cup. Place in the freezer and freeze for at least 2 hours, or until solid.

Peel away the paper cups to serve.

Makes 8
Per serving: 80 calories, 0 g fat

Fancy and Fun!

Maybe it's dubbed "super-premium," but this ice cream bar looks both paltry and dull compared to either the rich, colorful Summer Fruit Pops or the fancy fantasy of this Carousel Ice Cream Cake. In fact, the only way the ice cream bar exceeds the fruit pops or cake is in calories and fat content—which are off the charts. Think of it this way: You could enjoy both a slice of cake and a fruit pop and still not come anywhere near the calorie count of the ice cream bar. As for fat, the ice cream bar holds an astonishing 22 grams of the "bad" kind; the fruit pops and carousel cake have absolutely no fat at all.

1 super-premium ice cream bar (4 ounces)
330 calories **22** grams fat

1 Summer Fruit Pop
80 calories O grams fat

OR

**1 slice Carousel Ice Cream
Cake (see page 302)**
150 calories O grams fat

Photo on page 301

CAROUSEL ICE CREAM CAKE

Prep time: 15 minutes ■ *Chill time: 2 hours*

4 pints flavored fat-free frozen yogurt
   or soy alternative, such as
   vanilla, chocolate, and
   strawberry, softened

12–14 animal crackers

13 lollipops

1 plastic drinking straw

12 strips (8" each) thin decorative
   ribbon

Alternately layer the frozen yogurt into an 8" springform pan, smoothing the top. Place in the freezer for at least 2 hours, or until firm.

Unmold the frozen yogurt onto a serving plate. Press the animal crackers around the sides of the cake. Insert one of the lollipops into the end of the straw, snipping off the straw even with the lollipop stick, then place on top of the cake in the center. Insert the remaining 12 lollipops around the edges of the cake in a circle. Attach the ribbon to the lollipops, tying one end to the center lollipop and the other to the outer lollipops, to resemble a carousel.

Makes 12 servings
Per serving: 150 calories, 0 g fat

CHOCOLATE-DIPPED FRUIT

Prep time: 10 minutes ■ *Cook time: 5 minutes* ■ *Chill time: 30 minutes*

4   ounces semisweet chocolate

¼   cup water

¼   teaspoon ground cinnamon

1   pint strawberries (about 16)

8   dried apricots

3   bananas, each cut into 8 slices

Line a baking pan with waxed paper.

Place the chocolate, water, and cinnamon in a saucepan and cook, stirring, until melted.

Dip one-third of each fruit piece into the chocolate mixture. Place on the prepared baking pan and refrigerate for 30 minutes, or until ready to serve.

Makes 48 pieces
Per piece: 20 calories, 1 g fat

Chocolate-Dipped Fruit

There's more to chocolate than the candy bars on the front shelf at the grocery store or supermarket. That means there are more ways than one to satisfy your chocolate craving. The way shown here gives you the rich chocolate taste you yearn for along with the nutritional bonus of fruit—at fewer calories than the commercial candy.

1 Reese's Peanut Butter Cup
170 calories **8** grams fat

VS.

7 pieces
Chocolate-Dipped Fruit
140 calories **7** grams fat

SUPER CELEBRATIONS

*H*osting special occasions doesn't have to be detrimental to your Picture-Perfect Weight-Loss eating plan. You can be merry—*and* eat and drink—without worry, if you just do a little planning ahead. Use these party-pleasing menus as your springboard, and you'll soon see that you can entertain all you like and still get thin.

Cocktail Hour

Mushroom and Sun-Dried Tomato Phyllo Triangles, page 59

Roasted Red Pepper and Basil Dip, page 56

Gravlax with Mustard Sauce, page 72

Sweet-and-Sour Turkey Meatballs, page 65

Caramelized Onion and Roasted Red Pepper Pizza, page 70

Special Dinner for Friends

Mesclun with Pears, Pecans, and Blue Cheese, page 192

Roasted Lamb with Mediterranean Vegetables, page 188

Wild Mushrooms and Barley, page 228

Brussels Sprouts with Hazelnuts and Orange, page 222

Phyllo Cups with Ricotta Cream and Berries, page 258

Oscar Night

Mango and Black Bean Bruschetta,
   page 73

Mini Spinach Calzones, page 282

Pureed Veggie Terrine, page 110

Chocolate-Dipped Fruit, page 303

Raspberry Soufflé, page 259

Afternoon on the Patio

Citrus Teriyaki Shrimp Kebabs, page 64

Mediterranean Wraps, page 66

Curried Yogurt Dip, page 58

Cold Cucumber and Yogurt Soup, page 78

Stuffed Tomatoes, page 214

Creamy Lemon-Lime Cheesecake, page 270

Seafood Feast

Baked Crab Wontons,
   page 65

Chilled Roasted Red Pepper Soup with
   Basil and Crab, page 84

Grilled Peppery Salmon with Garlic
   Greens, page 146

Chili Shrimp with Fruity Relish,
   page 158

Assorted steamed vegetables

Pan-Grilled Pineapple with Mango
   Sorbet, page 264

Kid's Birthday Party

Fruit Kebabs with Strawberry-Ginger Dip, page 280

Celery and carrot sticks

Turkey Burgers with Secret Sauce, page 289

Baked french fries

Caramel Popcorn, page 299

Carousel Ice Cream Cake, page 302

Super Bowl Matchup

Five-Bean Chili, page 124

Roasted Garlic Pizza with Arugula and
Sun-Dried Tomatoes, page 118

Lime and Spice Chicken Drumsticks,
page 291

Warm Apple Compote with Frozen Yogurt,
page 251

Summer Barbecue

Spicy Grilled Chicken Breasts, page 167

Grilled Barbecue Tofu Kebabs, page 121

Old-Fashioned Potato Salad, page 197

Summer Skillet Vegetables, page 216

Trio of Melon Ices, page 256

Sunday Supper

Greek Chopped Salad, page 193

Pan-Grilled Chicken with Grapes and Thyme, page 168

Garlic and Chive Mashed Potatoes, page 213

Steamed asparagus with lemon

Roasted Pears with Chocolate Sauce, page 266

Autumn Harvest

Carrot and Ginger Soup, page 85

Turkey Cutlets Milanese, page 172

Mashed Sweet Potatoes and Apples,
    page 213

Citrusy Pumpkin Pudding, page 252

Winter Warmup

Winter Greens, Pear, and Goat Cheese Salad, page 198

Roasted Pork Loin and Vegetables, page 184

Espresso-Chocolate Fondue, page 250

CREDITS

Photography

Recipes

Index

Underscored page references indicate sidebars and tables. **Boldface** references indicate photographs.

Conversion Chart

These equivalents have been slightly rounded to make measuring easier.

Volume Measurements

U.S.	Imperial	Metric
¼ tsp	–	1 ml
½ tsp	–	2 ml
1 tsp	–	5 ml
1 Tbsp	–	15 ml
2 Tbsp (1 oz)	1 fl oz	30 ml
¼ cup (2 oz)	2 fl oz	60 ml
⅓ cup (3 oz)	3 fl oz	80 ml
½ cup (4 oz)	4 fl oz	120 ml
⅔ cup (5 oz)	5 fl oz	160 ml
¾ cup (6 oz)	6 fl oz	180 ml
1 cup (8 oz)	8 fl oz	240 ml

Weight Measurements

U.S.	Metric
1 oz	30 g
2 oz	60 g
4 oz (¼ lb)	115 g
5 oz (⅓ lb)	145 g
6 oz	170 g
7 oz	200 g
8 oz (½ lb)	230 g
10 oz	285 g
12 oz (¾ lb)	340 g
14 oz	400 g
16 oz (1 lb)	455 g
2.2 lb	1 kg

Length Measurements

U.S.	Metric
¼"	0.6 cm
½"	1.25 cm
1"	2.5 cm
2"	5 cm
4"	11 cm
6"	15 cm
8"	20 cm
10"	25 cm
12" (1')	30 cm

Pan Sizes

U.S.	Metric
8" cake pan	20 × 4 cm sandwich or cake tin
9" cake pan	23 × 3.5 cm sandwich or cake tin
11" × 7" baking pan	28 × 18 cm baking tin
13" × 9" baking pan	32.5 × 23 cm baking tin
15" × 10" baking pan	38 × 25.5 cm baking tin (Swiss roll tin)
1½ qt baking dish	1.5 liter baking dish
2 qt baking dish	2 liter baking dish
2 qt rectangular baking dish	30 × 19 cm baking dish
9" pie plate	22 × 4 or 23 × 4 cm pie plate
7" or 8" springform pan	18 or 20 cm springform or loose-bottom cake tin
9" × 5" loaf pan	23 × 13 cm or 2 lb narrow loaf tin or pâté tin

Temperatures

Fahrenheit	Centigrade	Gas
140°	60°	–
160°	70°	–
180°	80°	–
225°	105°	¼
250°	120°	½
275°	135°	1
300°	150°	2
325°	160°	3
350°	180°	4
375°	190°	5
400°	200°	6
425°	220°	7
450°	230°	8
475°	245°	9
500°	260°	–